In loving memory of Basil A. Gillis:
mentor, strategist, liberator, and guide

but most importantly—Da.

TABLE OF CONTENTS

vii   *Acknowledgements*

xi   *Introduction*

1   *Chapter 1*
       In the Beginning

23   *Chapter 2*
       The Healthcare Privatization Myth

51   *Chapter 3*
       Why the Emergency Department Mattered

71   *Chapter 4*
       The Four Horsemen

145   *Chapter 5*
       The Reward Puppets

179   *Chapter 6*
       Covid-19 Makes the Case

215   *Chapter 7*
       The Road Forward

277   *Conclusion*

289   *Endnotes*

313   *Index*

ACKNOWLEDGEMENTS

This work would not have been possible without the support of my precious family team.

I would like to thank my brilliant daughter Genevieve, for her exemplary editing skills and direction. Thanks for extending your long workdays to include your mother, kid. May our disputes pertaining to the use of the Oxford comma finally rest in peace.

To my oldest daughter, Lynore, and my son, Conrad Jr., thank you for having such great faith in this project. Your opinions and encouragement made it possible for me to see this work through to the end.

To my husband of forty-seven years, Conrad MacNeil, thank you so much for your editing, constructive feedback, and constant encouragement. It never hurts to be married to a retired English teacher when you decide to embark on a journey such as this. Thank you for your overwhelming support.

I would also like to express my heartfelt gratitude to Friesen Press and their entire staff. Thank you, Bret Newton, for being the best literary consultant a person could meet. Thank you, Leanne Jensen, you are a publishing specialist extraordinaire. Many thanks to designer Geoff Soch, for your insight and patience. Sincerest thanks to editors, Rhonda Hayter and Katie Heffring, for your kindness and skillful diligence.

Thank you to the incomparable Noam Chomsky for answering emails from a fledgling author. I hope you know that your spirit helped guide me through. Your work, much like your integrity, is unrivalled.

Part of the impetus for starting this work came from my former boss Margaret Szabo. You selected and groomed an "A Team" of health care professionals during the last years of my career. Your progressive vision of long-term care and your undying devotion to that vision inspired me and continues to inspire me. I hope you recognize parts of your collaborative, integrated style in these pages. Thank you for your immeasurable leadership.

If you're lucky enough to have a mentor during your formative years, hopefully you'll encounter someone like Jean (Sullivan) Logan. Mrs. Logan, as her nurses respectfully referred to her, was the evening nursing supervisor at Camp Hill Hospital in Halifax from 1977–1992. Mrs. Logan practised patient-centred care decades before the term became a neologism. For young nurses like myself, she inspired us to exude professionalism in nursing. Her unyielding devotion and respect for all patients has been a mainstay of my own practise for over forty years. I'm not sure how this work could have been completed without her enduring influence. Wherever there are pro-patient sentiments on these pages, a thought about Jean Logan has preceded them.

To every single Canadian taxpayer, this book was written with you in mind. I remain forever mindful of the work you do every day to generate the funds that keep this system rolling. It's your system. You deserve better. It is my hope this work will spark the momentum that will improve the system for all of you. I hope in some small way, it reflects the respect and compassion you so deserve.

To all the patients and families who have suffered at the hands of our defunded system and whose stories line these pages, this work is your treatise. It is my hope it will somehow illuminate

ACKNOWLEDGEMENTS

your struggles and keep your stories alive and, in the forefront, as we challenge governments to reform Medicare. I commend you for sharing these painful and heartbreaking stories. I hope these pages will ensure that your suffering and loss will not be forgotten.

Finally, to all the patients I have had the privilege of caring for over the decades, this book would not have happened without you. While time has started to erase some of your names, your faces and our encounters are indelibly etched upon my soul.

INTRODUCTION

No other policy initiative in Canadian history embodies both the struggle and the triumph of the human spirit more than the creation of Medicare. While Canadians have a propensity to view the creation of Medicare as a stand-alone success story, its evolution was part of a larger expanded social program package. Canadians were weary from two world wars and the destitution that followed the 1929 stock market crash. Western Canada had a set of unique circumstances that gave rise to broad, interrelated social-welfare initiatives, including a universal public health care system. From its inception, Medicare has always had its detractors. Despite this, Canadian legends like T. C. Douglas and his party rewrote the political history of the country. When Saskatchewan was impoverished and drought-stricken, they aligned with farmers and labourers to form a new political party known as the Co-operative Commonwealth Federation. The CCF pushed through large swaths of social reforms, including Medicare. The creation of the CCF, their ascendancy to power, and what they accomplished with minimal monetary and media support are achievements that remain unrivalled in Canadian history.

Opponents of Medicare have been unrelenting in their pursuit to dismantle Canada's crown jewel of public policy, but Medicare had a few good years during the social revolution of the 1960s and '70s. As the 1970s emerged, business and corporate classes, upset with government regulation, high corporate taxes, and the expansion of unionism, fought back. Neoliberalism—the emergence of pro-corporate power, deregulation, and low corporate taxes—swept across North America. By the 1980s, the writing was on the wall. Public systems were a disease on the economy. Consumerism and capitalism were now king. Armed with its new transcontinental trade agreements, neoliberalism became the *capo dei capi* assigned to "clip" public health care systems.

While neoliberalism enjoyed unbridled success within the US system, Canada remained a more elusive target. Ensconced in an egalitarian spirit and a symbol of pride, Medicare wasn't about to succumb without a fight. Although still swinging, Medicare is damaged and currently on the ropes. Neoliberal forces have created a hallucinogenic version of health care. Defunding, deregulating, defrauding, and *deliberate* disintegration have manipulated Canadians into despising the system they once cherished. Canadians are being convinced that Medicare is unsustainable, unfixable, and cost-prohibitive. There is a reason for that. Neoliberalism has the rescue medication locked within its assault armamentarium—privatization. The last stage of the takedown has begun, and the slow but steady infusion of privatization now flows unobstructed through the veins of Medicare.

Covid-19 has made the case of just how toxic a concoction this infusion has become. Its fallout is indicative of the systemic nature of these problems.

Has Medicare lost? As a registered nurse, I believe there is a path forward. My belief, amassed from forty-six years of nursing experience, is that we have one opportunity left. That opportunity requires a complete cultural shift in how health care services are managed in the future. It requires us to come together as funders to rebuild a system that is accessible, flexible, modernized, and integrated. Progress must shift to take on a whole new meaning. Part of that shift requires reaching back into the past and eliciting the strength and determination of our forefathers.

Analyzing the evolution of Medicare will afford us the tools required to salvage the system. This challenge exceeds the quick fixes we have witnessed thus far. It extends far beyond the reactionary, political expediency of throwing "good money after bad." The rescue plan includes defying neoliberal dogma. We must stop this direct infusion of deceit by countering it with a humanist antidote supported by evidence. This book seeks to rally Canadians to lead that fight.

Catherine Gillis-MacNeil

Chapter 1

IN THE BEGINNING

This man called Douglas-well, how'll I put it? He's a good deed in a naughty world...He was motivated by an ideal... To call him a politician, as you'd call Bennett or Diefenbaker a politician, is to insult him. He was and is a dreamer and a humanitarian, incorruptible, genuine and intellectually honest.

—Jack Scott, *Vancouver Sun*, 1960

"Time is muscle."[1] This was a phrase written on an algorithm poster in an emergency room where I worked years ago. The algorithm outlined the necessary steps required to get a heart attack victim from triage to the cardiac-catheterization lab for treatment. The expression implied if the team wasted any valuable seconds, heart muscle could languish. The urgency between time and health has not diminished. Whether it's initial seconds of CPR lost, a decision to avoid the emergency department, or leaving a persistent ache to go unattended for one more day—time affects outcome.

We, as health care providers, have always battled that inextricable link between time and outcome. Nowhere is that connection more pronounced than in the time remaining to save our public health care system. If swift and strategic action is not taken, Medicare will soon be on irreversible life support. In this sense, time has become unusually critical.

Thunderheads are circling the Canadian health care system. While the pro-business hounds of privatization have fought to commodify the most granular aspects of health, the spirit of Canadian collectivism has managed to outpace the hounds. But the chase is closing in. Over time, government at federal and provincial levels has made Medicare less and less of a priority. It continues to voluntarily defund the system and Canadian taxpayers continue to be defrauded by all political parties. In its American-like obsession to shift our public health care service to the vagaries of market forces, government has left the system unprotected and vulnerable. This has subjected hundreds of Canadians to harm, unnecessary suffering, and premature death. The conscious defunding that has created chaos across all Canadian emergency rooms has set the stage for the final *coup-de-grâce*: privatization. The plan of making the system as inaccessible and onerous as possible is almost complete. The terminal blow—conceding that the system is too expensive for us to sustain publicly—is but a step away.

Patients are not the only victims. Defunding and defrauding have created workplaces that are short staffed, disorganized, and frenetic, resulting in a frustrated, exhausted workforce that often feels abandoned. It's a workforce struggling to hold together a chaotic non-system. In addition to defunding and defrauding, deregulation has also crept through the public system, making it an easy mark for the private conglomerates circling it.

Canadians need to act now before our time runs out. We must ascend to the levels of humanitarianism and collectivism of the people who came before us and espouse the tenacity of predecessors like Douglas, Woodsworth, and Coldwell. A legacy bereft of affordable health care is a frightening inheritance for all our grandchildren. After four decades at hundreds of bedsides, I can attest to how vital it is to have a robust public health care system. If we cannot reverse the tide of privatization of health services, we stand to undo the greatest policy initiative in Canadian history: Medicare. If we fail, future Canadians may find themselves, like our American neighbours, selling their blood to buy food.

No socio-political initiative in the past century has affected the lives of everyday Canadians more than the establishment of the Canadian Medicare system. A revered icon of Canadiana, Medicare's establishment sent an arrow through the air of international health care discourse, signifying Canada's devotion to equity. It afforded all Canadians access to medical services, irrespective of their ability to pay, signifying Canada's ethos as a compassionate, egalitarian nation.

Canadians have responded with a genuine appreciation of Medicare. In virtually every report, every poll, and every election since Medicare's inception, the value of having a publicly funded health care system has been articulated without hesitation by Canadian voters. As recently as June 2019, in an Ipsos poll conducted on behalf of the College of Family Physicians, half of all Canadians ranked health care in their top three issues ahead of climate, taxes, poverty, education, and immigration.[2]

In 2004, the Canadian Broadcasting Corporation launched a television program to determine who should be considered the greatest Canadian of our time. It came as no surprise when Medicare pioneer, Tommy Douglas, scored high on a list of influential nominees. Polls were conducted via email, written correspondence, and telephone until midnight November 28,

2004. The following night, Douglas was announced the winner. Iconic marathoner for cancer research Terry Fox; Canada's fourteenth prime minister, Lester B. Pearson; hockey legend Wayne Gretzky; co-discoverer of insulin, Sir Frederick Banting; and world-famous environmentalist David Suzuki were among some of Douglas's formidable competitors.[3] From this list of notable luminaries Canadians again had voiced their reverence for the founder of Medicare and, by default, the system he helped create.

But the road to Canadian egalitarianism wasn't always paved with reverence. Its path was strewn with strife, unpredictability, strikes, and fierce political battles. Early twentieth-century Canada was less than an ideal place to live. Socio-economic conditions were starting to reflect some of the darkest times in history. The political winds of change were blowing with an unprecedented turbulence. Canada was still a vast geographical landmass sparsely populated with communities separated by rugged terrain and challenged by an austere climate. The confederation of Canada was still new with its regional communities linked by a strong centrist government. People of different languages, traditions, and backgrounds were cast together and connected primarily by the common thread of an evolving national identity. It is against this backdrop that the historical evolution of Medicare emerged. There were also specific influences that caused public health insurance in this expansive country to become rooted as a universal seed.

Socio-Economic Influence

Despite Wilfred Laurier's affirmation for "sunny ways," much about early twentieth-century Canada was less than sunny. At the time, much of the Canadian population was struggling.

This was particularly true for Canadian farmers subjected to the vagaries of a harsh climate. Immigrants were attempting to find their way in a vast new land. Urban factory workers were subjected to draconian working conditions that included monotonous labour, long hours, and low wages. Miners and industrial workers experienced serf-like treatment at the hands of feudally modelled companies. Factions of returning World War I veterans found themselves disabled. Others became unemployed. As Canada transitioned from its voracious war economy to a post-war one, the Roaring Twenties were just beginning. Most of us envision the 1920s as a time of flappers, fun, and frolic. But the twenties were not fun times for everyone. While Canadians exhibited a general happiness that the war had ended and lives were returning to normal, working conditions had deteriorated. War-associated costs influenced inflation and the cost of living rose. Workers who had previously supported the war effort by working long hours for reduced wages found their post-war situations had not changed. Many working conditions in post-war Canada remained bleak. Miners continued to toil on their knees under three- and four-foot mine ceilings for a starvation wage.

In this pre-Medicare milieu, health care was not yet a public responsibility. Federal jurisdiction presided over the most basic of public health services while provincial jurisdictions regulated hospitals. Canadians succumbing to illness at this time were attended to by families, charitable organizations, community, and various church groups. Any access to physician services had to be paid out of pocket. This network was a private market system.

Unionism in Western Canada had burgeoned markedly after 1897.[4] During these times, the growth of union vitality and militancy there was unrivalled in other parts of the country. By 1919, significant precursor developments in the West led to the formation of an influential labour movement and social reforms that would later give birth to Medicare. These labour issues were instrumental in ushering in a new social order. The labour strife in jurisdictions like Saskatchewan paved the way for social reforms that would eventually come to include a publicly funded health insurance system. Saskatchewan would become a leader-jurisdiction, making it truly "the heart of the heartland." Although workers across Canada were collectively struggling, author and historian Clare Pentland explains that Western Canada had a unique social climate that made it ripe for unprecedented reforms. The West had suffered more casualties of war than other parts of Canada. Men in Western Canada enlisted and subsequently died in inordinate numbers. As profiteers amassed fortunes, conscripted men began to view their sacrifice as futile as they gained a collective awareness of their own exploitation from a labour perspective. "In general, it left a sense of injustice, sacrifice, and entitlement that contributed to the fervour and brittleness of western behaviour."[5]

A second feature of Western Canada's uniqueness was how unionism developed. Western unionism developed as a distinct philosophy of policies and practices invented and designed to protect the rights of workers. In Canada's expansion after 1897, the West was the vanguard of labour reform, with Winnipeg as its centrifugal force. As Pentland explains, "… the land was wider and rawer than in the East, the scale of operations larger, the capitalists more ruthless and often absentees."[6]

A third distinctive feature was Western Canada's workforce. Pentland described this as "the most wide awake and informed labour force in the world. They worked well, but wanted a just reward, and readily formed unions to get it."[7] Isolationism, related to natural and geographical forces, rendered many

Western Canadian communities relatively insular. The immense dedication to work and the culture of production was met with an equally tenacious, industrial style of unionism. Between 1900–1919, wages failed to keep pace with the cost of living and wages for certain groups like western mine workers, fell drastically. Workers turned to unions to seek protection within these larger socioeconomic modes of production.

A fourth feature in the western landscape was the emergence of the political philosophy known as syndicalism. While it became a dominant labour philosophy of the 1900s, conditions in Western Canada made workers turn to it naturally. Syndicalism advanced transferring ownership and control of the means of production and distribution to workers' unions. It favoured unification of the working class by way of direct action such as striking. It also purported to be grass roots: composed for and of "the worker." As Pentland recalls, "The meanness of employers, geographic isolation and, frequently, the remoteness or hostility of government, left workers squarely dependent on their own resources, and led them to look favourably on the syndicalist devices of direct action and the sympathetic strike, and on the solidarity of the working class…"[8] This confluence of distinctly western features would create a landscape that spawned one of the most profoundly influential labour strikes in Canadian history.

The Winnipeg General Strike of 1919 was a salient antecedent to the formation of a political movement that emanated directly from western workers and their early-twentieth-century situation.

Pentland insists, "A great general strike, like a revolution, exposes the anatomy of a society…"[9] In early May 1919, metal-trade workers in Winnipeg staged several strikes. They were negotiating with employers for improved working conditions, better wages, and job improvements. By May 15, 1919, discussions by western labour union leaders broke down and a general strike ensued. Shortly afterwards, 30,000 additional workers left their jobs in support of the metal workers. Public-sector employees of all stripes joined the strikers in an unprecedented show of support.[10] The strike closed factories, halted retail trade, and crippled transportation routes. Polemic perceptions ensued. Strikers and their supporters viewed the strike as a peaceful, collective means to achieve bargaining rights and adequate living wages. Employers and their supporters viewed the strike as a revolutionary force designed to usurp economic control. In June of 1919, the Mounted Police charged into the striking crowd, which resulted in thirty-plus casualties, numerous arrests, and two fatalities. Labour leaders were arrested, including a protestant minister by the name of J. S. Woodsworth. Woodsworth would later form an alliance with Medicare architect Tommy Douglas as one of the founding leaders of the Co-operative Commonwealth Party (CCF). By the end of June 1919, no match for the suppression tactics of government and employers, the strikers were forced to return to work.[11] The strike left hungry workers little choice but to terminate their efforts. But the defeat of the Winnipeg strikers proved to be a Cadmean win for government. Two years after the strike, Canada mandated a minimum-wage standard for workers. The strike had also given rise to continued political discussions and social action that eventually led to the formation of the CCF, the party that would eventually launch Medicare.

Any exuberance of the Roaring Twenties came to a crashing halt in the fall of 1929. Sweeping social disillusionment gripped the world after the stock market crash. That disillusionment shifted socio-economic orientation around the world. There was no work and no money, and inflation was soaring. Family fortunes were lost. Homes and farms were abandoned. Citizens stood in long soup lines to be fed. Others traversed the country in boxcars seeking any source of employment. Western Canada—in areas like Saskatchewan—was really hit hard. In a parallel disaster, the prairies also succumbed to years of drought. In some jurisdictions in Saskatchewan, ninety percent of the population had no income.[12]

The rich suddenly found themselves poor, and the poor increasingly destitute. Naivety had been seared away on the First World War battlefields. Resentment rapidly replaced resilience. The Great Depression heralded a social turning point for Canada. Municipalities were forced to bear the brunt of social and medical services, provinces soon found themselves unable to shoulder the cost of medical services, and physicians faced stacks of unpaid bills. There became a growing demand for government to step in and provide a social minimum for Canadians.

Pressure began to mount from the citizenry and from professional associations. As Canadian author Antonia Maioni points out, "Although unpaid service was already a problem for doctors in the 1920s, it reached crisis proportions in the 1930s. The Canadian Medical Association (CMA) attempted to push governments to set up medical relief to alleviate the financial burden of non-remunerated care. The most drastic action came in Manitoba where physicians in Winnipeg temporarily withdrew all but emergency services to relief recipients to protest the absence of a medical relief policy that would offer payment to doctors."[13] The situation became so dire in rural Saskatchewan that the government began to provide some assistance to doctors, and by 1933, the Saskatchewan Medical Association formally endorsed health insurance.

Out of the economic adversity of the '30s came an epiphany.

Canadians had seen (and lived) the result of what happens when the health of a society is left solely to the devices of market forces. A decade earlier Canadians had marched off to war. War profiteers had made inordinate amounts of money and soldiers had seen how government could—when forced by a crisis—administer to the wounded and medically indigent. But once the war had ended, those medical services were unavailable at home. With no social safety net and people suffering from the grim economic conditions of the '30s, Canada suddenly seemed like a ruthless place to live.

This socio-economic reality began to change the way Canadians envisioned their society. As author Linda McQuaig reinforces, "If there was one lesson that Canadians had learned from the bitter days of the depressions of the '30s, it was the vulnerability of all Canadians—particularly those with children—to the swings of the economy. What Canadians wanted was a system that would protect them from the arbitrary dictates of the marketplace."[14] The greatest economic devastation had led to a transformation of the Canadian perspective. By 1939, Canadians found themselves marching off to another world war, but as author Michael Bradley asserts, "Canadians didn't march off to World War II with the blind and naive patriotism that characterized World War I. They marched off, but out of a sense of grim duty and with a wary and somewhat cynical eye on their government and military leaders."[15] The socio-economic conditions had permeated the diaphanous veil of war-time governmental propaganda. The winds had changed and were about to blow a bluster across the West and, eventually, across all of Canada.

IN THE BEGINNING

Political Influence

Although it was in post-World War II Canada that Medicare took its first great exhalation, the embryonic cells of Medicare had started to take form in the '20s and '30s. Coerced out of socio-economic necessity, organizations such as the Saskatchewan Anti-Tuberculin League were formed in 1911. By 1929, the league was providing tuberculosis care to patients free of charge, rendering Saskatchewan the first Canadian province to do so. In 1919, British Columbia had pushed for reforms allowing for health insurance coverage. Federal participation led to ongoing Royal Commissions. By the time discussions resumed, the effects of the Depression had ransacked the country. Although a health insurance bill did pass in the BC legislature in 1936, discussion dragged on until the end of the decade. When BC Liberals were returned to power in 1937, they formally sacked what would have arguably been their greatest progressive health reform package.[16] In 1933, the Saskatchewan Medical Association was also lobbying for health insurance to help cover their stock-piled costs resulting from the Depression. Although health insurance permeations had meandered throughout provincial and federal agendas prior to World War II, it wasn't until after the war that a Canadian public health care system would finally become a reality.

Thomas Clement Douglas was born on October 20, 1904, in Falkirk, Scotland. His parents immigrated to Canada (Winnipeg) in 1910. The Douglas family had no way of knowing when they arrived in Canada that their six-year-old boy would one day leave an indelible mark upon Canadian history. It was one hundred years after his birth, when Tommy Douglas would go on to be voted, by Canadians of all stripes, the greatest Canadian in history.

At the age of six, Douglas suffered a knee injury that left him with chronic osteomyelitis. Frequently on crutches, he was pulled to school on a sled by two immigrant boys who spoke little English. Their kindness seems to have left a lasting impression on him for years to come. Not able to afford the expertise of specialists, the Douglas family feared Tommy would eventually lose his leg. A serendipitous meeting with an orthopaedic surgeon who spotted young Douglas in a hospital ward altered Douglas's future forever. The surgeon, Dr. R. H. Smith, gave Tommy an operation in exchange for the opportunity to instruct his students during the procedure. The operation was successful. Afterward, Douglas, who went on to play sports, was changed by the echoing reality that his leg had been saved by a stroke of luck from a chance encounter.[17]

Douglas later entered the Baptist ministry. He studied at Brandon College and financed his studies by preaching at small churches on the weekends. In 1930, he was ordained and eventually took up residence at the Calvary United Church in Weyburn, Saskatchewan. Throughout the '30s, Douglas and his wife engaged in numerous community organizations. They opened their family home to youth in need and organized a local job agency to help people find employment. To help people left destitute by the Depression, his church basement was filled with bedding and second-hand clothes supplied to him by affiliate churches. As a grass-roots local communitarian, he actively became involved in the 1931 Estevan Mine Strike. During this strike, miners working and living in deplorable conditions clashed with mine owners over the formation of a union related to wages and working conditions. Before the strike, miners had had their 37.5 cents per hour wage reduced to 32.5 cents by mine owners.[18]

The beleaguered miners had accepted this, supplementing

IN THE BEGINNING

their meagre earnings with farming during the summer. But drought hit the prairies and the supplementary farm work also dried up. By 1931, the miners were paid by coal weight and were often cheated by owners who skimped on the weight.[19] The miners were also forced to buy goods from the company store, whose prices were notably higher than other stores. This kept them and their families hopelessly indebted to company-store owners. Seeing no way forward, the miners organized a union, and by September 8, the union went on strike to improve working conditions. Professional organizers (with alleged support of Soviet Russia) came from Saskatoon to support the miners. This alarmed corporate interests, who in turn persuaded the government to dispatch the RCMP to Estevan. A by-law was passed prohibiting demonstrations, but this was never communicated to the striking miners. A clash between the miners (and their supporters) and police broke out and rapidly escalated into a riot. Three men were shot and killed by police. Soon after the strike, Douglas was labelled as a communist for affiliating with the striking miners.[20]

After Estevan, Douglas grew frustrated by the frequent occurrence of strikes and violent responses associated with the demands of workers and farmers and he wrote to J. S. Woodsworth, a Winnipeg Labour MP (Winnipeg Strike). Woodsworth got a similar letter from a Regina alderman, M. J. Coldwell. Eventually, the three men would meet to discuss the labour injustices of the day. Their meeting resulted in the birth of the Co-operative Commonwealth Federation (CCF) party. The three drew up the Regina Manifesto united in one belief—there had to be a coalition of farmers and labourers in lieu of pockets of unconnected workers acting in a reactionary fashion. The CCF worked relentlessly to secure prairie co-ops; advance security of tenure for farmers and labourers; make the federal government accountable for unemployment; and design and support the socialization of provincial and later, pan-Canadian, health services.[21]

It wasn't an easy road. These compassionate social reformers were naive to the rigours of political dogma. On many occasions, political resistance to Douglas and the CCF became personal. Liberal saboteurs attempted to pour sugar and sand into the gas tank of his car. On another occasion, they attempted to destroy his car by loosening wheel nuts. Decades later, Douglas's daughter Shirley reaffirmed that her father (and the CCF) were never given equal radio time compared to other political parties of the day. One of the most prominent political speeches in Canadian history given by Douglas pertaining to the Farm Security Act of 1944 had to be communicated over commercial radio stations. CBC Saskatchewan had refused to broadcast it.[22]

Proponents of capitalism formed committees and sub-committees to construct CCF resistance. Simpsons department store even offered to help distribute anti-CCF propaganda. Despite these attempts, in 1935, Douglas was elected as a federal MP, a position he held until the 1940s.

As World War II began, Douglas and the CCF wanted to ensure "there would be no conscription of men without an equal conscription of wealth"[23] and unlike the First World War, Douglas didn't want thousands of young lives to be sacrificed for "capitalist war economics." By late in the war, the CCF was the most popular party in the country. During the election of 1944, Douglas eagerly returned home to Saskatchewan to fill the position of provincial CCF leader. He defeated the Liberals in a landslide victory. Forty-seven out of the fifty-two seats were won by the CCF, with sixty percent of the armed forces vote cast in favour of the CCF that year.[24]

Throughout history, there remains a critical interplay between war and health. The process of triage, for example, was born on the battlefield. In post-war Canada, the effects of war influenced the development of a universal health insurance. Canadians returned from World War II wounded and distrustful—with no inclination to be left to the punitive dictates of market forces. They had lived that reality and they had no plans of returning to similar levels of exploitation. They wanted the government they had served to take some degree of ownership for the deprivation that soldiers, labourers, farmers, and their families had endured.

After passing the Farms Security Act in 1944, Douglas and the CCF focussed their efforts upon the implementation of health insurance. The CCF procured the expertise of a group of physicians that conducted surveys on people's health needs and on the programs that could best meet those requirements based on the resources they had. The CCF was met with stiff opposition from the province's doctors, but on New Year's Day in 1947, fresh with a mandate from the people, "The Hospital Insurance Plan" was implemented.[25] The first patient under the plan was a new mother having a child—a testament to the inclusive and progressive nature of the Douglas plan.

In 1948, Douglas and the CCF were returned to power based largely on support for the Hospital Insurance Plan.[26] Douglas would eventually win five consecutive provincial elections over the course of his career. The final step for comprehensive Medicare was initiated soon after the election of 1948. It wouldn't be until 1959 that Douglas would announce the expanded Medicare package that "… included a comprehensive system of insurance for all health needs,"[27] consisting of more than just coverage of hospitalization costs.

By July 1, 1962, Saskatchewan launched the first government-run health insurance for hospital and doctor visits. But there would be more challenges ahead for Douglas and the CCF. The dark days of the Depression had disappeared as had the stacks of unpaid medical bills. In 1959, the climate of Canadian post-war prosperity helped reshape physician remuneration. The new Medicare scheme did not allow for extra billing provisions, and physicians viewed this as an overt form of government control.

The Saskatchewan College of Physicians and Surgeons (SCPS) launched a full assault on Medicare that included mandating their members to cover the cost of college literature containing anti-Medicare propaganda. The doctors used scare tactics based on "suggestions" emanating from the college. SCPS also published doctor-to-patient speeches like the ones that outlined how menopausal women might find themselves admitted to mental facilities should Medicare be enforced:

> In addition to suggesting to middle-aged women that menopausal tension "might" be justification for "referring" them to a mental hospital under Medicare, the good doctors of Saskatchewan were fond of telling pregnant women that "this might be the last pre-natal check-up they could have" before Medicare was enforced.[28]

Physicians organized rallies supported by business, where they carried effigies of Tommy Douglas hanging from a noose. In the end, the doctors (with support from the Canadian Medical Association) went on strike the day Medicare was launched on July 1, 1962. They did so by withdrawing all but emergency services to the people of Saskatchewan.

Douglas confronted the doctors directly and flew in British doctors to cover the strike. He also went one step further, indicating that he was more than willing to make the interim status of the British doctors permanent if the doctors of Saskatchewan continued to strike. The strike developed into a public-relations nightmare for the Saskatchewan College of Physicians and Surgeons.

Douglas insisted that the SCPS cease their scare tactics and get back to treating patients.[29] Ethical concerns surrounding the withdrawal of care mounted. Three weeks later, as their public support waned, the Saskatchewan doctors returned to work. They accepted the novel billing format via Medical Services Insurance (MSI) in exchange for what some historians would eventually call "the great compromise": doctors retaining their rights to act as autonomous contractors. Fee-for-service had taken its first breath.

After more delays and protracted federal-provincial cost-sharing discussions, single-payer health insurance finally emerged. It burgeoned from province to province, and by 1972, all of Canada had implemented universal public health insurance. Douglas and his followers had prevailed. Generations of Canadians would be forever in their debt.

Canadian sponsored health insurance was also largely influenced by Canada's political ties with Britain. Canada had a long history as a British colony and had close ties to Britain during the war. The Canadian parliamentary system was modelled after the British parliamentary system. The cooperative system on the prairies was also ensconced in British tradition.

Throughout Europe, post-war reconstruction grew to represent a litany of social packages that would protect society from the whims of the market forces that had caused so much destitution during the Depression. Emerging from the ashes of World War II, Britain saw society as needing to be better protected and interconnected vis-à-vis a social welfare system. This was in glaring contrast to the United States, which associated the welfare state with "handouts" and weakness and as counterproductive to market forces.

Leonard Marsh, who studied under Sir William Beveridge in Britain, pioneered social reform in Canada. Marsh's policies were based on Beveridge's blueprint of the British welfare state. Most historians agree that *The Report on Social Security for Canada,* authored by Marsh (1943), paved the way for the welfare state in Canada. As Marsh explains:

> ... social security payments are not money lost. The social insurances, and even some straightforward disbursements like children's allowances, are investments in morale and health, in greater family stability and from both material and psychological viewpoints, in human productive efficiency. They demand personal and community responsibilities... [and] in the eyes of most of the people who are beneficiaries, give a more evident meaning to the ideas of common effort and national solidarity.[30]

Geographical Influence

Canadian pioneers settled mainly in four areas of Canada. These included: Nova Scotia, the St. Lawrence River Valley, the prairies, and the Fraser River Valley along the Pacific Coast. These areas were most conducive to mixed farming, which could sustain food production and formed the basis for ancillary industries like fishing, mining, and manufacturing.[31] They were widely separated by rough terrain, vast distances, and mountain ranges. A harsh climate added to the isolation. In such bleak conditions, early settlers discovered that their survival required interdependence, and so these early Canadians turned to each other for support, which came in the form of neighbours, relatives, churches, and community organizations. Neighbours became use to helping each other even when their own resources were limited. In rural areas, this was particularly true. On the prairies, major relief came in the formation of cooperatives adopted from the British system. As industrialization spread, young adults set out in search of work in more urban areas, often sending money home to support families. Charities, missions, and churches helped the misfortunate and in coal mining towns like Glace Bay, strong unions developed to advocate for workers living in abject poverty. Snowdrifts, droughts, rugged terrain, vast distances, and mountains demonstrated to early settlers that collectivism was an essential element of survival. It therefore came as no surprise when discussions surrounding a health care system arose, Canadians would gravitate towards a system that was collective, egalitarian, and compassionate in nature—a system reminiscent of two immigrant boys who once pulled a disabled Tommy Douglas across the frozen Saskatchewan snow.

Federalism

Federalism offers both deterrents and advantages for policy development. During times of austerity, it affords federal politicians the opportunity to contract their political and economic involvement. This permits each level of government (federal and provincial) to engage in a jurisdictional tug-of-war stalling ownership and thwarting progress. Federalism, with its specific emphasis on policy development, also has the ability to foster competition among its provinces.

As Canadians, we have all witnessed multifarious examples of this, like the time Newfoundland and Labrador premier, Danny Williams, ordered Canadian flags to be removed from all official buildings in his province after a battle with Ottawa. The move was in retaliation for the federal government offering the premier what he felt was an unfair deal pertaining to offshore energy royalties and equalization payments. Williams felt his province was being unfairly targeted by the equalization formula process, whereby the richest provinces redistribute funds to the poorer provinces like Newfoundland.

In contrast, the structure of federalism allows for provincial experimentation and innovation as new political ideas and policies incubate. This federalist feature gives provincial policies the time to grow while "ironing out the wrinkles" during the development of new ideas. Such was the case with the implementation of hospital insurance within the province of Saskatchewan. Although a salient example of provincial innovation and policy development, the road to public health insurance within Saskatchewan wasn't an easy one. However, by the time the plan was ready to be implemented throughout the rest of Canada, the majority of challenges surrounding the policy had been resolved by the province. It remains for historians and Canadians alike to decide whether universal health care within Canada would have been as successful without the initial Saskatchewan "experiment."

The vast and sparsely populated Canada became the first country in North America to implement a national, publicly funded health care system. Dire socio-economic situations, tumultuous political developments, post-war reconstruction plans, geography, and a federalist structure were all contributing factors in giving the system breath. The development and acquisition of publicly funded health care in Canada is a story rife with heroes, struggles, determination, humanitarianism, and idealism. It is a dynamic past that's worth remembering, more so today than ever—as we face the countervailing forces that now seek to destroy it.

Chapter 2

THE HEALTH CARE PRIVATIZATION MYTH

*The strength of the pack is the wolf,
and the strength of the wolf is the pack.*

—Rudyard Kipling

The health of a nation is akin to a living, breathing ecosystem. If a society cannot agree upon universal health services, it revokes the possibility that anything more comprehensive can be achieved. If it lacks the primal cohesiveness to care for the sick whether they can pay or not, it has already succumbed to the most pervasive of diseases.

Severely injured wolves have been so attended to by their pack that they have recovered from broken jaws and limbs. Wolf hunters are aware that they can exploit the pack's extraordinary level of loyalty to their sick. When a lone wolf is caught in a trap, the pack may risk all to rescue the injured wolf. Is the level of loyalty and standard of care in the current American health care system below that of the wolf pack?

One of the most damning indictments about the privatization of health services is that it creates unnatural divisions within society. Privatization of health services contravenes the natural communitarianism espoused by the wolf pack. The pack could teach US legislators a thing or two.

One cannot assert that they live in "the land of the free" or "the home of the brave" when treatment of the sick rests solely on their ability to pay. Privatization is an insidious disease. It reinforces that some are worth saving while others are not. It is an ominous reminder that "a house divided against itself cannot stand."

The privatization of health services is a disaster in terms of cost; infant/neonatal/maternal mortality rates; overall disease burden; life expectancy; bankruptcies related to health costs; and the number of people that die because of lack of access to health services. This has been evidenced throughout the decades. Despite this, the suffering persists. The same forces that dominate American health care services have expanded into Canada. This is a development Canadians must resist.

As Canadians turned towards collectivism and the formation of the welfare state, Americans turned towards individualism and the formation of a pro-capitalist society. That is not to say they didn't attempt to formulate a public system of health insurance—they did, several times. Like Douglas in Canada, they were also met by the competing forces of big business, professional medical associations, American conservatism, and the Dixiecrats. Where Douglas and his Canadian cohort succeeded, numerous American governments failed. Corporate interests prevailed, leaving the allocation of health services within the United States abandoned to market forces. This complete submission to the market made the United States an international outlier in the provision of health care services.

Much of the US system is predominately privatized,

unregulated, and run by large corporate conglomerates. The question remains, why, in those early days, were US legislators unable to implement some variation on universal health insurance? Paradoxically, American society maintains a sycophantic obsession with individualism and "freedom" of choice. Yet millions of Americans are anything but free to access the health care they deserve because many services remain far beyond their financial reach. In a society that prides itself on individualism and freedom, how did health care services become so enslaved to corporate forces? World-renown linguist and philosopher, Noam Chomsky, articulates this contradiction. In an interview for *Truthout* with C. J. Polychroniou, Chomsky, explains how the origins of corporate America helped shape this dichotomy:

> ... the political economy and social structure of the United States developed in a kind of *tabla rasa*... mass killing of the indigenous nations cleared the ground for invading settlers... that led to the rise of a society of individual farmers, and also, thanks to slavery, substantial control of the product that fuelled the industrial revolution: cotton.

Chomsky continues:

> American society lacked the traditional social stratification and autocratic political structure of Europe, and the various measures of social support that developed unevenly and erratically. There has been ample state intervention in the economy from the outset... but without general support systems. As a result, US society is, to an unusual extent,

business-run... the business community is also set on containing or demolishing the "political power of the masses," which it deems as a serious "hazard to industrialists."

This is evidenced by Chomsky's explanation of the US labour movement:

US labor history is unusually violent... labor remains relatively weak in the US in comparison to similar societies. It is constantly battling even for survival as a significant organized force in the society, under particularly harsh attack since the Reagan years."[32]

David Himmelstein, professor of public policy at City University of New York, and Karen Palmer, professor of health science at Simon Fraser University, appear to endorse Chomsky's theory. According to Himmelstein, if there's one all-encompassing reason why a country like the US didn't develop a universal health care system, it's because, "... there hasn't been a labor party in the US that represents the working class." Karen Palmer also reaffirms, "It is the core value of the labor party to bring social solidarity."[33]

When pressed about why Americans continue to allow "concentrated private capital to undermine necessities of life in the interests of profit and power," Chomsky indicates that there is a profound democratic deficit in an atomized society, lacking the kind of popular associations and organizations that enable the public to participate in a meaningful way in determining the course of political, social, and economic affairs. These would crucially include a strong and participatory labor movement and actual political parties growing from public deliberation and participation instead of elite-run candidate-producing groups that pass for political parties.[34]

Chomsky also refers to America's leading twentieth-century social philosopher, John Dewy, when speaking about the current state of corporate dominance in the US: "Power today resides in control of the means of production, exchange, publicity, transportation and communication. Whoever owns them rules the life of the country."

Dewy believed, "until these institutions are in the hands of the public... politics will remain the shadow cast on society by big business."[35] As long as US corporate forces continue to turn huge profits, they are not likely to relinquish their death-grip on what is currently an American health care plutocracy. Politicians aren't likely to help either. As reporter Annalisa Merelli points out, "Both the GOP and the Democratic Party are under the influence of the medical-industrial complex: In 2016, hospitals and nursing homes contributed over $95 million to electoral campaigns in the US, and the pharmaceutical sector gave nearly $250 million."[36]

Theodore Roosevelt, who had served as a Republican president from 1901–1909, had limited success in getting Congress to act on any health laws. He eventually broke away from his traditional Republican Party after he lost the nomination to William H. Taft in 1912. Upset by the Republican Party's shift to the right, Roosevelt and a few of his colleagues formed a new, progressive party later referred to as the "Bull Moose Party." The party's platform was built on Roosevelt's "square deal," which was a progressive set of domestic reforms that included a national health service. The party was also intent on removing the influence of big business from politics, which they asserted dominated both main political parties and was the root of corruption within the political system. Although he campaigned vigorously, Roosevelt lost the election once he was no longer supported by "big business."[37]

In 1913, Democrat Woodrow Wilson was elected president and aspired to have a National Health Insurance plan, but this did not occur during his presidency.

Franklin Roosevelt attempted to add health insurance to his 1935 Social Security Act legislation. As the bill neared completion, Roosevelt abdicated from the idea of including health insurance, fearful it would squash or stall the entire legislation. In the end, it was left out of the 1935 bill "… due in large part to the opposition of business and the medical profession allied with conservative interests in congress."[38] In 1944, Roosevelt focused on an expansion of the Economic Bill of Rights that included the right to medical care and the ability to achieve good health. Roosevelt died before these rights could be incorporated into the constitution.

Roosevelt's successor, President Harry Truman, seemed equally committed to the creation of a national health insurance system. But by 1946, he also had made little headway due to stiff opposition from a Republican Congress and the American Medical Association. Merelli reminds us the AMA set out on a campaign using "anti-communist sentiment to terrorize people against the spectre of 'socialized medicine.'"[39]

Maioni confirms, "Truman tried no less than three times to press forward health insurance legislation, but as with Bill Clinton, his failure would be a crucial factor in the Republicans' regaining of Congress and, eventually, the presidency. It would also be the reason that the Democratic leadership was wary of re-embarking on a doomed path."[40]

The US and Canada embarked on divergent paths towards the development of their respective health care systems. Canada combated countervailing forces of universal single-payer, while the US did not. Returning to Chomsky's assessment, we are reminded that Tommy Douglas's CCF party was directly from the people. He and his cohort had lived the poverty of their time first-hand. In glaring contrast to the US political system of the day, the CCF sought to limit corporate profit, not expand it. They were a party that rallied behind struggling farmers, workers, labour rights, the indigent, and the sick. They were representative of their constituents. To date, there has not been a party in US history comparable to Douglas's CCF. The Democratic Party, which boasts ties with unions according to Merelli, has "always had a strong pro-business soul which prevented it from focusing primarily on the needs of the working class."[41] Among other reasons, America's inability to develop a party emanating directly from the people contributed to its failure to secure a universal public health care system. Chomsky's theory prevails—until the American people decide they have had enough.

It seems as if the American people have a long fuse. The private system is fraught with gross inequality, poor outcomes, burgeoning costs, financial anxiety, and unnecessary suffering. Privatization must be recognized as a failure in the allocation of health care services. To those forces seeking to privatize health care elsewhere, you need not look towards your imagination, speculate costs, or ponder outcomes. It's all readily available. Every disturbing feature.

In 2018, the US continued its lead in outspending all its

Organization for Economic Co-operation and Development (OECD) counterparts. As a percentage of its GDP, it spent 16.9 percent, almost twice as much as the average OECD country. The OECD average spending on health (as a percentage of GDP in 2018) was 8.8 percent ($5,055 per person). The US spending was considerably higher compared to the average, where the other members have predominately universal health care systems. France came in at 11.2 percent, Germany 11.2 percent, Sweden 11 percent, Canada 10.7 percent, Netherlands 9.9 percent, Australia 9.3 percent, New Zealand 9.3 percent, and the U.K. 9.8 percent. Despite its run-away spending, the US had the lowest life expectancy, highest suicide rates, highest chronic disease burden, and an obesity rate that was twice as high as the OECD average. [42]

The US GDP for 2017 was a staggering $19.39 trillion. Not only does health spending in the US briskly outpace the other OECD countries as a percentage of a GDP, but it's also a percentage of an unimaginable amount of money. That is just part of the story. When we talk about coverage and efficiency, the story becomes darker. While Canadian Medicare covers every citizen, the story south of the border is quite different. In 2018, despite the astronomical spending (even after the application of the Affordable Care Act), the US system had 28.5 million people uninsured.[43] That amounts to approximately seventy-seven percent of the entire Canadian population. The statistics around children without access to health care services are equally frightening. For the same year, 4.3 million children under the age of nineteen remained uninsured.[44] To put that into a Canadian perspective, if the total populations of Prince Edward Island, Nova Scotia, New Brunswick, Newfoundland and Labrador, the Yukon, Nunavut, the Northwest Territories, and Saskatchewan were all children, they would all be uninsured. That would still leave another half a million children uninsured. That means if a child has a suspected appendicitis, strep throat, unexplained fever, or even Covid-19 symptoms, uninsured families must really weigh if they can afford to take their child to be seen by a health care professional. This financial anxiety may lead parents to play a waiting game, a game that could prove to be deadly when a critically ill child is put at such risk. This race to the bottom is what market forces do best when they seek to commodify the uncommodifiable.

In 2017, as the US economy galloped along at its astonishing pace with declining unemployment rates and a robust performance, the number of children uninsured rose by about 276,000. According to a study released by Georgetown University's Centre for Children and Families, this reversal is the first in a decade of previous gains.[45] This is further proof that even during record economic gains, market forces do not distribute health care services equitably.

According to the US Census Bureau, employer-based health insurance remains the most common type of health insurance in 2017, covering 56 percent of the population.[46] This means that 56 percent of the population live with the jarring reality that a job loss translates into loss of health insurance. People employed in stressful job situations or jobs they are ill-suited for may be unable to move as they fear losing their medical coverage.

When we look at the underinsured, the situation remains dismal. According to a Commonwealth Fund study in 2016, twenty-eight percent of adults in the US aged nineteen to sixty-four were underinsured. That amounts to about forty-one million people.[47] That number represents the entire population of Canada plus an additional four million people. Underinsurance can seriously harm a family's livelihood. For citizens opting for low-cost plans, this means the lower the premiums, the more likely you are to pay much higher deductibles. Lower premiums could mean mandatory diagnostic tests are not covered, and if you do not have additional funds or savings, costs can mount rapidly. This could rapidly leave the underinsured person or family in serious economic peril.

Unlike Canada, medical debt in the US is the number-one source of personal bankruptcy in the country.[48] Researchers Sarah Cliff and Margot Sanger-Katz maintain Americans owed about $140 billion in unpaid medical bills in 2020. As shocking as that may seem, it does not include medical debt that Americans are currently paying in instalments or have placed on credit cards or credit lines. When you add this debt to the $140 billion sitting in collection agencies, the number is much higher. Many of the debt-ridden are people who have insurance, but the sky-high deductibles coupled with escalating premiums have plummeted them into bankruptcy. Sarah Gantz, of the *Philadelphia Inquirer,* relays a story of cancer patient Sharon Kelly, whose high-deductible insurance plan required her to pay $7,000 out of pocket. Halfway through 2019, she was diagnosed with cancer and had to spend the second half of the year paying her deductible only to start all over again in January of the following year. As the bills grew, Ms. Kelly was forced to stop her chemotherapy treatments and stop going to the doctor. Despite being insured, the costs were just too overwhelming. There is also no cap on out-of-pocket expenses for patients registered in Medicare Advantage plans.[49]

In the richest country in the world, with such a robust economy and with over seventeen percent of that GDP being utilized for health spending, why are so many people uninsured, under-insured, or bankrupt from medical expenses? Where is the money being spent?

Despite having utilization rates like other countries, the US continues to spend almost double the amount of money compared to the other high-spending countries.

> ... administrative costs of care (activities related to planning, regulating, and managing health systems and services) accounted for 8 percent in the US vs a range of 1 percent to 3 percent in other countries. For pharmaceutical costs, spending per capita was $1,443 in the US vs a range of $466 to $939 in other countries. Salaries of physicians and nurses were higher in the US; for example, generalist physician salaries were $218,173 in the US compared with a range of $86,607 to $154,126 in other countries.[50]

In study after study, the inordinate and burdensome weight of US administrative costs are stark. This troubling phenomenon is demonstrated by researchers in an article in *Health Affairs*. In a formidable attempt to analyze and cross-compare US health administrative costs to the administrative costs of other nations with various health care systems, the researchers assembled a team of international health policy experts. They studied the administrative costs of eight nations: Canada, Netherlands, United States, England, Scotland, France, Germany, and Wales. For each of the other countries, the researchers reviewed detailed documentation surrounding hospital expense categories and then mapped the data against the US categories. To remain accurate, where uncertainties were revealed, Medicare auditors were consulted. The highest hospital costs devoted to administration were in the US, coming in at 25.3 percent. Scotland and Canada, with single-payer systems, were the lowest at 11.59 percent and 12.42 percent respectively. The authors further concluded reducing US per-capita spending for hospital administrative costs to Scottish or Canadian levels would have (in 2011) saved a staggering $150 billion. The study suggests reducing administrative costs in the US would best be accomplished using a simpler and less market-oriented payment scheme.[51] Billing protocols within for-profit institutions remains complex and cumbersome. This is because there are multiple payers, multiple interfaces between insurers, multiple employers, complex accounting structures, collection departments, and a myriad of different forms and payment schemes. Hospital administration costs continue to rise. "US hospital administrative costs rose from 23.5 percent of total hospital costs ($97.816 billion) in 2000 to 25.3 percent ($215.369 billion) in 2011. In the same time period, the hospital administration share of the GDP rose from .98 percent to 1.43 percent. The proportion spent on administration by Canadian hospitals fell slightly from 1999 (12.9 percent) to 2011 (12.4 percent)."[52]

In a heartbreaking 2019 interview with Nicole Smith-Holt, the mother of twenty-six-year-old Alec, Smith-Holt tells CBS correspondent Anna Werner that her son died because he couldn't afford his insulin. When Alec turned twenty-six, he was no longer covered by his parents' insurance plan. He had just moved into his own apartment. His parents did not know that Alec was struggling to pay for his insulin. When the cost of the drug became too high, he started rationing his insulin supply.[53] That approach became deadly. On June 22, 2017, Alec attempted to purchase insulin but was short money. He made a decision to wait until his next payday. Three days shy of that pay day, on June 27, 2017, young Alec Smith was found dead in his apartment after lapsing into a diabetic coma.

Between 2002 and 2013, the price of insulin has tripled in the US, and since 2008, several of the top insulin producers raised the price of the drug ten times. The attorney general for Minnesota at the time of Alec Smith's death launched a lawsuit against the top three insulin manufacturers alleging "deceptive, misleading, and misrepresentative list prices."[54]

By the end of April 2019, caravans of young type-one diabetics were making the ten-hour trip from the US to Canada to buy insulin. Insulin is about one-tenth the cost in Canada compared to the US. Lija Greenseid was with the travellers and spoke to CBC's Carol Off. When asked about the cost, Greenseid said, "So, a vial of NovoRapid in Canada costs about $30 US, and in the United States … costs about $300." Greenseid also told CBC that her friend was paying $600 per month for her insulin in the US. But that isn't all, she goes on to explain that many of the shoppers do have insurance, but they have high deductible plans. In her case, she paid $27,000 in health insurance in the preceding year, but the first $7,000 had to be paid directly out of pocket.[55]

These are the lucky ones with health insurance plans. In the richest country in the world, young type-one diabetics are driving to the land of universal health care in caravans, trying to stay alive.

Profit is driving the cost of insulin. Due to sluggish regulatory environments, US drug companies can keep raising the cost of the life-saving medicine. Author Julia Belluz explains, "… the US is an outlier on money spent on the drug, representing only 5 percent of the global insulin market and generating almost half of the pharmaceutical industry's insulin revenue."[56] While the profiteering and escalating costs persist, people will continue to suffer many of the disastrous consequences of untreated diabetes. Or, as in Alec Smith's case, die from them.

Alec Smith is not the only young person who has died from drug rationing. On April 26, 2017, twenty-two-year-old Antavia Worsham was found dead in her apartment by her brother. She had been working two jobs to try and pay her staggering insulin costs. Antavia was paying $1,200 to $1,300 per month for her insulin and, like Alec Smith, was trying to ration supplies. Her mom says, When my son found her in her bed, she had a pen in her bed, but it was empty." Antavia didn't have any insulin left.[57]

On June 28, 2019, twenty-one-year-old Jesimya David Scherer-Radcliff from Minnesota also died from insulin rationing. Alec's mom, Nicole Smith-Holt, attended his funeral. She reaffirmed big pharma's complicity in the deaths of both boys: "My son and Jesy, they were murdered. They were killed by Big Pharma. The cause of death should actually be on their death certificates, corporate greed."[58]

Twenty-seven-year-old Josh Wilkerson was another victim of corporate greed. He had matured out of his stepfather's insurance plan at twenty-six and, as a type-one diabetic, required insulin. Struggling to pay his rent, his student loans, and his $1,200 medical costs, Josh started rationing his insulin. The groom-to-be was found in a coma by his fiancée, Rose, after he failed to return her calls. His blood sugar was at a lethal level of 1700. A brain scan revealed he had suffered from brain swelling after a series of strokes. Shortly afterwards, he died. When asked what she would say to the board of insulin producer Eli Lilly, should she be afforded the opportunity, Erin Weaver, Josh's mother, replied, "According to your own website you claim to follow three core values: 1. Integrity, 2. Excellence, 3. Respect for people... in your goal toward a higher profit-margin, you have allowed yourselves to become murderers!! Does that fit into ANY of your three core values?"[59]

By the end of 2018, insulin-maker Eli Lilly readjusted its 2019 revenue estimates: "Lilly said its revenue was expected to be between $25.3 billion and $25.8 billion for the coming year also above estimate of $24.77 billion."[60] In addition, Lilly's tax rate fell to eighteen percent in 2018 down from 20.5 percent in 2017, thanks to new tax laws. This will allow Lilly to access more than $9 billion of cash and investments.[61]

It's not just insulin. Other drugs, like medications for many chronic illnesses are also soaring out of control due to the non-regulatory, free-market system. For patients with chronic debilitating neurological diseases like multiple sclerosis (MS), this has become an overwhelming burden. Like insulin, out-of-pocket costs for drugs used to treat everything from MS to epilepsy continue to soar. Specialists are sounding alarm bells, asserting those patients like young Alec Smith are trying to ease their financial burdens by skipping doses and rationing. It is worth reinforcing that many of these patients also have insurance plans, but deductibles and premiums still pose considerable financial obstacles. Judy George explains, "Out-of-pocket costs for prescription drugs to treat neurological disorders rose dramatically from 2004 to 2016, with MS medications showing the fastest increase, according to an analysis of private insurance claims."[62]

"The average out-of-pocket costs for people taking MS drugs soared twenty-fold over the study's twelve-year period…" according to doctor Brian Callaghan and colleagues of the University of Michigan.[63]

In the richest country in the world, medications to ease chronic illness are for many unattainable. If family deductibles are $14,000, in addition to soaring maintenance premiums, does this type of price gouging even constitute insurance? The exorbitant drug costs and overwhelming administrative and labour costs give rise to countless resultant systemic flaws. When the buyer is illness and the seller is privatization, the health and welfare of a nation are inevitably doomed.

As a busy working mother of three in the 1990s, I read Linda McQuaig's book *The Wealthy Banker's Wife*. In Chapter 1 of the book, she outlines how for-profit centres had sprung up across the US. These centres, where customers could go to sell their blood, predominated in poorer neighbourhoods.[64] The commodification of blood resonated with me. I wondered how such unbridled profiteering could translate into literal "blood money." I remember staring at blood products in ICUs after that, thinking, thank goodness I live in Canada where this does not exist. I remember thinking Canadians were fortunate to have a universal health care system, where this did not occur. As we are now aware, this is no longer the case.

There is a booming corporate enterprise in the US. It's called blood selling. In poor neighbourhoods across the country, people line up to donate their plasma for thirty to forty dollars per donation. In a country rife with wage stagnation and glaring income disparity, selling your blood is now a reliable income to help feed your family or pay rent. The centres are run by for-profit corporations, and if the stats are any indication, the multi-million-dollar industry is booming. It is a $19.7 billion global industry for the biotech companies that run these for-profit clinics.[65] Nicholas Scheffler tells us, "There are 601 plasma donation centers in the United States and 80 percent of these are located in America's poorer neighbourhoods. Since 2005, the number of donation centers has more than doubled."[66]

In the beginning, people frequented these centres for something extra, such as helping to finance a down payment. There is ample evidence to suggest people today are not selling their blood for anything extra but that more and more are doing so just to get by. ABC reporters, Alexa Valiente, Mark Abdelmalek, and Lauren Pearle profiled some low-income Americans who regularly sell their blood plasma. One of the donors has two small children and donates twice a week. On one occasion, he admitted to donating plasma to get $7.50 to buy his daughter a bathing suit and a cake for her birthday. Another donor also has two young children and works at Burger King. He also donates twice a week for the additional money. He told the journalists that he switches arms: "Right arm I use Friday. Other I use Sunday. I switch up every time… It's a 21-gauge needle, so it's pretty thick."[67]

Obviously, the blood products are sold to recipients who can buy them or who have insurance plans that cover the cost. What happens if the donors themselves are uninsured or too poor to purchase a blood product they need? In a perverted twist of market logic, the blood of the poor can be harvested for a profit but is only given to those who can afford to buy it. Poor Americans are supplying blood to a market that excludes them. In a dystopian distortion such as this, for-profit centres continue to flip large profits while draining the blood of America's poor.

Regularly donating blood also carries with it a second associated hazard. Donating blood is an invasive procedure. As a nurse, I wondered how the donors would finance any treatment they might require as a result of the clinical risks associated with regular blood donation (infection, scar tissue, anemia, and the like). In a false economy such as this, donors are placed at increased risk yet remain socio-economically confined to poverty.

With respect to health care access, the story is also grim and may appear foreign to Canadians. The choice between paying your rent or accessing medical help has yet to be fully thrust upon present-day Canadians in the same way. In a system where lack of access is a reality, those consequences are deadly.

Envision Canada's beautiful Northwest Territories with an estimated population of 44,445 people in 2018. Then try and envision this entire population vanishing every year. That's how many people are dying every year from lack of access to health care in the US. It's sudden death and unnecessary suffering that could have been avoided. It's years of productivity lost. It's dreams, hopes, and futures dissolved. It's marriages, friendships, and family units all irrevocably broken. It is also—preventable.

It seems reasonable that if you are trapped in a cycle with no access to health care, your prognosis will be adversely affected. Realizing the significant relationship between access and mortality, researchers have long sought to place a number on how many patients die due to lack of access within the US system.

David Cecere, of Cambridge Health Alliance, cites a new study that finds 44,789 deaths occur annually as a result of lack of health insurance. "The study, which analyzed data from national surveys carried out by the Centers for Disease Control and Prevention (CDC), assessed death rates after considering education, income, and many other factors, including smoking, drinking, and obesity. It is estimated that the lack of health insurance causes 44,789 excess deaths annually." This study asserts that common disease killers such as kidney failure have now been surpassed by deaths associated with lack of medical insurance. It's another one of those astonishing statements. As a Canadian nurse, I found it difficult to comprehend. In the United States of America, lack of access to health care now kills more people than kidney disease. The study's co-author, Dr. Stephanie Woolhandler, also adds, "Historically, every other developed nation has achieved universal health care through some form of non-profit national health insurance. Our failure to do so means that all Americans pay higher health care costs, and 45,000 pay with their lives."[68] Until health care privatization is dismantled, a population equivalent to that of Canada's Northwest Territories will continue to vanish every year.

Georgeanne Koehler knows first-hand what it's like to be a family member of one of those vanishing patients. Her brother Billy died because his implanted defibrillator ceased to work after the battery stopped working. Billy suffered from an arrhythmia and required the device to live but a new battery cost thousands of dollars. This was a purchase Billy couldn't afford after losing his job and its accompanying health insurance, back in 2003. Billy eventually secured another job delivering pizzas, but this job didn't offer insurance. His attempts at buying a private health insurance plan were thwarted at every turn. Insurers cited their reason for denial of coverage was because he had a "pre-existing condition." In a heart-crushing admission, Georgeanne told journalist Arthur Delaney, "He drove two blocks, came to a stop sign, put his car in park, and slumped into his steering wheel."[69] Billy Koehler died because a battery change on a life-saving device was something he couldn't afford. He was denied that chance of survival because multi-million-dollar insurance companies refused him coverage. It's how life ends in a health care plutocracy.

So, what are the people to do? In a system that leaves the Billy Koehlers behind, is there any recourse if you are sick? There may be one last hope. You can try your luck at waiting in line for a travelling health caravan. If you are lucky enough to be seen, your care may be administered in a field, a stall, or in a tent.

Stan Brock founded Remote Area Medical (RAM). He was

a humanist, born in Lancashire, England. Older readers may remember Stan's name from the TV series *Mutual of Omaha's Wild Kingdom,* where he appeared as a co-host.

At seventeen years old, Stan went to work in British Guiana, where he managed the world's largest cattle ranch, called Dadanawa. He eventually became a bush and transport pilot. One day, after suffering an injury, he realized medical help was almost a month away on foot. That realization led to the idea of a travelling medical clinic, named Remote Area Medical (RAM), that would deliver health and dental services in unserved, poor areas like Haiti and Puerto Rico. His non-profit RAM delivered medical and dental services to remote third world locations where people could die from lack of access to basic health care. One day, Stan Brock received a phone call from a most unusual source: a social worker working in Hancock County, Tennessee. That call led his RAM expeditions straight into the heart of Tennessee and the privatized US health care system. After agreeing to take RAM to Hancock County, where the only dentist and hospital had closed shop, Stan became inundated with subsequent requests to service other areas of the United States.[70]

In his book *Deadly Spin,* author Wendell Potter, former VP of health insurer Cigna turned whistle blower, describes one such encounter with a RAM expedition in Wise County, Virginia, in 2007. In what the author calls a life-changing event, Potter relays the astounding scene: "… On the day I was there, the first day of the clinic, eight hundred people had lined up before dawn to be sure they could get in when the gates opened at five-thirty am."[71] Potter continues, "… I felt as if I'd stepped into a movie set or a war zone… As I walked around, I noticed that some of those lines led to barn and cinder block buildings with row after row of animal stalls, where doctors and nurses were treating patients... Except for curtains serving as makeshift doors on the animal stalls, there was little privacy... dentists were pulling teeth and filling cavities... doctors and nurses were doing pap smears and mammograms, surgeons were cutting out skin cancers, and gastroenterologists were conducting sigmoidoscopes."[72] In the richest country in the world, this is what privatization had produced: animal-stall health care.

Since then, the RAM clinics are still going strong, as Potter explains, "Because the need of the services that RAM and its volunteers provide shows no sign of abating."[73]

Far from the health care being administered in the stalls and barns of rural America, statisticians and researchers keep reminding us that the performance of the US system continues to fail. When compared to other OECD countries, the US has one of the lowest life expectancies. In 2015, the US had an average life expectancy of 78.6 years, lagging behind eleven other countries whose average was 82.2 years.[74] The same is true for US infant and maternal mortality rates. According to Forbes, "The U.S. is the only industrialized nation in the world where maternal mortality is rising. The U.S. has nearly the highest maternal mortality rate among high-income countries. Each year 700 American women die during pregnancy, childbirth or subsequent complications... with respect to infant mortality, the U.S. ranks thirty-three out of thirty-six OECD nations. In 2018... more than 21,000 infants died. Compared to countries with a similar GDP, the U.S. mortality rate is much higher." In 2018, the US rate was 5.6 infant deaths per 1,000 live births compared to countries like France and the UK, which had 3.8 deaths per 1,000 live births.[75]

According to healthsystemtracker.org, a DALY (disability adjusted life years) is "a measure of disease burden that takes into account years of life lost due to premature death as well as years of productive life lost to poor health or disability." The US continues to have higher age-adjusted disease burden rates than those of comparable countries. Since 1990, the disease burden rate in the US has dropped by fourteen percent, while comparable countries have seen an average decrease of eighteen percent.[76]

Despite the US spending much more on health care than comparable countries, the performance and the outcomes of its system remain uniquely dismal.

In both Canada and the US, business and professional physician associations have repeatedly thrown their support behind the privatization of health care services. Canadian business owners and physicians may want to think carefully before endorsing such a plan. In a for-profit model such as the US system, business owners may find themselves weighted down in a transactional quagmire of administrative red tape and costs. This includes dealing with big insurance conglomerates, tracking and maintaining the health histories of employees, filing endless forms, and dealing with the constant costs of rising employer health-insurance premiums. Those employers not interested in providing employee health insurance may experience the constant jumping of employees from their employment to a competitor who does supply insurance. These job-hopping costs employers more money, as employees become increasingly transient. The ability to start a new business may also be stifled, as leaving a job that supplies health insurance may be a disincentive to entrepreneurship. Are Canadian businesses really prepared to add dealing with insurance conglomerates such as Cigna or Aetna to their daily agendas?

What are the labour-market effects when employer health

premiums continue to escalate? The *National Bureau of Economic Research* in the US warns us about the delicate balance between rising benefit costs and employment: "Economic theory suggests that if workers fully value their health insurance benefits, they will bear the burden of higher premiums in the form of lower wages... but if firms are limited in their ability to offset higher benefit costs through lower wages—for example, by minimum wage laws or union contracts—then rising premiums may cause employers to reduce their work force or shift employment to employees who do not receive benefits, such as part-time workers."[77] It seems doubtful that Canadian employers would be willing to reduce the Canadian labour force to part-time, benefit-free earners. Part-time, benefit-free workers would have much less disposable income, particularly if they are forced to buy private insurance coverage. These cascading negative cash flow effects will only hurt, not help, business. Local small and medium business owners stand to lose the most.

The personal bankruptcy rate related to medical costs in Canada is close to zero. That is because our costs, for the most part, are covered by our collective tax revenues. In the US, the story is much different. Over sixty percent of personal bankruptcies are related to medical-expense costs or work loss related to illness. Academic research has demonstrated that "66.5 percent of all bankruptcies were tied to medical issues... an estimated 530,000 families turn to bankruptcy each year because of medical issues and bills..."[78] Privatization of health services has the potential to introduce Canadians to a whole new level of financial disparity, a disparity that will adversely affect economic growth. Canadian business owners know a bankrupt society doesn't have much purchasing power. If you are bankrupt or utilizing all your financial assets to cover health insurance premiums, there's not much left to spend on goods and services.

These negative economic effects have the potential to do one more thing—send people towards more welfare and social-safety-net programs. This increased burden further depletes tax dollars that could be spent on expanding public services like health.

Physician associations pushing for increased privatization should also proceed with caution. Although they may perceive the privatization model as being more financially lucrative, this endorsement requires a sober second thought. Medical malpractice is a booming business in the US system, where there exists a highly litigious environment. This is what happens when citizens are forced to pay soaring high premiums and deductibles directly out of pocket. When people become ill and the expenses mount, they demand every bang for their buck, much like we would with a home or car insurance claim. Patients may put undue pressure on physicians to do unnecessary diagnostic testing that is potentially harmful. This phenomenon, where physicians feel compelled to appease patients by carrying out unnecessary tests and treatments for fear of litigation, has been dubbed "defensive medicine," and it drives health care costs higher. Several studies have demonstrated the astronomical costs associated with unnecessary testing in order to avoid litigation. A study in the Archives of Internal Medicine estimated the yearly cost to avoid litigation in the US at about $60 billion. Another study pegged the 2008 costs of defensive medicine at $45.6 billion. A study by the Harvard School of Public Health estimated medical malpractice liability costs to be $55.6 billion, the bulk of which was related to defensive medicine costs.[79] The defensive medicine worry is not nearly as prevalent in countries that have universal health care systems.

Dealing with insurance conglomerates is another level of

frustration that Canadian physicians have yet to experience. In the US, physicians who know the best course of action for treatment of an illness often find themselves at the mercy of insurance executives. Options for the patient are not based on what the physician thinks is best practice or evidence-based but is often predicated on what type of insurance coverage the patient has and what is financially acceptable to the insurers. In Canada, a discussion about a vaginal hysterectomy versus an abdominal hysterectomy is one held privately between the physician and the patient, not in an insurance board room with brokers. In the US, if the coverage isn't available and the patient cannot afford the recommended treatment, this puts added stress on the physician to convince the insurer what is clinically most appropriate. This advocacy can be very time consuming for physicians. Patients may be left with cheaper treatment options or none at all. The physician's recommended treatment choice takes a back seat to affordability. Medical latitude regarding treatment is ultimately restricted by costs.

If your family physician is like mine, you may occasionally hear him or her complain about their endless stack of paperwork. The next time they comment, you may want to reassure them they are not as unfortunate as their US counterparts. As a physician in the US, the administrative burden of dealing with multiple insurers is heavy. US physicians must deal with multiple insurers, a litany of billing guidelines, collection companies, and the cost of constantly transferring medical records between providers to sort out insurance claims. Compared to a single-payer system like Canada, where physicians are dealing with one insurer, the US system is considerably more onerous. This burden costs physicians thousands of dollars. Try to imagine being a family-practice physician with 2,000 patients. Your paperwork involves dealing with Medicare, Medicaid, a litany of individual insurance companies, patients with varying deductibles and premiums, and people who are uninsured. Add to that differences in state coverages and the complexity multiplies exponentially. Dealing with this administrative bulk not only detracts from valuable patient time, but it can also impose a hefty overhead cost to one's practice. How costly is that administrative burden? According to Austin Frakt, a lot. Citing a study in *Health Affairs* that surveyed physicians and their administrators about billing, the findings maintain "this time costs an additional $68,000 US, per year, per physician (in 2006)." Frakt also tells us, "like the overall cost of the US health system, its administrative cost alone is No.1 in the world."[80] Ultimately, these administrative costs are down-shifted to the patient.

In study after study in medical journals, blogs, the Bureau of Statistics, and public health journals, the facts are indisputable. The US system of health care remains an outlier, preforms poorly, and costs more than any of its universal single-payer counterparts. The level of corporate control and abject profiteering is obscene. It is a system based on runaway greed without morality. It is responsible for the wholesale slaughter of not only young diabetics, but the elderly, the poor, the disenfranchised, the underinsured, the uninsured, thousands of children, those with chronic debilitating diseases, and millions of hard-working, middle-class Americans who are paying soaring premiums and deductibles. The government of the United States should be more worried about the deleterious domestic effects of this health care plutocracy than any other foreign distraction. It is an enemy like no other. It kills Americans methodically and consistently on home soil. It is pervasive and precise in its attack. It is a huge medical-industrial complex with an unfettered practice of medical extortion. It remains the greatest enemy within.

To the forces that seek to transform Medicare into this system, let these facts be a sharp warning. As the curators of Medicare, we have a responsibility to protect it from the forces that seek to exploit it for profit. Those forces have set up shop in our back yard. The first cracks in the landscape are now well-defined fault lines. The ground is shifting. As with any ground collapse, the first foreshock is felt before the larger seismic event. That foreshock is the crumbling of the Canadian emergency services sector because its performance is a systems indicator.

Chapter 3

WHY THE EMERGENCY DEPARTMENT MATTERED

But then Thucydides wrote that Themistocles' greatness lay in the fact that he realized Athens was not immortal. I think we have to realize that Canada is not immortal; but if it is going to go, let it go with a bang rather than a whimper.

—Pierre E. Trudeau, testifying before the Senate, Submissions Group on the Meech Lake Accord, 1988

January 16, 2006 was a pivotal day in my career. On that day, I arrived at the Dartmouth General Hospital Emergency Department as the new health services manager of the emergency department. I accepted the position thinking I was aptly prepared for whatever this job encompassed. It was here I discovered that prepared or not, the disintegration of the Canadian health care system had already gripped emergency services.

I vividly remember my first day. Alarms sounded erratically. Linen carts and garbage cans were overflowing. The waiting-room doors were stuck in the open position. The staffing board had multiple circled vacancies. Staff were running about as if invisible to each other. Others darted to computer stations, clicking through screens of information and flashing icons. Phones rang asynchronously. Porters circuitously shuffled patients on stretchers. On the periphery, visitors and families wandered aimlessly, looking at wall signs. Others sat motionless at curtained bedsides. Alarming EKG monitors expelled rhythm strips that dangled from the monitors onto the floor. The dull hum of casting saws murmured in the background. On the minor treatment side, orphaned in-patients lay in wait—many of them for days. Paramedics lined the back hallway, guarding their unloaded stretcher patients like sentries. Here they waited for any sign indicating that they could place patients into beds and attend to other calls. The department was illuminated by blinding overhead lights. I soon learned this was a typical day in a busy city ER.

Consider the emergency department a seismograph for the health care system. It responds to all the ground motions of the system and, like a seismograph, records the energy from the ground shaking. Emergency departments began to feel these foreshocks decades ago. Policy makers would have been wise to heed them. Emergency department staff across the country had passionately and persistently articulated their concerns. Front-line workers issued warnings about the state of deterioration. This included their inability to meet emergency-department standards and do their jobs effectively. Warnings also came from patients, doctors, families, and patient advocates. Stories of sub-standard care and poor patient experiences flooded social media and news outlets across Canada. Public outcry was met with a callous indifference.

Howard Ovens, emergency department chief of Toronto's Mount Sinai Hospital, maintains, "Arriving at a crowded emergency department increases your risk of bad outcomes. It increases the risk you'll bounce back to the emergency room and increases the risk you'll die if you're admitted."[81]

A consistently overcrowded emergency department also affects other services within the hospital. As competition for beds mounts, health services squabble for valuable bed space. Our emergency department was constantly attempting to borrow surgery beds for admitted patients. Surgeries had to be cancelled or rescheduled. These cancellations had real consequences for the patients prepared and scheduled for surgery.

The emergency department is often the community's first point of contact with medical care. Negative outcomes in the emergency department have been known to indelibly tarnish a hospital's reputation. If a community's emergency department is consistently unable to provide adequate and timely services, it negatively affects the entire community. Lack of confidence in one's emergency department influences sick patients to avoid emergency care. In these cases, the results are often disastrous.

With its unrelenting pressures, unpredictability, and doors that seldom close, emergency departments across Canada are stressful at the best of times. Yet Canadian emergency departments are equipped to function well when the health care system is reasonably funded, robust, and flexible. The collapse of Canada's emergency departments is a prologue for the disintegration of Medicare.

As every measure of emergency department efficiency began to decline and stories of sub-standard emergency care grew, governments looked the other way. When government response did occur, it focused blame solely on the emergency departments instead of acknowledging the problem as part of a larger system collapse. Many provincial solutions were knee-jerk "responses" that were void of any long-term planning. Consequently, more money and resources were channelled into the wrong directions for the wrong reasons.

Like its counterparts across the country, the emergency department that I managed continued to spiral into a state of chaos. Despite the skillfulness and dedication of the staff, the situation worsened. Benchmarks for emergency care were seldom met. Overcrowding was an ongoing challenge. Left-without-being-seen (LWBS) rates were below national standards. Ambulance off-load delays (of patients) were considerable. Staff felt like the care they were administering was inadequate and the overcrowding situation was unrelenting. Stress increased while staff morale bottomed out.

During my tenure, the department went through numerous process reviews. We engaged in training to maximize the department's logistical efficiency. We regularly collaborated with our health-district counterparts, in-patient managers, and department heads. We pored through decision-support data, looking for answers in the form of statistical analyses. At one point, the department had twenty admitted patients with nowhere to go. This included one ICU patient on a ventilator. This was our reality—housing entire in-patient units and ICU patients within the emergency department. Around it, we frantically kept emergency services going.

When I attended conferences across the country, members of other jurisdictions relayed similar experiences of overcrowding. We agreed that the slow death of emergency services was upon us.

After an exasperating first year, I had to attend a mandatory district staff gathering at the Cunard Centre in Halifax. The invitation had been extended to approximately 600 staff

WHY THE EMERGENCY DEPARTMENT MATTERED

members from various departments throughout the health district. Transportation was provided via a private bus service that shuttled hundreds of staff to and from the venue.

At the time, the emergency department was still experiencing severe challenges. Staff vacancies, relentless overcrowding, ongoing patient complaints, and endless lines of sick people continued to consume us. The last place I felt I should be was at an expensive gathering celebrating the accomplishments of our district health authority. But attendance was mandatory. Staff from almost every hospital department were present. The CEO was there, as was the VP of medicine, and the hospital board members. Front-line staff were obligated to be there while their positions had to be back-filled. The gathering was opulent, with JumboTron screens playing scenes from around the health district. Large tables of fresh fruit, snacks, coffee, and bottled water adorned the room.

The CEO gave an election-style speech in the centre of a massive room. She outlined the district's successes and how it was doing such great things. A physiotherapist took the stage to encourage the crowd of 600 people to take a break to do jumping jacks.

There we were, in the Cunard Centre, all jumping in the air like children. Except we weren't children. We were managers, department heads, administrators, nurses, doctors, and front-line staff all being remunerated by tax dollars. As the surgery manager and I darted out for some air, we speculated about what taxpayers would think. She wondered how many surgeries might be cancelled due to lack of beds that day. I worried about the current state of overcrowding in the emergency department. The jumping jacks ended. It was time to go back in.

I had to regularly attend costly programs aimed at process

improvement while watching the front lines in the department flounder. Policy makers were subsumed in rhetoric. Discourse centred around buzzwords, clichés, austerity planning, consultancy, competition, and restructuring. The health district exchanged notions of nurturance and caregiving for a new corporate vernacular. These were the days of the accelerated corporate craze. It penetrated every aspect of hospital care. We convened around board tables, hypothesizing about what would improve flow in our hospitals. Kafkaesque administrations were everywhere.

We covered walls with hundreds of sticky notes and were instructed to use crayons to "brainstorm" ideas on paper tablecloths. We sat in circles with "talking sticks." There was a district motto called "the promise." Milestones of "the promise" were developed. There were the 2013 milestones. Then there were the 2016 milestones. Eventually, the milestones vanished altogether. We aspired to be a "haven for patient-centred care." We were mandated to attend leadership courses wherein external consultants were billed at the taxpayers' expense. In these sessions, we were instructed to develop our personality "colours" and profiles. The consultants gave us pseudo leadership names. Mine was "Majestic River." Except nothing I was doing felt majestic, and little was flowing through emergency departments anywhere within the district.

In one of our meetings at my own hospital, a process engineer proclaimed, "Nothing is off the table, and no one is allowed to be negative." My presentation of the continuous challenges within the emergency department was met with Oz-like suggestions from the group. One process engineer pondered if patient flow could be accelerated by asking emergency department physicians to enter their own admitting data when the admitting clerk went to lunch. The look of complete shock on my face was interrupted by a light tap upon the boardroom door. It was the charge nurse, Mary. It was early afternoon. We were now approaching sixteen admitted patients with no places for them to go. The room murmured with the group's chatter. Meanwhile, Rome burned.

My cohort reported similar experiences across the country. Suddenly, believing in Carrollian logic was the main requisite for managing health. The facetious lingo and toxic positivity of corporate strategies permeated hospitals everywhere. We were required to sign "our promise" to comply. On one occasion, the management group received a supply of stress orbs. Round squeezable objects were purchased for all managers to squeeze whenever they felt stressed.

The CEO continued to post vignettes on our health authority intranet espousing to the new and improved "future state." She asserted that patients in the health district would soon find themselves in a health care utopia. According to this vision, patients would be able to sign in and select their physicians and book appointments from their home computers. Patients would be "engaged" and regularly apprised of their care. Our district would be the "haven for patient-centredness." A "Mecca" of citizen engagement.

"Working in silos" was a popular buzz phrase that was counter to the promise. The promise affirmed we would all have a "shared vision of healthy people and healthy communities." We would all "care with our hearts as well as our hands and our minds." There was no room for critical thinking or negativity if you signed onto the promise because we had committed ourselves to this corporate "love-in," where we would pursue "our shared human experience." We alleged to be one big happy corporation that promised "safe quality care."[82] Except there was one serious problem. The promise was not grounded in any kind of reality. While it looked good on paper and sounded idyllic, it was never a reflection of the struggles front-line staff faced every single day. The promise represented one thing: It was an affirmation of fealty to the propaganda being circulated. As time ticked on and pressure within the system mounted, the entire concept eventually went down in a large ball of flames, taking with it every last tax dollar that supported it. Nirvana never arrived.

We are now long past the promised utopia. Service has deteriorated beyond our wildest dreams. Booking doctors' appointments has become more cumbersome. Doing so from one's home computer is a non-reality. Currently 4.8 million Canadians do not have a regular care provider.[83] At the time of this writing, there are 100,590 people in Nova Scotia without access to a family physician.[84] Emergency departments remain one of the only outlets for patients without access to primary care. In regions like the Cape Breton Regional Municipality in Nova Scotia, the situation has gone from challenging to dangerous. Ambulance offload conditions in many jurisdictions are listed as code critical, signifying times when there are no available ambulances to serve communities. Heartbreaking stories surrounding emergency department disintegration abound. Signs of systemic deterioration are omnipresent, reinforcing the absurdity of making "promises" that can never be kept.

By the time I entered the emergency department, the concept of regionalization was well over a decade old. Forced by a deficit crisis in the 1990s, the provinces and territories looked to the process of regionalization to integrate and coordinate hospital and community-based services. Regionalization promised to improve the health of constituents within defined geographic regions.[85] Provinces like Nova Scotia were rapidly re-structured into regional health authorities. The regionalization of Nova Scotia resulted in nine separate health authorities, each with its own bureaucratic structure. Each authority had its own CEO and board.

These structures operated for years promising equity across provinces, increased citizen engagement, economic efficiency, and greater accountability. Critics of regionalization claimed it fractured the governance relationship with physicians because they were provincially remunerated (MSI) and not by the regions where they worked. Medical specialists were also bound by the limits of regionalization. Their contributions were filtered through organizational bureaucracy. Citizen engagement did not increase with the regionalization of health authorities as promised. Professionals and bureaucrats continued to dominate health care decision-making. Competition between services provided in urban and rural jurisdictions flourished, thus making these services less integrated and less equitable. The shortcomings of regionalization adversely affected emergency services across the country.

Today (and millions of tax dollars later), many regional health authorities have been disbanded for super-health boards, like those in Alberta and Nova Scotia. The top brass who once championed the restructuring schemes have either reinvented themselves or retired. Many left with massive payouts and lucrative pensions. The cost of merging Alberta's regional health boards into one super board amounted to about $80 million.[86]

Jack Davis, former CEO of Calgary Health Region, was paid $1.7 million in severance and $4.028 million under his executive retirement plan. The plan included a pension of $300,000 annually for the rest of his life. Davis is just one of eight CEOs included in the province's payout.[87]

The story was similar in Nova Scotia. Documents there revealed that $5.7 million was spent on severance for the "talking circle" gurus. This was in addition to $3.3 million spent on consolidating IT systems and $873,000 more to new mediation and communication consultants.[88]

During the mid to late '90s, the proliferation of health care consultancy flourished. By the year 2007, a string of highly paid consultants occupied every corner of health care. Nova Scotia was no exception. It became routine to hire an endless platoon of consulting services for every problem that plagued the system.

Corpus Sanchez Consultancy was one such firm. The British Columbia-based group was hired to do yet another operational review of the health services in Nova Scotia. That report, *Provincial Health Services Operational Review* (PHSOR), cost taxpayers one million dollars. It followed on the heels of countless other reviews from 1994 through to 2006.[89]

The report provided 103 recommendations and emphasized the "health care system in the province is at a crisis point and stressed to capacity."[90] The PHSOR report indicated that not all small hospitals were offering *true* emergency care and, instead, "… EDs are used as substitutes for primary health care clinics and doctor's offices."[91] Former Conservative premier Rodney MacDonald had accepted all the recommendations but did not believe that "… the system was in full crisis."[92]

Other key recommendations centred around expanding primary care and the use of data to help guide health care decisions. Recommendations also outlined the need to refocus emergency departments on administering *true* emergency care through "the provision of alternative, non-emergent service mechanisms" and to re-deploy funding into primary-care services, recruitment, and retention of health care providers. PHSOR suggested the development of a rural health strategy designed to move non-emergent care from emergency departments into more appropriate settings.[93] This would help citizens access desperately needed primary care and take the pressure off emergency services.

Former Liberal minister of health and wellness Monique Begin famously remarked, "Canada is a country of perpetual pilot projects."[94] The remark seemed to imply we haplessly continue to hire experts and consultants to repeatedly solve the same problems. The compilation of costly reviews like those of Corpus Sanchez are often filed into obscurity where the only action they ever really see is an unending accumulation of office dust.

In a section of the Corpus Sanchez report *Changing Nova Scotia's Health care System: Creating Sustainability Through Transformation*, the consulting group reinforced the need for data to be a driving force for change. They refer to a culture of "analysis-paralysis" within the system and asserted "across the system there is a need to build a culture that uses data to support care and financial decisions. Currently, data are not leveraged to support key operational and strategic decisions."[95] The consultants were not the first group to articulate the need for a culture change within the Canadian health care system.

When it comes to innovation and evidence-based action we can't seem to get out of our own way. The political infringement on the structure and administration of the health care system smothers innovation and any chance of real leadership.[96] The inability of government to acknowledge this reality continues to adversely affect emergency services across Canada.

In January 2009, our director and district chief of emergency services at the Queen Elizabeth II Health Sciences Centre decided enough was enough. With eighteen admitted patients in his ER and ambulances lining the hallways, Dr. John Ross called a "code orange." The code is usually reserved for external disasters involving numerous casualties, such as the Swiss Air crash of 1998. It stopped all regular hospital operations to focus primarily on the disaster—an overcrowded emergency department. All resources shifted to placing admitted patients from the emergency department into beds. Eight hours later, the ER was mainly cleared. It was both a statement and a bold move by frustrated staff who clearly felt that they had no other option. In a *Globe and Mail* article dated January 24, 2009, the chief said, "… the breaking point, after years of building frustration, came Sunday and Monday when his department's hallways filled with patients with nowhere to go."[97]

The hospital CEO's response indicated that: "… We have a duty administrative process in place to call."[98] It is likely that calling a senior bureaucrat would not have cleared the department. Senior administrative staff have always been on call for trouble-shooting resolutions to acute hospital problems. Conversations with them rarely translate into direct, actionable crisis intervention. The CEO's recommendation reinforced the level of disconnect between those of us on the ground and those in their administrative towers.

One salient point about the Halifax code orange of 2009 was a point made by Dr. Ross in the *Globe and Mail* article. In making a pitch to increase the number of beds available for general treatment as opposed to specialized treatment, Dr. Ross questioned the health authority's decision on not acting quickly to restore one such clinic known as the Community Medicine Service. It had closed in the summer because the founding physician had left the area. Dr. Ross said, "Those ten to twelve beds would

WHY THE EMERGENCY DEPARTMENT MATTERED

have provided crucial relief on Sunday and Monday, providing general practitioners who could look after the ER patients."[99]

Shortly after the code orange, the district chief stepped aside from his duties. Other internal positions were realigned. For a while the boldness of calling the code orange kept the spotlight focused on the critical situation within the Halifax emergency department and other emergency departments across the country. But any relief resulting from the calling of code orange was short lived.

In September 2020, over a decade had elapsed since Dr. Ross called his code orange at the QE II Health Sciences Centre in Halifax. In the same month, retired school principal Kelly MacPhee collapsed at home. Mr. MacPhee's apartment was six minutes from the hospital. His wife made three frantic calls to 911. It took the ambulance forty minutes to arrive. When the ambulance arrived, it was too late; Mr. MacPhee had succumbed to a heart attack. The paramedics came from a jurisdiction eighty-four kilometres away because Mrs. MacPhee was told that there were no available ambulances in Halifax at the time. She also told *CTV News* that her husband had told her he felt he was dying and spent the last thirty minutes of his life "in terror" asking her, "Where are they?"

A freedom of information request showed the average ambulance offload time at Dr. Ross's former emergency department was ninety-one minutes—the longest offload time in the province. Ambulance crews lined the emergency department's hallways, and yet trucks were unavailable to respond to Mrs. MacPhee's urgent calls six minutes away.[100]

Long after the dust had settled on Dr Ross's 2009 code orange, studies and reviews of emergency services persisted. With repeated stories of paramedics lining the hallways of Nova

Scotia emergency departments, the US-based *Fitch Report* was ordered in October 2018 and released two years after its original delivery date in March of 2021. This report cost taxpayers $145,000. It came with sixty-eight new recommendations, many of which bore an eerie resemblance to the Corpus Sanchez recommendations of 2008.

The predominant finding of the *Fitch Report* was that Nova Scotia paramedics were "spending too much time in non-productive, non-emergency activities." It also indicated that to remedy the situation, "it will take the entire health system working together in a coordinated way to improve things."[101] Twelve years after the code orange and thirteen years after the $1 million Corpus Sanchez review, the *Fitch Report* gives new credence to the words articulated by Monique Begin, "We have solved every single problem in our health care system ten times over, but we seem incapable of scaling up the solutions."[102]

The downfall of emergency services throughout Canada is only part of the story. The real culprit lies within a deteriorating health care system as a whole and the inability of the government to act. The inaccessibility to patient care, dwindling resources, lack of primary care, defunding of hospital beds, collapse of the long-term care sector, and lack of staff have contributed to the collapse of emergency services across the country.

The real struggle for emergency departments began about thirty years ago. An article from *Healthy Debate* (2017) reaffirms this observation. The authors state, "Many feel ED overcrowding began to be a problem in the early 1990s, when budget cuts led to the number of available beds being cut by about a third across the country. Canada has dropped from having four acute-care beds per 1,000 people in 1990 to 2.1 per 1,000 people in 2013. That makes us third last out of 34 OECD countries."[103] This was compounded by a growing aging population and a lack of infrastructure to support home care for seniors, creating a "perfect storm," leaving Canada's hospitals packed with sick seniors in beds designated for acute care.

A *Globe and Mail* article (2017) described the effects of the combined loss of beds and a surge of sick seniors within the province of Ontario: "The Sault Area Hospital's acute-care section has had the second-highest average occupancy rate of any hospital in Ontario over the past five years... Many experts assert that eighty-five percent is the ideal occupancy rate for accommodating surges of patients. The hospital's average occupancy rate was just over 106 percent between 2012 and the end of last year; it peaked at 120.8 percent in the winter of 2015." This leaves a zero-surge capacity for new patients coming into the emergency department. The article goes on to say that this was one of six hospitals that averaged occupancy rates over a hundred percent and one of eighty-nine in the province, whose acute-care occupancy rates were above the eighty-five percent. Ontario's community hospitals such as Trenton, Exeter, Dryden, and Huntsville are feeling the same pressures.[104]

A rising tide of seniors with chronic complex illnesses continued to fill hospital beds. The overall lack of community infrastructure left Canadian seniors with nowhere to go. Grant explains, "Doctors and health-policy experts say that a lack of co-ordination between primary care, hospitals, home care and long-term care in Canada's fractured health care system is certainty part of the problem…" [105]

Health reporter, André Picard, indicates that the aging boomer dynamic coupled with the lack of long-term planning and a deficit of long-term care beds is the perfect combination for severe overcrowding.[106]

Data from the *British Columbia Care Providers Association Report* demonstrates that the statistics are solemn. BC is short 3,000 beds with a waitlist for long-term care of 1,379 people, 340 of whom are still in hospital beds. It is estimated that the province needs 45,000 new beds over the next twenty years. Approximately 19,000 new health workers will be required to staff these new beds. In view of this demand, only 120 new beds have been added this year. Other jurisdictions are facing similar challenges. In Ontario, the waitlist for long-term care is 34,000. In Nova Scotia, one-third of hospital beds are occupied by patients waiting for long-term care. These long-term care patients have been medically discharged but wait in "valuable" acute-care beds.[107] With this type of congestion, it is clear to see how the country's emergency departments continue to collapse inward.

Emergency departments across the country sounded alarm bells. Policy makers would have been wise to heed those warnings. They instead sought politically expedient solutions that coincided with election cycles. Long-term initiatives based on data and valuable input from front-line clinicians were not a priority. It remains difficult to say where it will all end for the brave staff who continue to provide emergency services amidst this unalloyed chaos. It also remains difficult to say where government's "analysis-paralysis" will leave patients who so desperately need evidence-based action that will work.

There is one last staggering statistic that puts the scope of the problem into perspective. "Nationwide there are 7,550 alternate level of care patients—the equivalent of twenty-five hospitals with 300 beds each..."[108] It is beyond comprehension that Canada's emergency departments are providing emergency services around this sobering reality. Austerity and privatization proponents argue that there's simply not enough money. Budgets are exhausted. Privatization or a parallel private/public system is the only way to rescue Medicare. It's a well-defined pattern. Ignore the public system and soon funders will come to understand only privatization can save us. In fact, leave it to slide long enough and far enough until the funders beg for privatization.

On August 12, 2019, I was able to catch an 11:30 p.m. broadcast on the local news. One of the first stories was a feature about local emergency room closures. Dr. Margaret Fraser was commenting on the situation at the Cape Breton Regional Hospital Emergency Department, where she works. The news story centred around the fact that one-third of the province's emergency departments were closed due to physician and nursing shortages. As a result, the Cape Breton Regional Hospital in Sydney was shouldering the brunt of redirected emergency services. Dr. Fraser asserted that the increased wait times had impactful consequences for patients. It meant that people were at higher risk of having cardiac arrests in waiting room and triage areas instead of being seen. Like many times before, Dr. Fraser reinforced that staff could only work to the point of exhaustion for so long. A frustrated Dr. Fraser also indicated that she could go almost anywhere else in Canada and make more money. Despite that fact, she and the rest of the team at the Cape Breton Regional Hospital persist.

Emergency services across the rest of Canada are experiencing the same pressures. In January 2019, the chair of *Improving Health care and Ending Hallway Medicine* in Ontario, Dr. Rueben Devlin, sent a letter to Premier Doug Ford and the Ontario minister of health saying, "The concern is that on any given day in the province, there are at least 1,000 patients receiving health care in the hallways of our hospitals. At the same time, the wait to access a bed in a long-term care home is 146 days, and this can vary significantly depending on where you happen to reside in Ontario."[109]

At the Valley Regional Hospital in Kentville, Nova Scotia, three emergency-room physicians decided that they had also had enough. After several exasperating meetings with local administrators, the trio left their local ER, citing an ongoing untenable work situation.

Doctors Rob Miller, Rebecca Brewer, and Keith MacCormick had been trying to explain how the lack of long-term care beds and lack of primary-care providers adversely affected their ER. The persistent overcrowding was not manageable for them anymore. In a *CTV News* report, the doctors asserted that at a time, in the last year, they had twenty-four admitted patients in a twenty-bed unit.[110] Dr. MacCormick planned to leave by January 2020; Dr. Miller, by February 2020. Dr. Brewer would be significantly reducing her shifts.[111]

In a startling move in November 2019, the Campbellton Regional Hospital closed services due to its overcrowding issues. The hospital's medical management team announced it was closing obstetrics-gynaecology, surgical, and outpatient clinics due to severe overcrowding. Forty-two stretchers were serving as hospital beds because there were simply no more regular beds available. The team acknowledged that the crisis was multifactorial... "and has a lot to do with beds being used for long-term care cases."[112]

In fact, listed occupancy rates from hospitals around the country may even be worse than they seem. How is that possible when a hospital's occupancy rate is already listed at ninety-nine or one hundred percent? This is because not all beds within the system can accommodate all the admitted patients that require them. If you're running a facility and the only two empty beds are paediatric cribs, birthing units, or ICU beds and the occupancy rate is ninety-eight percent, none of the ten or fifteen adult medical patients waiting in ER hallways can access those beds. For obvious reasons, you cannot put a sick adult patient in a birthing bed or a child's crib. The same usually holds true for specialized ICU beds. So, the true occupancy rate, accounting for those admitted patients in hallways, closets, or other unconventional spaces where we now hold patients, may be 115 percent or 120 percent.

In addition to this obstructive congestion, ERs are seeing increases in visits per annum, driven by a persistent lack of primary-care services. Barbara Garratt went to Southlake Hospital emergency department in February 2019 as a sixty-year-old woman with stage-four cancer and she waited from Tuesday until Friday to get a bed. She finally received a bed in the cardiac unit, leaving twenty-five more admitted patients behind her in the ER. A spokesperson for Southlake's emergency department said, "Southlake's Emergency Department was designed for 70,000 visits per year, but saw 113,000 patients last year..."[113] In case after case, emergency rooms are experiencing the weight of a collapsing health care system. Surge capacity continues to diminish with every passing year.

On March 2, 2021, a local news story broke about New Brunswick Grade 10 student Lexi Daken. With a history of anxiety and depression and a previous suicide attempt, Lexi ran into problems in late February 2021 and staff at her school became concerned about her mental health. On February 18, 2021, Lexi was taken to the Dr. Everett Chalmers Hospital ER in Fredericton, New Brunswick, by her school guidance counsellor. Lexi waited eight hours and was eventually told a psychiatrist was unavailable. A week later, the sixteen-year-old committed suicide.[114] It is almost unimaginable that fifteen years after I first stepped into an emergency department, stories like Lexi's continue to emerge.

Emergency departments across the country could have been rescued. The fall of emergency services across the country should have raised alarm bells eliciting support, reform, and funding infusions for the system. Instead, governments chose to hold the line on spending, clinging to the ways things have always been done. With health care managers at the mercy of politicians, the ability to carry out transformative change remains impossible. Since improving care isn't the true priority of the system, the plight of emergency services remains unchanged. Canadian emergency departments continue to be unfairly forced to carry the weight of a collapsing health care system upon their shoulders. Until broader "system issues" are resolved, stories like those of Lexi Daken and Kelly MacPhee will continue to be front page news.

Chapter 4

THE FOUR HORSEMEN

One of the facts of history is that battles do not stay won. Those that matter have to be waged again and again.

—Stanley Knowles

Medicare has always had its detractors. Namely, capitalists, professional physician groups, pro-business interests, corporate lobbyists, and, of course, the elites who still wonder why their tax dollars should fund a system that they neither need nor want. Fortunately for Medicare, its evolution was so purely Canadiana, it won't succumb without a fight. It is that hope that Medicare proponents such as myself cling to, as the narrative to privatize the system continues to expand. That narrative has gone from a largely values-driven focus to a corporate-driven one. We've been led to believe that everything happening to Medicare is related to its unsustainability. We've been force-fed the story about demand outstripping revenue. It's a narrative designed to cater to the current political economy where capitalism is king, and all public services are up for grabs. It's a narrative built on fear, fanned by greed. It's reinforced by allowing the public system to decline. That decline is strategically sustained by conscious defunding, defrauding, and deregulation. The result is a deliberate system of disintegration. This permits neoliberal solutions to move in and save the day. It also creates the illusion that these solutions are the only salvation.

Against mounting opposition, Tommy Douglas and the architects of Medicare stayed the course. As long as Douglas lived, he remained acutely aware of who the enemies of Medicare were. He knew corporate interests would continue to haunt the sustainability of the universal single-payer system. But what Douglas and his cohort could not have imagined is the zeal with which the new political order of neoliberalism would attack all Canadian public services, particularly Medicare. None of us could have imagined the degree of destruction that would ensue.

In its ruthless pursuit to reduce every aspect of our lives to what author Stephen Metcalf aptly described as "the bloodless paragon of efficiency known as the free market,"[115] neoliberalism has engulfed the Canadian Medicare system.

Fuelled by Keynesianism, post-World War II Canada saw the rise of the worker. Union strength grew and with that strength came an increase in the standard of living. Supported by income and benefit security, workers gained increased confidence. As Jim Stanford tells us, "A confident working class won a larger and larger share of the economic pie: in Canada, the labor share of the GDP grew steadily through the post war era, peaking in the late 1970s."[116] Worker confidence permeated workplaces. These changes restricted corporate autonomy. This was the era of high corporate taxes and regulation for employers. Enmeshed throughout this era of strong unionism and worker confidence was an active wave of social turbulence fuelled by rebellion against the establishment. Social acts of rebellion spread across North America. It was the age of anti-war protests, civil rights marches, women's liberation movements, the Kent State shootings, Woodstock, and the development of a very vocal and determined counterculture. All of it worried the power, the authority, and the autonomy of the corporate world. Pursued by interventionist governments, regulations, and power to the people, corporations sought to shake off what they perceived were the chains of constraint and a "surplus of free-thinkers supporting democracy."

The election victory of Mulroney in Canada (and Reagan and Thatcher in the US and Britain) ushered in a new economic world order. By 1981, interest rates had shot up to the historical high of 22.75 percent, and as Canadian economist and author Jim Stanford explains, "monetary authorities showed they were willing to sacrifice the course of the whole economy in order to impose this painful new doctrine. They demonstrated that reducing inflation and preserving the value of financial wealth (which suffered badly during the turbulent 1960s and 1970s) was now the number one priority of economic governance."[117] With the ratification of the free-trade agreement in 1989, the stage had been set. The free-trade deals paved the way for large multinationals to have increased access to Canadian markets. They also set the stage for the privatization of public-health services. With the advent of globalization, Canadian businesses identified less and less with a domestic agenda and more and more with a continentalist agenda fuelled by international competition.[118] That doctrine was reinforced by Liberal finance minister Paul Martin, who, by the 1990s, took up where Mulroney left off. He continued the neoliberal scourge by further cutting social programs like employment insurance and federal health transfers to the provinces. Canadian provincial health care systems have never recovered from the massive restructuring of this era.

Unions also became targets as corporations sought to

regain power. Gains made by unions in the '70s were stripped. Eventually the right to strike by health care workers was countered by essential-service legislation. Employee benefits, such as sick time, began to evaporate. Armed with its new-found power, Canada's corporate sector began a full-out assault on deficit slaying. Preying on the good intentions and fiscal responsibility of law-abiding citizens, the corporate sector equated a federal state of fiscal doom and gloom with the private finances of Canadians, a comparison, however absurd, that resonated with cost-conscious taxpayers. This incessant corporate cry associated any public spending with waste and self-absorption. Suddenly, anything we paid for collectively was unaffordable. We were told the only real solution to prevent the country from going over a fiscal cliff lay in the expansion of private enterprise and the contraction of public programs. As Stanford reminds us, "Neoliberalism represented a multi-faceted, deliberate, global strategy by elites (in both the financial and the real spheres of the economy) to turn the whole ship around."[119] The ship did get turned around. By 2010, there appeared to be a new social order. It involved a growing disparity between the rich and the poor fuelled by everything corporate. Real wage growth (in terms of inflation) declined and corporate coffers grew. We experienced the subprime mortgage crisis in 2008, which was driven largely by corporate greed and the high-risk practices of Wall Street.

In 2012, we witnessed an unprecedented request by then Bank of Canada governor Mark Carney, who insisted corporate Canada should do more with their large stockpiles of money (dead money). Taking a swipe at Canadian firms, Carney insisted they should reinvest their billions of dollars back into the economy and create jobs, rather than sitting on piles of cash. At the time, "Statistics Canada's numbers showed non-financial corporations with a cash hoard of $526-billion at the end of the first quarter of 2012..."[120] That same year the Conservative government of Stephen Harper reworked the federal funding formula to the provinces by announcing that starting in 2016–17, the annual six percent cash transfers would be replaced by a 3.9 percent transfer or by a three-year average of nominal GDP growth. Altering the federal funding formula in this way meant federal transfers would be reduced from 20.4 percent to 18.6 percent by 2025—a cut of $36 billion over a ten-year period.[121]

As corporations were stockpiling cash and transfers to the provinces were being cut, the Harper government also took another astonishing step. In 2006, it dropped the federal corporate tax rate from 22.1 percent to 15 percent, further reducing revenue by about $12 billion annually.[122] The clawbacks and revenue reduction amounted to billions of dollars that easily could have been poured into the maintenance and expansion of public health care.

One of the main objectives of neoliberalism is to strip the welfare state of any real power. This is done by aggressive defunding and cutting taxes, creating the need to slash services. Beyond being an extremist, pro-business agenda, neoliberalism is a total social reordering. It transcends right-wing fiscal austerity obsession. It seeks to reduce what capitalists perceive as "an abundance of democratic involvement." According to author, Stephen Metcalf, "... neoliberalism is not simply a name for pro market policies... it is a name for a premise that, quietly, has come to regulate all we practice and believe: that competition is the only legitimate organizing principle for human activity."[123] In short, as Sam Gindin, adjunct professor of political science at York University, explains, "[It's] capitalism working without a working class opposition."[124]

Superimposed on a public health care system, the tenets of

neoliberalism have the potential to become deadly. We need look no further than the American health care system to understand the severity with which this unbridled dogma has limited health care services. In the shakedown, there are four essential components: defunding, defrauding, deregulation, and deliberate disintegration.

Defunding

Canadians may think of their Medicare system as a straightforward single-payer model, but there is much about the payment scheme and financial support for Medicare that is more complex and convoluted than meets the eye. Primarily a provincial responsibility, Medicare in Canada has been described by some as thirteen separate single-payer systems (ten provinces and three territories), each with its unique features and a surprisingly lack of uniformity. Although the provinces have the relegated responsibility of providing health services, all provinces rely on federal transfer payments to help shoulder their health care costs. All are governed by the five principles of the Canada Health Act (1984). In this sense, the nature of Canadian federalism (as it relates to the provision of health services) inextricably bonds the two jurisdictions. It gives the provinces the major load of health care responsibility and budgeting and the federal government major health care legislative powers. In addition to this assortment of funding, a portion of Canada's health care system is paid for privately. In 2018, sixty-nine percent of health care was publicly funded in Canada. This percentage comprised all hospital care and medically necessary services. The remaining thirty-one percent of health care costs were privately covered by Canadians either as straight out-of-pocket expenditures, as co-payments, or in the maintenance of private insurance plans.[125] These private payments covered services currently not included under Medicare, such as physiotherapy, occupational therapy, optometry, homecare, factions of long-term care, dental care, and pharmaceuticals. In 2018, $254.6 billion went to pay for total health care services in Canada.[126]

Canadians need to know everything we pay for collectively is cheaper. Although the current political rhetoric would have you think otherwise, it simply isn't true. That is why the bombast surrounding lowering taxes and having more money in hand is misleading. When you cut taxes, forcing service reduction, those services must then be paid for privately by individuals. Except for the ultra-rich, everyone loses when this occurs. The privatization of the US health care system is a pristine example of this tenet.

When the Pearson government initiated the national universal health care system in 1966 Ottawa cost-shared close to fifty percent of the provincial cost of services. By 1977, the Trudeau Liberals recoiled from that arrangement, replacing it with a block-funding scheme that doled out grants to the provinces on a per capita basis.[127] This eliminated the open-endedness of the previous cost-sharing accord and directly shifted the budgeting for health care to the provinces. With cost containment on the brain of the federal conservatives during the 1980s, transfer growth was further restricted to the provinces. In 1989, the transfers were frozen.[128] With double-digit interest rates, the transfers frozen, and the recession soaring, the provinces struggled to maintain all social programs including health care. By the 1990s, the federal Liberals replaced the block transfers with the Canada Health and Social Transfer program. Those were particularly dire times for those of us working in health care as the provinces attempted to transition through the new payment scheme. Their reaction was both autonomic and acute as Maioni explains, "The impact on provincial health systems was immediate and intense, with negative growth in spending, hospitals closings and, in some cases, rapid restructuring of delivery as well."[129] For those of us who were at the bedside, this era was a watershed moment for health care service delivery in Canada. We woke up to find ourselves in the middle of a neoliberal nightmare from which we have yet to awaken. Medicare had crossed the Rubicon.

According to CIHI, this period in the 1990s was a time of "significant change in the Canadian health care system, as provincial governments restrained expenditure growth in most programs in order to balance budgets."[130] From 1993 to 1996, health expenditures allocated to hospitals dropped from 37.4 percent to 33.7 percent. In 1988–89, the number of beds approved by provincial governments peaked at 179,256. During the three years between 1993–94 to 1996–97, the number of beds dropped by 20.7 percent and expenditure decreased by 5.7 percent. By 2000–2001, the number of beds levelled out at approximately 115,000 with some small year-to-year variations.[131]

As governments tried to slay the deficit dragon from the 1980s to the '90s, corporate tax rates continued to fall. The corporate income tax rate in the 1960s and '70s was about thirty-seven percent. In 1980, it was reduced to thirty-six percent. By 1990, the corporate tax rate was at twenty-eight percent.[132] Both Liberals and Conservatives have consistently lowered the corporate tax rates while slashing public spending on health care. This down-shifting to provinces and municipalities placed further stress on cash-strapped provinces to fund health care.

Provinces across the country responded dramatically. This period in health care will forever be remembered as the age of bed closures, rapid restructuring without forethought, and downsizing on steroids. It was the golden age of consultancy, nightmarish staff shortages, the proliferation of private/public/ partnerships (P3s), and the answer to everyone's health service delivery problems—regionalization.

In Nova Scotia, there were about 4,300 hospital beds when the Nova Scotia Liberals took power in 1993. Within the first two years of former Liberal premier John Savage's reign, 1,200 hospital beds were closed. By 1999, there were only 3,127 beds remaining, a loss of 1,680 beds.[133]

In Alberta, former Conservative premier Ralph Klein devoted most of his tenure to deficit slashing. Under his stewardship, health services within Alberta were robustly re-structured. From 1992–2000 per capita spending declined. There was an elimination or reduction of 14,753 positions in health care. Regionalization of Alberta health care services occurred, and a hospital was leased to an American for-profit health group. The old Calgary hospital was demolished in 1998. Calgary's Salvation Army hospital, Grace, and another, Holy Cross, were also closed. Budgets were slashed and Klein pushed legislation to permit the purchase of health services from private providers. He also became an ardent proponent of a parallel, private/public health care system.[134]

There were similar stories throughout the rest of the country. In New Brunswick, former premier Frank McKenna (1987–1997) consolidated fifty-one hospital boards into eight regional corporations and the growth in health care spending dropped from ten percent in 1987 to under one percent in 1997. In 2003, New Brunswick nurses' union president Linda Silas confirmed there had been a reduction of 700 nursing positions in the province since 1993.[135]

In Ontario, former Conservative premier Mike Harris

(1995–2002) and his government forfeited $15 billion per year in revenue from cut taxes that could have funded public health care. Between 1995 and 2003, more than 11,400 beds in Ontario were cut. More than one out of every three of Ontario's acute and chronic-care hospital beds were closed. Between 1996 and 2000, thirty-nine hospitals were ordered closed. Forty-four hospitals were amalgamated. Six psychiatric hospitals were closed. Tens of thousands of nurses, health professionals, patient-support services, and care workers were laid off or had jobs eliminated by attrition. User fees for drugs were initiated for seniors. An assortment of health care services was privatized.[136]

In British Columbia, former Liberal premier Gordon Campbell became famous for his slash-and-burn tactics related to public health care. Private clinics mushroomed and ancillary hospital services were contracted out. As a result of sub-standard practices related to for-profit cleaning companies, infection rates increased. Campbell expanded the P3 model of building hospitals, which involved private funding, consultants, and catering to expensive corporations. He engaged in a campaign of closing rural hospitals. He gave tax breaks to the rich and to corporations. He had an incendiary relationship with health professionals and their unions, which culminated in a 43,000-person strike. Campbell legislated the strikers back to work and imposed a fifteen-percent wage cut.[137] Later, the province became noted for a protracted legal case in which the owner of a private British Columbia surgical clinic (Cambie Surgeries Corp.) was found guilty of overcharging patients. In response, he filed a charter challenge alleging the Canada Health Act violated the Canadian Charter of Rights and Freedoms by limiting patients to public health care. In 2020, British Columbia's highest court struck down that claim. After the loss, clinic owner Dr. Brian Day said he fully expects the case to be appealed and go all the way to the Supreme Court of Canada. Dr. Richard Klasa, a retired oncologist and a board member of Canadian Doctors for Medicare, later claimed, "For-profit health insurers are salivating to be able to get into the Canadian market."[138] Paradoxically, one of the earliest provincial signatories to Medicare appears to be determined to dismantle the core of Canada's public health care system.

Largely driven by a public outcry and the 2002 *Romanow Report*, new funding to the provinces was eventually increased. But by this time, so many services had been slashed or so negatively impacted, the cash infusions were not enough to restore service to anything close to the pre-Paul Martin era.

By 2004, the provinces and the federal government had agreed on a new, ten-year initiative. New cash would be injected into the system and there would be a consistent six-percent increase for the period of 2006–2014. In 2006, the Conservatives won the federal election. By 2011, they had decided to change the rules of the game, retreating from the former spending promises made by the Liberals. By 2016, the Canadian Institute for Health Information (CIHI) was asserting that 2016 was the sixth year in a row in which health care spending had not kept pace with inflation, aging, or population growth. As Michael Hunt, director of health spending and strategic initiatives at CIHI explained, "Our trend in health care spending since 2010 is really about very moderate growth… if you were to adjust for population growth, aging, and inflation, there has been very little growth on a per-person basis in health care spending, overall, across the country."[139]

Between the years 2000 and 2004, Paul Martin cut the corporate tax rate to twenty-one percent. That was a precipitous drop of six percentage points in three years. In 2006, the federal Conservatives further reduced the rate to fifteen percent.[140] At a time when a robust corporate tax rate would have significantly increased revenues, health care was facing a full-on assault. The aging baby boomers and their parents were needing to access the system that they had funded for years. There was one huge problem, though. Both Liberal and Conservative governments had siphoned off that money to big corporations.

It didn't seem to matter that the Liberals were elected as the new federal government in 2015. Surprisingly, they held firm to the Conservative's transfer reduction plan. By 2016, the two levels of government were engaged in another dispute about federal transfers. The parliamentary budget office had already warned the provinces that Ottawa wanted to reduce its contribution to the provinces in the form of transfers for health care. The provinces would have to come up with a way to manage the increased financial burden of providing health care within their respective jurisdictions. NDP health critic Don Davis pointed out, "It's a curious thing for them to hold the line on… they've vastly ballooned their spending in all sorts of areas. To me it's a misplaced priority for them to draw a firm line in the sand on health care."[141] While it appears that the federal government remains intent on holding the province's feet to the fire on funding, both levels of government appear to have money for just about everything else. The problem with that, of course, is that the funders (taxpayers) want health care to be a priority.

In both health policy and rhetoric, the tenets of neoliberalism are omnipresent. From the supply-side economics of Mulroney in the '80s to the scorched-earth tactics of the Liberals in the '90s, our public health care system has taken so many hits, it is unlikely to rebound unless swift action is taken. It also appears that despite the reverence for Medicare, the attacks on the system are far from over.

The Ontario government of Doug Ford continues to impose funding cuts that have significantly affected health care services in that province. The government cut funding to public health budgets by $200 million, then reversed the cuts, cancelled mandatory annual inspections of long-term care facilities, rejected proposals to increase nursing staff, passed Bill 175, which increases for-profit delivery of homecare, and rejected pleas to increase rehabilitation services for patients who are currently paying out of pocket.[142]

In New Brunswick, the 2018-elected Higgs Conservative government started out of the gate by announcing the closure of six rural overnight emergency departments. After ten p.m., patients requiring immediate emergency care from these jurisdictions would have to make the trip to the Saint John Regional Hospital. Public backlash was swift. Opponents insisted the regional hospital was overloaded twenty-four hours a day and lacked the surge capacity to handle new emergencies from the surrounding areas. After intense criticism and persistent public pushback, Higgs reversed the decision.

In Alberta, United Conservative Premier Jason Kenney thought privatization of health services was a reasonable way to reduce costs within the Alberta system. When asked about privatization in a news conference at an Edmonton seniors' home in 2019, Kenney asserted, "We're not going to let ideology get in the way of our focus, which is timely patient care."[143] Kenney also backed away from a three-percent increase in health spending made by his NDP predecessor. According to Mike Parker, HSAA president, Alberta health care workers have heard this discourse before. The freeze suggested by Kenney could mean a $1.2

billion cut to health spending.[144] Kenney also convened a blue-ribbon panel headed by former Saskatchewan finance minister Janice MacKinnon. The panel was convened, ostensibly, to tackle Alberta's spending issues. In a move reminiscent of the Klein era, MacKinnon's recommendations included slashing public-sector spending, making use of private clinics to deliver health services, renegotiating fees paid to doctors, and, if necessary, using, "... the hammer of legislation to bring doctors in line."[145]

In Nova Scotia, the outgoing Liberal government of Stephen McNeil (2013–2021), cut funding to long-term care two years in a row. The one percent cuts to one hundred long-term care facilities had significant impacts. In Dartmouth, Nova Scotia, the 111 bed Oakwood Terrace lost $82,000 in the 2015 cuts and $86,000 in the 2016 cuts. Administrator Anthony Taylor told CBC the McNeil government "... has cut more money from this nursing home than any other government has done to this home in the thirty-four years we have existed." It meant Oakwood had to let their scheduling person go, cut a reception position for evenings and weekends, and greatly reduce overtime. Halifax's Northwood also took a substantial hit. CEO Janet Simm said the 2015 cut amounted to $360,000 from their budget, while the 2016 cut amounted to a $600,000 shortfall. In response to the government's cutbacks, a long-term care facility in Port Hawksbury, Nova Scotia, issued layoff notices to employees in its cooking and cleaning departments.[146]

The McNeil government didn't stop there. The government took an adversarial approach in dealing with the province's nurses. At one point, it attempted to legislate them into the union of the government's choice. It also passed Bill 37, which stripped close to 40,000 health and community services workers of their right to strike and Bill 30, which ended a strike by the province's home-support workers. Bill 30 mandated that no further strikes could start until an essential services agreement between the union was in place. Despite the attacks on the province's public service sector and the cuts to long-term care, in February 2020, the McNeil government announced it would be dropping the corporate tax rate by two full percentage points, and the small-business tax rate by one half of a percentage point, foregoing $81 million dollars in revenue.[147] Eighty-one million dollars vanished and, with it, all the health care services it could have funded, such as help for the beleaguered long-term care sector.

The descent of the Canadian health care system from 1980 until present has been deliberate, divisive, and devastating. With the initiation of the neoliberal trade deals of NAFTA and the WTO general agreement on trade, the corporatization of the Canadian health care system was complete. There was also a vigorous trend to shift services outward into communities. Although I fully support the expansion of community health services, neither the infrastructure nor resources to support such services preceded or followed the transition. As a result, thousands of Canadians are paying for these services directly out of pocket or can't afford them at all.

Outsourcing also became popular. Canadians awoke to find multiple hospital-services related to laundry, cleaning, dietary, lab, and maintenance all contracted out to private companies. As Colleen Fuller tells us, "In 2015 alone, one health authority, Vancouver Coastal Health, forked over nearly $35 million to Sodexo, a French food services and facilities management company, amidst rising complaints about the awful food in in BC hospitals… so our tax dollars are helping to line the pockets of Sodexo shareholders, the largest of whom is the Bellon family of France. Pierre Bellon, the company founder, is on the *Forbes* list of the richest 500 billionaires in the world with a net worth of $4.1 billion."[148]

The defunding of the public system is only scheduled to worsen. The six percent unconditional yearly cash transfers are gone. Governments have promised to use tax dollars to fund the public health care system. Instead, those funds continue to help line the pockets of shareholders. In doing so, the government has forced the funders to pay more out-of-pocket expenses and accept drastic service reductions. This defunding deception for pecuniary corporate gain is the first phase of public system deconstruction. The second, includes the defrauding of billions of vital tax dollars.

Defrauding

The persistent cry of "no money for health" is a bogus claim. Health care is not cheap, nor are health care services free anywhere in the world. But there is more than enough revenue in this country to make health care the priority Canadians want it to be.

If there isn't enough money to support Medicare, then we can assume a few sound economic principles have all been exhausted. We can assume that governments everywhere have set stringent priorities to funnel what revenues they do have towards the most crucial of public systems: health care. We can also assume that they have acted in the most fiscally responsible manner, not wasting money on frivolous, useless projects that render little or no value to the public. We can also conclude, if revenue is an ongoing issue (which we are constantly told it is), that all opportunities to increase revenue have been exhausted and that revenue extraction has been applied equitably across the board.

Yet nothing could be further from the truth. We all know if money were tight, the squandering of billions of tax dollars would not occur. When you consistently reduce taxes for the country's richest, foregoing billions of dollars in revenue, surely the "no money" argument must be contrived. Otherwise, why wouldn't you apply the tax laws fairly and gain the additional revenue? The squandering of tax dollars on meritless schemes and the foregoing of billions of dollars in revenue while defunding public health care is a large Ponzi scheme.

In 2013, *Maclean's* magazine did a brilliant job outlining some of the ways governments wasted valuable tax dollars. The article "99 stupid things the government did with your money" is a collage of ridiculous spending by all levels of government. It clearly demonstrates that the fiscal stewardship of vital tax dollars has been in serious trouble for a long time. It also reinforces, with every irritating example, why the argument of "no money for health care" is weightless. One more thing about the *Maclean's* article: Since 2013, the vigour and extent with which governments have continued to waste tax dollars has not abated. It has only accelerated. We could fill these pages with ongoing erratic and wasteful spending—all lost revenue that should have been poured into Canada's public health care system.

Examples noted in the *Maclean's* article:
- In December 2011, with the hope of staving off the closure of Bowater Mersey paper mill, Nova Scotia's provincial government handed $24 million to its owner, in return for a swath of company land. By June the mill had gone out of business.

- The Bank of Canada spent nearly $40,000 to promote its new twenty-dollar bill. That spending included $35,832 to a company to design and install seven-story images of the new polymer note on the bank's headquarters in downtown Ottawa.

- When Swedish giant Ikea opened its first store in Winnipeg, the city and province offered a combined $22 million in subsidies. Ikea's annual sales of $32 billion are about three times what the province brings in annually from all forms of taxes, fees, and transfers.

- In Ottawa, the federal government spent $1.5 million to maintain a massive 108,000 square foot warehouse known as Plouffe Park, which was set to be demolished. It also poured another $5.5 million into the former headquarters of Agriculture Canada, though the building has been empty for years.

- A CBC news analysis found that $20 million doled out by Newfoundland to attract out-of-province business generated just fifty-eight full time jobs.

- Alberta's conservative government dropped $70,000 on a caucus retreat to a luxurious lodge to brainstorm how to trim the province's $3 billion deficit.

- Agriculture Canada handed $826,000 to Cardinal Meat Specialists Ltd. to help the meat-processing company research a sausage that doesn't burst open when its cooked... the parliamentary secretary for agriculture said a grant to develop a less-explosive sausage was critical to the government's focus on "jobs, growth, and long-term prosperity."[149]

Although we could continue with endless more examples, the point is this: Every day, across this country, our vital tax dollars are squandered in an inexhaustible orgy of unaccountability. This amounts to billions of lost dollars. With this degree of apathy towards tax dollars, there is absolutely no way we can believe that there isn't enough money in the system to fund Medicare.

A recent debacle in my home province of Nova Scotia also reinforces the level of tax-dollar disregard. The Yarmouth ferry service in Nova Scotia runs between Bar Harbor, Maine, and Yarmouth, Nova Scotia. In 2019, the ferry system in Yarmouth cost Nova Scotian taxpayers $13.8 million in operating subsidies and $8.5 million in updates to the American side of the terminal. Yet the ferry didn't make one single crossing during the 2019 season.[150]

We should also mention Canada's $20 billion loss from its involvement in the now-defunct Afghanistan War or the federal Phoenix pay-system debacle, which will cost upwards of another $3 billion to fix. All money that could have been redirected to health care.

The truth of the matter is that there is money for health care—lots of it. It's being defrauded from Canadian taxpayers. The argument that there isn't enough money to support a robust, public health care system lacks all fiscal and moral credibility.

All stripes of government have consistently lowered corporate tax rates while claiming there is no money for health. At the peak of Canadian industrial expansion and economic development in the 1960s, the corporate tax rate was forty percent.[151] Despite running large deficits, today, the corporate tax rate in Canada stands at fifteen percent. Irresponsibly wasting massive swathes of tax dollars is one form of defrauding the public. Simultaneously reducing vast amounts of corporate revenue to bolster shareholder's profits while running deficits is another.

The numbers speak for themselves. By 2011, Canada's corporate tax hit an all-time low of fifteen percent. By dropping the corporate tax rate in 2011 from 18.5 percent to 15 percent, Canadians lost $6 billion in revenue per annum. That's roughly a $1.75 billion loss for every percentage point decreased.[152] Over the past nine years, that translates into a $54 billion dollar loss. Corporate tax reductions (while running deficits) have been paid for by cuts to public services like health care. Over sixty years ago, the amount of tax paid by people and corporations was about equal. Since then, the amount of corporate taxes has dropped significantly. In 2015–16, Canadians paid $145 billion in income tax. Corporations paid $41 billion.[153] The amount of tax being paid (as a proportion of their profits) by Canada's largest companies has been dropping for years. An analysis of the financial filings of Canada's 102 biggest corporations showed these companies have avoided paying $62.9 billion in income taxes over a six-year period. Those corporations also benefitted from tax loopholes. In an average year, these 102 biggest corporations pay $10.5 billion less than they would if taxes were paid at the official corporate tax rate.[154] Imagine how $10.5 billion per year could have helped Medicare across the country. Think about the plight of Dr. Margaret Fraser and the staff of the Cape Breton Regional Hospital. Think about what an investment of $10 billion could have done for Cape Breton Island or Northern Ontario. Why are we constantly being told there isn't any money to support public health care? It's because in a neoliberal world, corporate wealth is king and public services are disposable. Neoliberalism is strengthening the power of the wealthiest one percent. That one percent doesn't care if Medicare survives.

While Canada appears to have trouble coming up with

money for public health care, Canadian corporations remain flush with money and enviable profits. In 2016, Canada's top five banks (BMO, RBC, CIBC, TD, and Scotiabank) booked $44.1 billion in pre-tax profit. That same year, they avoided $5.5 billion in taxes. From 2010 to 2015, Statistics Canada confirms their pre-tax profits soared by sixty percent. In the same timeframe, the banking sector's tax rate had dropped by almost the same amount.[155]

Canada's elite are also dodging billions in taxes due to a myriad of loopholes, shelters, and exemptions. In a report by the Canadian Centre for Policy Alternatives (CCPA), senior economist David Mcdonald asserts, "the richest 10 percent of Canadians enjoy an average of $20,500 a year in tax exemptions, credits, and other loopholes." Some of the key findings include: "The cost to the federal government for all preferential personal income tax treatments, not just for the rich, has ballooned from $90.3 billion in 1992 to a projected $152.3 billion in 2018. That's a 69 percent cost increase since 1992. Preferential treatment of personal capital gains cost federal coffers $6.1 billion in 2017. That's 1,415 percent higher than in 1992. The cost to Ottawa for preferential corporate tax treatments also ballooned, rising from $13.5 billion in 1992 to a projected $23.1 billion by 2018. That's a 71 percent cost increase since 1992. Thanks to preferential tax treatments ranging from personal income taxes, corporate taxes to RRSP enticements, and GST exemptions, the federal government will lose $202.5 billion in foregone revenue in 2018. That tax expenditure cost is up from $120.9 billion in 1992."[156]

The Canada Revenue Agency asserts Canadians have hidden up to $240.5 billion in foreign accounts, dodging $3 billion a year in federal tax. According to a CBC article, both domestic and foreign tax dodging puts Canada's tax gap at about "$14.6

billion a year based on 2014 data." Coincidentally, that number represents the entire federal deficit for the 2018–19 year. Even with excess spending, the federal government could have eliminated their entire annual deficit by closing that tax gap.[157]

On October 3, 2021, a global consortium of media outlets released information outlining the financial records of world's wealthiest citizens who hold assets through tax havens. The list included former world leaders, celebrities, billionaires, athletes, and public officials around the world. Much like the *Panama Papers* and the *Paradise Papers* before them, the *Pandora Papers* demonstrated that the wealth hidden off-shore continues to elude taxation systems around the globe. After the 2016 *Panama Papers,* world leaders were vocal in calling for a crackdown on tax-avoidance practices. It would appear some of those leaders are also part of the problem. A report by *CBC News* has identified at least 500 Canadian residents listed in the records. A 2020 report by the Paris-based OECD, lists the total size of offshore assets held in 2019 by eighty-four countries was $11.3 trillion. As Zach Dubinsky explains, "… the complexity and secrecy of the offshore system make it impossible to know how much of that is tied to tax evasion and other crimes and how much has been reported to authorities."[158] What is certain is that there are glaring loopholes that enable the rich everywhere, including in Canada, to dodge paying their fair share of taxes. If Canadian politicians and leaders were serious about funding health care, they could start by closing those gaps and redirecting the recovered revenue towards our public health care system.

There are other ways the Canadian public is being defrauded. Massive cutbacks and re-structuring of health care by the federal Liberals in the 1990s meant many services shifted from the more expensive hospital-care model to a more affordable community-based one. A fundamental flaw with this early restructuring was that the services were switched without the appropriate infrastructure in place. We are still trying to play catch-up as more and more services are off-loaded to the community setting while lacking the resources and infrastructure to support them. Many of the community services involved in this transition of care were not included in the basket of goods initially covered under Medicare. The shift from funded, institutionalized care to largely unfunded community care is a furtive form of privatization. I believe in the principles of primary care. I support collaborative health care teams and the need to shift episodic hospital care to fully funded, community-based care. As funders, we cannot ignore the fiscal reality of that conversion. Canadians are paying taxes that were originally designated to cover the cost of Medicare. Transitioning those services into an arena not covered by Medicare and forcing people to pay out of pocket is another form of defrauding.

Billions of dollars in tax revenue are lost every year due to a grossly inequitable tax system. A litany of tax exemptions and loopholes for the rich, coupled with the tax-dodging actions of multinational corporations, also costs Canada billions of dollars in additional lost revenue. Not holding these individuals to the same level of fiscal accountability as ordinary Canadians is the cruellest form of defrauding. It's a defrauding system that mandatorily extracts hard-earned tax dollars from ordinary Canadians while being completely lenient with Canada's most affluent. Politicians continue to hoodwink Canadians further by reinforcing the promise that Canadian tax dollars will be utilized to support and maintain Medicare. That is not what is happening. Less and less of the tax revenue obtained from ordinary Canadians is going towards sustaining Medicare. While these glaring inequities continue to exist, the argument that Canada lacks enough revenue to sustain Medicare cannot be taken seriously. Governments continue to reinforce this fiscal illusion. Canadians need to open their eyes to the realities of such rhetoric.

Defrauding is the second weapon in the neoliberal attack on public services. The third is deregulation.

Deregulation

Canada's proximity to the largest for-profit medical industrial complex places the sustainability of Medicare in an unenviable position. Coupled with the vastness of the country and the patchwork of provincial and territorial health care systems, the job of protecting Medicare from commercialization has become formidable. Increased efforts to privatize the public system have already attracted foreign commercial participation. For obvious political and economic reasons, US health insurance conglomerates are circling the Canadian market with an unambiguous eagerness.

Historically, government regulations have kept us safe. Since Canada's entrance into the free-trade agreements with the US in 1989, government regulations have been dissolving at a worrisome pace. This erosion continues with the revamping of NAFTA into the 2018 new trade deal between Canada, the US, and Mexico (USMCA). Neoliberal governments are hell bent on continuing down the path of deregulation. They repeatedly tell us deregulation will make us more economically competitive and will reap cost savings. The devolution of government regulation is a key tool in the neoliberal tool chest. Abdicating government regulative authority to corporatization has a concerning downside—it adversely affects public safety.

In 2000, many residents of Walkerton, Ontario, fell ill after drinking their own tap water, which was contaminated with E. coli. Seven residents died. In 2006, an overpass in Laval, Quebec, collapsed, killing three people, and in 2008, a tainted-meat outbreak at Maple Leaf Foods left twenty-two people dead. In Walkerton, we later found out that the provincial government had been lax in enforcing water-quality regulations. In the listeriosis outbreak involving the Maple Leaf tainted-meat case, the union representing the food inspectors said they didn't have enough meat inspectors to appropriately monitor the plant. One hour before the collapse of the Quebec overpass, drivers had called emergency services after witnessing large chunks of concrete falling onto the road beneath the structure. When government regulations are lax, safety suffers.

Over and above the weakening effects that commercialization imposes on our public health care system, there is another concern Canadians should be wary about. Canada's involvement in NAFTA and the WTO trade rules, as they pertain to protections of our health care system, may not be as ironclad as we think. As journalists Jim Grieshaber-Otto and Scott Sinclair point out, "It is an uncomfortable, but inescapable, reality that every important change to Canadian health care policy must now be vetted to ensure that it does not unnecessarily expose the health system to trade treaty litigation and potentially crippling sanctions."[159] From a health-policy perspective, the authors reinforce the need for due diligence and vigilance to ensure that commercial trade treaties do not erode Canada's current system or interfere with any future health reforms. This is particularly true for areas where creeping privatization and commercialization have already taken hold. The authors leave us with a serious warning about allowing increased commercialization of

Canadas public health care system through for-profit models and private funding: "... Commercialization weakens the protective effect of the trade treaty safeguards for health at the same time it facilitates the entry of foreign investors and service providers into newly created markets in health services... thus once foreign investors and service providers become involved in Canada's health care system—and the more they become—the more difficult and costly it will be to limit or reverse the trend towards commercialization."[160] Sadly, this phenomenon is now well underway as Canada's deregulatory efforts continue to accelerate.

In November 2018, a new NAFTA emerged. The new trade agreement, dominated and spurred on by the Trump government, refastened the three economies of the United States, Mexico, and Canada. The USMCA contained small gains for Canada but also lingering concerns. One area of concern centres around the patents on biologic drugs. The patents will now be extended to ten years, up from eight. Biologics are some of the most expensive drugs on the market. They are at the forefront of medical advances today and include drugs that treat cancer, tissues for transplants, and gene therapies. According to the Council of Canadians Trade campaigner Sujata Dey increasing the patents to ten years "... will also make the prices impossible for a public drug system—pharmacare—to bear. Already, increasing the biologic patents from five to eight years was estimated to come at a price of $800 million a year."[161] The USMCA also makes it easier for drug companies to extend their patents by making minor changes in how drugs are administered or by making minor component changes. This process, dubbed *evergreening*, also prevents regulators from accessing the patent drug company's test data when seeking approval for generic brands.[162]

Also worrisome is the new language on regulation. The new agreement requires the three country participants to ensure that any new international regulations "do not create unnecessary obstacles to international trade."[163] This predisposes the idea that trade will take priority over health regulation. USMCA is also filled with language around cooperation and refers to "risk-based handling" of regulations. Sujata Dey says risk-based handling "... means the onus is on individuals not on industry to prove harm. Regulatory cooperation allows companies to bypass parliamentary processes and come up with its own rules."[164] In many ways, the new USMCA reinforces many of the unmodernized features of the old NAFTA. It includes a corporate-centric focus and strong language around deregulatory cooperation rules. Other subtle changes may place considerable constraint on Canada's ability to enact health regulations.

Should the blood running through your veins be a commodity? Should every living part of you be available to sell on the market? If so, who gets to sell and who gets to buy? In terms of blood products, the latter question is easily answered. The poor are always the sellers. As discussed earlier, such is the case in the US, where the proliferation of private, for-profit blood centres has turned into a flourishing business. At these facilities, donors exchange their blood for an average of $30. That $30 plasma is then flipped into approximately $300 worth of a wholesale immunoglobulin product.[165] Destitute Americans continue to use the money to pay for subway fare, medication, food, and rent. For some, selling their blood is their sole source of income. Canada has now joined the "blood money" pack.

I was a front-line clinical nurse throughout the tainted-blood scandal of the 1980s and 1990s. In the early 1980s, approximately 2,000 Canadians were infected with the AIDS virus and upwards of 30,000 more were infected with hepatitis C from tainted blood. A Royal Commission of Inquiry was eventually created, chaired by Justice Horace Krever. The 1200-plus page *Krever Inquiry* was released in 1997. It outlined the convoluted sequence of events, overt negligence, and disastrous decisions within the public-health system that led to what Krever called "a nationwide public health calamity."[166] The report also emphasized that all blood collection should be "voluntary and unpaid, except in rare circumstances," and that "the malfeasance was systemic, driven in part by the profit motive."[167] Krever also added that Health Canada "must regulate in the interest of the public—not that of companies engaged in commercial activities."[168] Post Krever, Canada's blood system became safer, more rigorously regulated, and much more transparent. With the emergence of private plasma centres within Canada, donors like those in the US can now be paid for donating their plasma. It would seem, this is the exact scenario Justice Krever warned us about so many years ago. In what appears to be a complete shun of the Krever blueprint, Canada is now in the blood-brokering business. It remains inconceivable that in my lifetime, I would live to see such a major deregulatory shift within the Canadian health care system.

The World Health Organization (WHO) also endorses voluntary non-remunerated blood donation. WHO has gone on record to say, "An adequate and reliable supply of safe blood can be assured by a stable base of regular, voluntary, unpaid blood donors. These donors are also the safest group of donors as the prevalence of blood-borne infections is lowest among this group."[169]

The concerns of Horace Krever and the World Health Organization were not enough to stop Health Canada from turning its head in February 2016. That's when Canadian Plasma Resources (CPR) set up shop in, of all places, Saskatoon, Saskatchewan. That the birthplace of Medicare is now the home to a private blood-brokering clinic is a current, jaw-dropping Canadian reality. There is also a second centre in Moncton, New Brunswick. Today, the Moncton facility proudly asserts it is meeting all its targets. It's making 300 appointments per week for Canadians who want to sell their plasma. The clinic aims to boost that number to 1000 paid donors per week. The plasma collected in Moncton is not used domestically because it doesn't stay in Canada. It is potentially distributed across one hundred countries, mainly throughout Europe.[170]

Advocates for the for-profit system assert paid facilities do not adversely affect public donation numbers, are regularly inspected, and are safe. Opponents of the system suggest the blood-brokering business is not safe and Canadians should continue to follow the guidelines set out in the *Krever Inquiry*. They also maintain for-profit plasma centres adversely affect the voluntary blood donation supply chain. There is evidence to indicate that this is a real concern. Eight short months after CPR was established in Saskatchewan, Canadian Blood Services announced what proponents for a public voluntary blood system feared. The Saskatoon operation was "impinging on Canada's plasma self-sufficiency." CBS called for governments "to put a pause on for-profit plasma collection…"[171] Yet in July of 2017, Health Canada went on to approve a second for-profit clinic site in Moncton, New Brunswick. Blood activists across Canada continue to believe the private selling of plasma for international markets is really just beginning. There are discussions happening at this moment to indicate that before too long, every province in Canada may be opening its doors to new for-profit paid plasma facilities. If this proliferation is allowed, there will be nothing stopping Canada from becoming a major player in the commodification of blood products much like the US. This not only threatens the safety and supply management of Canadian blood products but has the potential to also pull scarce human resources such as nurses, doctors, and lab technicians from the public system to the private system. The creation of this private/public/parallel scenario will deplete vital human resources within the public system, further adding to services delays, cancellations, ER closures, and wait times.

A 2017 *Maclean's* article reports "more than 850 pages of communication between Health Canada, Canadian Blood Services, and CPR between 2009–2016 raise new questions about blood governance and its ties to industry. They indicate that since 2009, CPR's parent has been working in partnership with German-owned Biotest AG, the world's fifth-biggest player in the plasma-proteins therapy market; in 2009 it told Health Canada that it planned to invest $400 million to spearhead a Canadian plasma industry… The documents reveal that over years Health Canada worked collaboratively with CPR itself…"[172]

There is also documentation to indicate that Health Canada wants to ditch the highly respected *Krever Inquiry* and replace it with the *Dublin Consensus Statement*. The Dublin statement was created at a 2010 meeting in Ireland when various groups met, including the Plasma Protein Therapeutics Association. The PPTA is the lobbying group for the plasma protein industry. The activist group BloodWatch dismisses the Dublin Consensus. BloodWatch's co-founder Kat Lanteigne claims, "The Dublin Consensus has no standing whatsoever in terms of rigorous evaluation… Krever, on the other hand, was a publicly paid and authorized legal mind that studied reams of evidence. So why would a regulator go with the Dublin report as their reference? The answer is that no appropriate, well-informed regulator would do so."[173]

One last word on the deregulation of Canada's blood service. The proliferation of paid-plasma centres within the US has been tied to questionable screening guidelines as destitute donors give false information to pass medical screening tests. In one example, a desperate paid donor reported, "I can't eat if I don't pass."[174] It is exactly this interplay between for-profit clinics anxious for a plasma supply and desperate donors anxious for remuneration that has Canadian blood activists worried. Is the abdication from Krever and the proliferation of for-profit plasma clinics in Canada a possible deadly combination? In my opinion, it absolutely is.

The silence around the proliferation of private health clinics within the Canadian public health care system is deafening. Passed unanimously in 1984, the Canada Health Act legislatively ensured medically necessary care would be grounded in need-of-service, not ability to pay. The act prohibits user-fees and extra-billing. Provincial governments have an obligation under the law to report such transgressions to Ottawa, who, in turn, can levy fines against the offenders. In theory, Ottawa and the provinces are supposed to stop this illegal practice. The complete opposite is happening. Over the past decades, private health clinics have insidiously sprung up across the country. Far from the impoverished neighbourhoods of the for-profit plasma clinics, an array of executive health clinics, private MRI clinics, surgical clinics, boutique clinics, and ophthalmology clinics now dot the Canadian landscape. Building and expanding on the falsehood that they are rescuing the public system from overload; private clinic owners are now charging patients for services previously paid by MSI. With increased proliferation, owners have become much bolder, charging user fees disguised as "membership fees." Those fees now range in the thousands of dollars. Often, additional testing is diagnostically unrelated to the patient's primary issue but performed anyway in a bid to reel in additional fees, bolster profits, and give patients the assurance they are getting every bang for their buck.

Regulator responses have been less than robust. When regulators have attempted to monitor for-profit clinic activities, access has not always been easy. Such was the case in British Columbia with the Cambie Surgical Centre and its specialist referral clinic. The centre refused auditors access to their files, and it wasn't until the BC government obtained a court order to allow them access that the facilities finally conceded. This underscores the difficulty in government regulation of these private clinics once they have secured a steady foothold within the public health care system.

From history and physicals to private appointments to MRIs and surgical procedures, Canadians are now paying hundreds or thousands of dollars out of pocket for quicker access and to jump the queue.

A few years ago, the *Globe and Mail* looked at several patient cases as part of an investigation into unlawful extra billing by Canadian doctors. They compiled data on seventy-one private clinics across the country. Their data indicated, "that at least 63 percent of 699 doctors listed as owning or working at those 71 private-pay facilities also work in the public system—an indication the rules against extra-billing are widely ignored." The *Globe and Mail*'s investigation suggested that both, "conflict of interest by doctors... and double-dipping are routine." Patients interviewed also asserted they paid the price asked by the clinics often because they were desperate to receive treatment. In some cases, the patients took out bank loans to pay the fees.[175]

Rosalia Guthrie was one of several case studies the *Globe* investigation reviewed. Rosalia injured her shoulder a decade ago. Her family physician in British Columbia referred her to an orthopedic specialist, where she was placed on a waitlist. Unable to stand the pain, Rosalia called the specialist back and was told by his receptionist that for a fee, she could see the doctor in his private clinic. Her specialist was a minor shareholder at the private clinic, but that was never disclosed to Rosalia. After paying the $500 fee to see the specialist at the private facility, Rosalia was also billed an additional $3,850 for an eight-page report the specialist wrote about her injuries. After paying the fees, she was operated on in a public facility by the specialist. The provincial health plan paid the surgeon an additional $401.67 for the surgery. When Mrs. Guthrie's doctor discovered she had to pay these out-of-pocket expenses to get treatment, he filed a complaint with the BC College of Physicians calling her fee "a simple bribe." The records of the investigation that ensued indicated that neither the conflict of interest nor the extra-billing issues were ever adequately addressed. The surgeon didn't tell the college he owned shares in the clinic, and apparently, the regulators didn't ask. The extra billing issue was not addressed by the BC college. Extra-billing issues are enforced by the government, not the regulator. The surgeon told the regulator Mrs. Guthrie had chosen to see him on her own and that his receptionist had simply given her another treatment option. In the end, the regulator noted it was "troubled by the issue of a patient who had been seen in a non-insured private consultation being subsequently placed in the queue for insured surgery in the public hospital… no regulatory criticism is warranted." It is worth reinforcing that after jumping the queue, Rosalia's surgery was performed in a publicly funded hospital, obviously precluding another tax-payer who was unable to pay the requisite user fees to jump the system. The province found so much worrisome extra-billing at Rosalia's clinic that they tried to shut it down.[176] These practices serve to significantly undermine the ethos of our publicly funded system.

Paul Dutton was another *Globe* case study. A gastroenterologist at the University Health Network in Toronto told Mr. Dutton he could get a colonoscopy faster at a private clinic, rather than wait on the public waitlist. There was just one catch, he would have to pay $495 to see a dietician first. The physician acknowledged the patient really didn't need to see the dietician but confirmed he couldn't get the colonoscopy at the clinic without paying the consultation fee. In the end, Mr. Dutton decided to wait for an opening in the public system, feeling the doctor was just trying to drum up business for the clinic. Like Rosalia Guthrie's family doctor, Mr. Dutton also filed a complaint with regulators. The decision outlined by the regulators referred to the fact that the physician had initially told the college he didn't own the clinic, nor did he get any part of the $495 fee. It wasn't until later that the doctor admitted he was, in fact, a shareholder. The physician was never penalized.[177]

Ninety-year-old pensioner Geraldine Henry, from Woodstock, Ontario, ended up paying $1000 for basic cataract surgery, normally covered under the Ontario Hospital Insurance Plan. She is another case study from the *Globe*'s investigation. Her daughter, Brenda Seaton, said they had already waited six months for Dr. Derek Lui to preform her mom's eye surgery and they felt they couldn't have waited much longer. The surgeon informed them he had used up all his hospital OR time for the year but added Geraldine could have the surgery at a private clinic if she was willing to pay. If not, she would have no other option but to wait. The Burlington Laser Eye Centre did, in fact, admit that it charges Dr. Lui's patients a fee. Dr. Lui argued that the clinic kept the $1000 fee, and he had no shares in the clinic, nor was he ever an employee of the clinic. He was simply an eye surgeon who used the private facility and later billed OHIP, as he normally would. What remains unclear is why the Burlington Laser Eye Clinic can charge patients a $1000 fee for eye surgery that is already covered by OHIP.[178]

Cost is another concern. Research has demonstrated that when patients do have procedures at private clinics, the cost is often higher than when those same procedures are performed in public facilities. The *Globe and Mail* looked at billing records for surgeries at the Cambie Centre in Vancouver and found costs for procedures performed there much more expensive than those performed in public hospitals. "For example, billing records for sixteen surgeries done at the private Cambie Surgical Centre in Vancouver, including knee replacements and a hernia repair, show that patients were charged as much as $17,000 each for their procedures. By contrast, health authorities pay somewhere between $1,500 and $7,600 for the publicly funded surgeries that they sometimes contract out to those clinics..." Shockingly, clinic owners readily admit that the paying patients really do subsidize the non-paying patients whose procedures are covered by government plans.[179]

One thing both doctors and patients agree upon is that wait times for medically necessary procedures are often unbearable. For desperate patients, paying out-of-pocket or borrowing money to have the procedure performed in private facilities often seems like the only option. The bigger question for Canadians is why are our publicly funded facilities not extending OR hours to address the long waitlists associated with certain procedures, most of which are already covered under MSI? Dr. Etches of Doctors for Medicare believes the blame lies with government: "The private clinics are now deeply entrenched in the health care system... and that lies at the feet of the politicians."[180]

Between the autumn of 2016 and the spring of 2017, the Ontario Health Coalition (OHC) compiled a body of research also related to the private clinic situation within Canada. The OHC, with support from other provincial health coalitions, called all the private clinics they could possibly locate. Collectively they surveyed 136 clinics in nine provinces. From their interviews they found eighty-eight clinics in six provinces that were "charging patients extra user fees and selling medically necessary services."[181]

The OHC found twenty-one boutique physician clinics across the country, ten in operation within Ontario alone. Executive or membership fees appeared well beyond what average Canadians could normally afford and fees varied from jurisdiction to jurisdiction.[182] According to the coalition, "In Alberta we were quoted a price of $1,775 for mixed medically necessary and unnecessary services... In British Columbia we were told a comprehensive health assessment would cost $1,850, and annual fees ranged from $895 to $3,495. In Ontario we were quoted prices that ranged from $1500 to $4000 per year. In Quebec fees were measured by the minute—the longer your consult... the higher the fee. Fees to see a doctor ranged from $95–$320... and an annual exam, we were told, would cost $400."[183] Since the Coalition's report, Halifax has also become home to a new boutique executive clinic selling executive memberships and access to on-site physicians.

MRI services are covered under the Canada Health Act. Despite this fact, the OHC found forty-seven private MRI clinics operating across the country, with Quebec having nineteen private MRI sites alone. Fees ranged from $600–$750 in Quebec to $900–$950 in Saskatchewan. Fees generally ranged from $800–$900, with added fees tacked on for additional body parts scanned, which could add upwards of $500 to the total test cost. The researchers were also told by several clinics to bring their public health card, despite the fact the clinic was charging the patients privately.[184]

The OHC researchers found thirty-two private surgery clinics across the country with BC having fourteen such clinics. In four provinces, patients were charged directly for services. As with the MRI clinics, researchers were again told they needed to bring their health card despite the fact they were also being billed privately. Surgery for a torn ACL was quoted as being between $5,000–$12,000, with BC charging $8,000+ and Quebec charging $7,000.[185]

Toronto has several posh, private clinics. Clinics such as Health care 365, the Deerfield's Wellness Centre, Medcan, the Cleveland Clinic, and Medisys all cater to an elite professional class or anyone able to dole out the extravagant annual membership fees. Executive health plans/packages range from $1500 per year to $3900 per year, depending on which clinic and which package you select. Some of the clinics are equipped with gymnasiums, floor to ceiling windows, valet parking, executive showers, 24/7 access to on-call physicians, complimentary breakfast buffets, complimentary lunches, and gourmet coffee. Private health assessments range from two to six hours, depending on the package purchased.[186]

In a 2017 investigation carried out by the *Toronto Star* and the Ryerson School of Journalism, reporters posing as patients visited several of the plush boutique clinics located within metro Toronto. They found sprawling surroundings like at the Cleveland Clinic located on the thirtieth floor of a high-rise on Bay Street. The 26,000-square-foot space overlooking Lake Ontario offers both privately and provincially funded services with an executive health package going for about $3000. Medcan also charges an annual "membership fee of $3,300," which can buy patrons a wellness plan and fifteen diagnostic tests. At Executive Health Care in York Mills, fees range as high as $4500 per year for specialized health packages. The reporters also asked about the clinic's service of charging an additional fee of $1000 for 24/7 access to a "primary care physician." A receptionist told the reporter you would have access to the physician throughout the year. When the reporter asked if the physician would be like a family doctor, the receptionist answered, "Yes." When asked if one didn't pay could they still go to the clinic, the receptionist replied, "No." Later, Dr. Elaine Chin, clinic founder and director, clarified that the $1000 additional fee covered strategy sessions with a naturopath, physician, and nutritionist and that "primary care" "misrepresents the service." Chin went on to explain, "The $1,000 fee should be appropriately renamed to 'year-round coaching fee' as it refers to ongoing strategy sessions that continue the work from the initial session."[187]

So, what are Health Canada and the provincial health ministries doing to regulate this flourishing private medical boutique industry within the public system? It would appear not near enough. With our current paucity of health professionals, the proliferation of private clinics only adds to the drain of doctors, nurses, and technicians from the public system. For-profit clinics create a competition for resources between the private sector and the public sector. This competition reduces staff in the public system, leading to more overcrowding of patients and longer wait times, creating—not abating—lower standards of care.

Closer analysis indicates that the rhetoric from private-clinic owners that private clinics will save public health care is not borne out by the evidence. As these clinics proliferate, fees charged to patients continue to rise. In some instances, services that Canadians are paying for via their tax dollars are now being charged out of pocket. There is also an indication that double-dipping is expanding, as clinics bill individual patients and provincial and territorial health plans for the same services.

With wait times such an issue, frustrated Canadians with the ability to pay to jump the queue are more likely to do so. "This is the challenge of allowing a fringe of private enterprise in what is supposed to be a comprehensive public service for medically necessary care," says Bernard Dickens, professor emeritus of health law and policy at the University of Toronto. Dickens also claims, "Waiting lists in the public system—made longer by physicians moving into private clinics—push many Ontarian's to bypass by paying."[188] In addition to adversely affecting staffing shortages and wait times within the public system, there are other ethical and legal grey areas. Often, after their elaborate and timely medical assessments, patients with any medical abnormalities are sent back to the public system to be treated. This enables patients who are financially able to fast-track diagnostic workups and bring results back to specialists or family doctors within the public system, who are compelled to treat them. This treatment is not based on any kind of an acuity scale. It's solely based on the ability to pay. Dr. Danielle Martin of Toronto has seen this in her own practice. "The first time a patient showed up with 50 pages from an executive physical, I was floored... and because largely insignificant abnormalities that had shown up were sent back into the public system to deal with."[189]

There are other issues around treatment necessity, quality of care, and enforcement of standards. Are patrons subjected to clinic tests and procedures they really need or are they being tested unnecessarily to bolster clinic profits? Are private-clinic standards equivalent to hospital standards, and should an emergency arise during a procedure, how safe are private clinics? How are clinic standards assessed and enforced?

A cardiac stress test is a diagnostic test done to measure the heart's ability to respond to external stress. Under controlled hospital conditions, the patient is made to exercise on a treadmill in a manner that makes their heart work harder. Vital signs are closely monitored, and the patient is connected to an electrocardiogram machine. Several for-profit clinics now offer stress testing, which traditionally has been performed within accredited public hospitals. In hospitals, stress tests are usually performed by internists or cardiologists, and patients are buttressed by code-blue policies, intensive care units, emergency departments, and emergency response teams. For the patient with suspected heart disease, being stress tested is not a risk-free procedure. During a hospital stress test, where the patient collapses or develops chest pain, the patient receives swift emergency care. The patient is usually attended to by a specialist or a full code-blue team with members who are familiar with emergency response systems. The patient is also surrounded by diagnostic equipment and can be transported to critical care areas within minutes, often within the same hospital. Contrast this situation with a private clinic: While public hospitals usually follow tight regulatory control, that regulation may be more difficult to oversee within a private, for-profit setting. While an attending clinic physician maybe administering the stress test and the clinic may have protocols, there is no guarantee that the emergency response systems are equal to those in an accredited public hospital. The attending clinic physician must be a skilled first responder. Normally private clinics do not have a team of emergency responders, each with a specific skill set. Clinic staff have the added responsibility of keeping the patient alive until a 911 team arrives. Ultimately, a clinic patient who deteriorates will require transport to the nearest hospital. The attending clinic physician may not have had the opportunity to practise critical-care skills like those members of a hospital emergency response team. Depending on the nature of the situation, private clinic staff may not have the same amount of experience when dealing with sudden patient deterioration. Hospitals, on the other hand, are quite familiar with this scenario. The deterioration of an acutely ill patient within a clinic setting has limitations. The clinic response is orchestrated around transporting the patient out—to a hospital. Having a health crisis within a private clinic setting is not equivalent to having a health crisis within a hospital setting. Patients, often seduced by individualized care and the lavish surroundings of upscale clinics, may not understand this crucial difference.

In January of 2008, Jean-Jacques Sauvageau went to a Montreal-area private medical clinic because he was having trouble breathing. The receptionist who greeted Mr. Sauvageau didn't notice his difficulty in breathing. When other patients did take note of the patient's laboured breathing, a doctor was sent to see him. According to a report released by Quebec coroner Catherine Rudel-Tessier, Mr. Sauvageau was pronounced deceased by the clinic doctor. CPR was not initiated. The doctor called 911, but as the coroner's report explains, Mr. Sauvageau was left on a chair in the waiting room surrounded by other patients. The report goes on to say that the 911 dispatchers asked clinic staff to perform CPR, but they refused. Afterwards, the coroner requested that the Quebec College of Physicians be called upon to clarify guidelines for private clinics, that all administrative personnel in the clinic be trained in CPR, and that the clinic improve its intake methods and oversight of its waiting room.[190]

Compare this scene to a similar scenario within a hospital emergency department. Upon arrival, Mr. Sauvageau would have been triaged by a qualified triage nurse, skilled in applying the Canadian Triage and Acuity Scale (CTAS) and skilled at identifying an emergency. From what we know, it seems the patient would have been assessed at a high acuity level. Such allocation would have rendered the patient an expedited emergency room assessment with rapid access to cardiac and oxygen saturation monitoring, intravenous lines, vital signs monitoring, emergency medications, and every available emergency support required to assist him in distress. Had the patient continued to deteriorate, the emergency room team would have proceeded to call a code blue, CPR would have been initiated, and the patient would have eventually been transported to an ICU. Without knowing the fine details of the patient's condition, it is difficult to say with certainty whether Mr. Sauvageau would still be alive today had he just walked into a public hospital rather than a private clinic. What is absolutely certain is that leaving any patient to be assessed by an untrained receptionist, forcing other waiting-room patients to advocate for someone critically ill, leaving a patient in the midst of a cardiac or respiratory arrest without life-saving CPR, and leaving a deceased patient in a chair surrounded by other patients does not constitute even a minimum standard of care.

Probably one of the most well-known examples of what can

go wrong when patients deteriorate within a lavish private clinic setting is the untimely death of celebrity Joan Rivers. Rivers entered a New York City clinic for what was to be a routine procedure and possible biopsy in 2014. Somewhere during the latter stages of the procedure, Rivers sustained a cardiac arrest. A lawsuit filed by the actress's family alleges that "the doctors at the clinic were reckless, grossly negligent and wanton and abandoned the eighty-one-year-old comedian when emergency procedures were necessary to save her life." After the procedure, with deteriorating vital signs, a code blue was eventually called. It wasn't until twelve minutes after the code blue was called that someone dialled 911. The complaint against the clinic goes on to say, "None of the medical personnel at Yorkville Endoscopy who were present during the procedures performed on Joan Rivers possessed the knowledge, training and ability to handle the medical emergency." Ms. Rivers' daughter, Melissa, told the Associated Press, "The level of medical mismanagement, incompetency, disrespect, and outrageous behaviour is shocking and frankly, almost incomprehensible."[191] A week after the procedure, the actress died, succumbing to brain damage she'd sustained as a result of lack of oxygen. Although the Joan Rivers tragedy did not happen within the Canadian system, it, like the story of Jean Jacques Sauvageau, serves as a chilling reminder of what can go terribly wrong when private clinics offering services outside publicly accredited hospitals encounter emergency situations.

In 2016, Ms. Rivers's family announced that the malpractice lawsuit against the New York endoscopy clinic and the doctors involved had been settled for an undisclosed amount. In releasing a statement about the settlement, Melissa Rivers remarked, "Moving forward, my focus will be to ensure that no one ever has to go through what my mother… went through and I will work towards ensuring higher safety standards in out-patient surgical clinics."[192]

Other aspects of the public system continue to be shifted to private companies. During the fetishistic health care cuts of the 1990s, everything from laundry services to food services within Canada's hospitals were systematically contracted out to cut costs. These cost-cutting measures often sacrificed quality service delivery.

There was a time when a patient's medical files were transferred safely from physician to physician, as family doctors retired, or patients changed locales. Today, the handling of medical files has, in many jurisdictions, been contracted out to record-storage companies. Eighty-seven-year-old Grace Cove and her ninety-two-year-old husband, Wyman, from Amherst, Nova Scotia, had their medical files sent to a medical-storage company in Ontario after their doctor retired. The company was willing to send the Coves their records but not until they paid $309. Their niece attempted to intervene on their behalf but was also told that if they couldn't pay up, nothing could be done. The couple eventually found a new family doctor but still had to secure their files so that their new doctor would have critical medical information related to their medical history.[193]

Wendy Doran from Thunder Bay was also quoted a steep fee of $617 from Record Storage and Retrieval Services INC to obtain her medical files. The patient saw a notice indicating the closure of her physician's office and it included information that directed patients to the record-storage company, should they need to obtain copies of their medical files. Although Ms. Doran's file was lengthy, the cost of $617 still seemed exorbitant. The company asserted there are several costs to consider when companies are requested to forward confidential medical files to patients—costs such as file disassembly, photocopying, removal of references to third parties, and scanning. While the company agreed to work with Ms. Doran to get her the information she required, they were by no means obligated to do so.[194] The service is not regulated and private record-storage companies are free to set whatever fees the market deems acceptable. With this type of deregulation on the rise, patients like the Coves in Amherst and Wendy Doran in Thunder Bay, are left trying to negotiate a fee process that prohibits them from obtaining their own medical information. Patients who need the transfer of crucial medical information to assist their new care providers but are hard pressed to pay the inordinate fees associated with retrieving it, should not be subjected to this type of deregulatory practice.

In 2017, long-term care residents in British Columbia woke up to find themselves paying rent to the Chinese government. That was the year the federal government approved the sale of Vancouver-based Retirement Concepts to the Chinese insurance company Anbang. Shortly after the sale, the Chinese government took control of the company, alleging Anbang's chairman had committed financial crimes. The chairman was eventually sentenced to eighteen years in prison for fraud and embezzlement.[195]

By 2019, Selkirk Seniors Village in Victoria had become the third home in British Columbia controlled by the Chinese government to be taken over by the local health authority. South Island medical health officer Dr. Murray Fyfe appointed an administrator after assessing a litany of complaints filed from the families of seniors living at Selkirk Village. According to a CBC article, "The complaints cited neglect, emotional abuse, staffing shortages, health and hygiene issues and dangerous facilities." Dr. Fyfe claimed the action was necessary to protect the seniors living at the home, saying, "Based on the number and nature of contraventions outlined in the final investigation summary, it is my opinion that action is required to protect the health, safety, and dignity of persons in care at Selkirk Seniors Village." One of the significant concerns related to care was a constant understaffing situation within the facility. Staff at the facility seemed to be transient. The facility struggled to retain staff because employees were being paid three to five dollars an hour less than employees in other facilities.[196]

Earlier in 2019, two other facilities owned by Retirement Concepts also met similar fates. Nanaimo Seniors Village and Comox Valley Seniors Village were also placed under health authority administration. Both cited neglect of residents and serious, chronic understaffing levels. In Nanaimo, Central Island's former medical health officer Dr. Paul Hasselback cited, "concerns about medication delays, inadequate treatment of wounds, and poor care that might have led to hospital stays" as some of the reasons why the health authority decided to move in. The Hospitals Employees Union also voiced concerns about on-going staffing levels at the Nanaimo facility, saying low wages paid to care aids and licenced practical nurses were at least part of the problem.[197]

At the 136-bed Comox facility, the story was much the same. The local health authority had to step in amid "multiple complaints from family members and investigations into allegations of neglect, disease outbreaks, emotional and physical abuse, and staffing shortages." An administrator was also appointed there after forty-five investigations and inspections, between March and August of 2019, revealed numerous licencing contraventions. Dr. Charmaine Enns, North Island medical health officer, said it was "an unacceptable risk and potential for harm to persons in care."[198]

At the time of this writing, a fourth facility in the chain of Retirement Concepts private-care homes has also been added to the list of homes taken over by local health authorities. Summerland Seniors Village, in the Okanagan town of Summerland, came under fire after licencing inspectors found numerous infractions there. Contraventions were found in areas of nutrition, care planning, and hygiene. As with the other three sites, a health authority administrator had also been hired to over-see resident care and the changes required to meet the health authority's licencing standards.[199]

The Retirement Concepts examples clearly illustrate the problems for-profit facilities pose when caring for some of the most vulnerable members of our society. They also demonstrate the importance that strict regulation plays within the for-profit sector. As all four of the examples demonstrate, the multiple violations that were uncovered came after health authority licencing staff inspected the facilities during routine inspections. Without this type of regulation, one can only shudder to think how much worse conditions may have become.

While the sub-standard levels of care were occurring at the Retirement Concepts facilities, the province of British Columbia was still funding them. So, you have a case where the Chinese government owns these sites, but the sites are also being funded by the taxpayers. Clearly most of the money is not going into direct patient care. So, where exactly is the money going? It's difficult to say because there isn't much transparency around how these facilities allocate their funds once they are received. It is likely that however the for-profit homes are spending their money, much of it has to do with increasing profit margins. Staff who have worked at both for-profit and non-profit homes will tell you much of the for-profit money appears to go towards construction and ostentatious building designs. British Columbia taxpayers need to keep asking why tax dollars are being forked over to for-profit facilities at the same rate they are for non-profit sites, even though resident care is below industry standards.

A February 2020 report released by British Columbia Seniors Advocate, Isobel Mackenzie, suggested public money given to for-profit homes is not being spent directly on resident care. The for-profit facilities are providing sub-standard levels of care at the same time they are underpaying or under-hiring employees and over-investing in construction. For-profit and non-profit homes receive about the same level of government funding in British Columbia. But as Mackenzie points out, "… in the 2017/18 fiscal year, BC's for-profit care homes failed to deliver 207,000 hours of care for which they received public funding… Non-profit homes, on the other hand, over-delivered by about 80,000 hours. Overall, the non-profit sector spends about twenty-four percent more per resident per year on direct care—or about $10,000 for each resident… for-profits have more money in profit. They have twelve times the profit that the not-for-profit sector generates." The report goes on to say what licencing inspectors had verified. Staffing levels were critical in some for-profit homes with "… operators who are paying up to twenty-eight percent less than the industry standard—and they're funded to pay the industry standard." Jennifer Whiteside, who is the secretary business manager with the Hospital Employees Union, was not shocked at the report's findings. Whiteside maintains, "The wage gap has led to a recruitment and retention crisis in the industry, which in turn affects seniors… the system is broken, and BC seniors and those who care for them are paying the price."[200]

After the chairman of Anbang was jailed, the Chinese government created the Dajia Insurance Group to take control of the assets related to Retirement Concepts. That a foreign-owned insurance company provides sub-standard care to seniors in Canada is now a jarring reality. Currently, Retirement Concepts has seventeen homes within BC, two in Alberta, and one in the province of Quebec.

The problems around for-profit long-term care facilities are not limited to British Columbia. In Alberta, families also had many complaints around the care their loved ones were receiving at Athabasca Extendicare. Allegations surfaced about staff forced to ration incontinence products, which were kept under lock and key. The facility's administration asserted products were locked because they were being abused. Canadian Institute for Health Information statistics indicate "that from 2017–2018 the home had a urinary-tract infection rate of 7.5 percent, much higher than the national average of 4.3 percent." Don Bryan described the care his mother, Sheila, received there as "despicable," saying she "endured repeated bladder infections, yeast infections, and skin rashes" during her four year stay there.[201]

Shannex INC. is also a private organization that owns long-term care facilities across Nova Scotia and New Brunswick. In 2018, Chrissy Dunnington died from an infection related to a bedsore at a facility in Halifax, Nova Scotia. Chrissy had spinal bifida and required long-term nursing care. Chrissy's family developed concerns about her care shortly after she arrived at the Halifax campus. In late 2017, the family was told Chrissy had developed bedsores. In January of 2018, the family was notified that Chrissy had developed a fever, most likely secondary to an infection related to a bedsore. A few days later, the family became very concerned about her deteriorating condition and insisted the doctor be called. Chrissy was eventually taken to the hospital, where emergency room staff asserted had, she not been taken to the ER that day, she most likely would have died. It wasn't until that ER visit that the family saw Chrissy's bedsore, which they described as "traumatizing." The bedsore opening had a hole so deep, bone could be seen.[202] Four weeks of antibiotic therapy could not save Chrissy Dunnington. On March 22, 2018, she died at the QEII Health Sciences Centre in Halifax. Chrissy Dunnington was forty years old.

Regulatory licencing inspections for water supplies, food distribution, infrastructure repair, and acute and chronic care facilities keep us all safe. Attempts to replace profit for safety must be countered by all Canadians. Legislation that permits more regulatory power to large corporations or allows them to self-regulate places public safety in a compromising position. As Trish Hennessy reminds us, "The more Canadians allow their governments to weaken the protective role of regulation and regulators, the more we expose ourselves to many potential threats lurking in the dark corners of the global marketplace."[203]

The privatization of Canada's hospitals began in earnest during the feverish cuts of the late 1990s. Searching for alternative ways to deliver much-needed infrastructure without breaking existing government budgets, the P3 model of construction (public/private partnerships) arose. It was initially thought if private resources could build public infrastructure with government oversight and collaboration, construction costs would be lower, and this would leave for-profit building consortiums to do what they do best—build. Government costs for large capital expenditures could then be spread out over decades and costs could be kicked down the road, something that seemed very enticing to reigning governments. If it sounds too good to be true, that is because it is. Private, for-profit consortiums build and finance infrastructure and end up owning public institutions like our schools and hospitals. The government then pays something akin to rent or lease payments to the consortium for non-clinical services and rent. The contracts are usually multi-decades long. Much like ending a car lease, at the end of the hospital lease agreement, government doesn't own the building. For-profit consortiums obviously are focused on profit. When this type of agreement is applied to hospital construction and maintenance, it has the potential to become a dangerous situation. Despite the mountain of evidence and a litany of boondoggles surrounding the P3 craze, Canadian governments of all stripes blindly continue down the P3 hospital path.

One of the first countries to embrace the P3 hospital obsession was Britain. Currently, Britain is trying to distance itself from the P3 hospital model after decades of over-costs and disasters. Sarcastically labelled "Perfidious Financial Idiocy"[204] by the *British Medical Journal*, P3s in the UK have been tried and ultimately abandoned. The statistics surrounding their abject failure are astounding and are outlined in an article by the Ontario Health Coalition:

> The first 18 P3 hospitals in Britain cost $53 million pounds (over $110 million) for consultants alone. P3s in Britain have led to a 30% reduction in hospital beds and a 25% reduction in clinical staff budgets. In the first British P3 hospitals in Cumberland, shortcuts in facility construction and design have created a shocking host of problems:
>
> - two ceilings collapsed because of cheap plastic joints in piping and plumbing faults—one narrowly missing patients in the maternity unit

- the sewage system could not cope with the number of users and flooded the operating theatre with sewage
- clerical and laundry staff cannot work in their offices because they are too small
- a transparent roof design flaw and no air conditioning mean that on a sunny day the temperature inside the infirmary reaches over 33 degrees Celsius[205]

So, why does Canada persist in pursuing the P3 pipe dream? The lure of cost deferment is very appealing to all governments because hospitals are huge capital undertakings. Governments see the P3 phenomenon as a way of providing the service without incurring the debt. For the moment, that is. Governments also see it as a way of providing the service, without incurring the immediate responsibility. That means both cost and responsibility are transferred to future taxpayers. The P3 model also enables future governments to disown the adverse outcomes, claiming they were not responsible for the original contracts. With the governments of the day gone and the new governments disavowing ownership, the real losers are the taxpayers. Critics have also asserted there are powerful financial institutions and government entities who are friendly to contractors. Contractors may inflate the costs because, ultimately, tax dollars will be covering the bills. In short, governments end up subsidizing consortium profits. Whatever reasons governments may have, the real concern is that taxpayers are footing the bill for public hospitals that are of lesser quality and much more costly than their public predecessors.

Canada's track record with P3 hospitals is dismal. It is laden with over-costs, delays, safety concerns, and multiple transactional errors. Brampton Civic Hospital was Ontario's first P3 hospital. The Brampton P3 was contracted out to multinational corporations to build, and all the hospital's support services are managed by the private sector. Supposed to be a joyous occasion and heralded as a shining new piece of infrastructure, the P3 Brampton hospital experience ended up being mired in controversy. About a year after it opened, auditor general Jim McCarter outlined what appeared to be a disastrous set of contract flaws and somewhat of an accounting nightmare pertaining to the Brampton project. In his own words, McCarter concluded, "Our work indicated that the all-in cost could well have been lower if the government had built the hospital itself." The project cost taxpayers about $194 million more than if the hospital had been built publicly. There was also the case of an additional $200 million in interest charges to finance the construction because governments can borrow money at lower interest rates than private contractors. The Auditor General's Report went on to outline several major flaws with the contract. In 2001, the original cost for a 716-bed hospital was estimated at $381 million, but by 2004, the estimate ended up being $525 million for a 608-bed hospital. Discrepancies surrounding the quotes were never clarified. Interestingly, the hospital opened with only 479 beds in service in the fall of 2007. There were also $63 million in modifications made that were directly related to lack of planning and "rushing the project." [206]

The interest rates the building consortia were given were about 120 basis points higher than government's borrowing rates at the time. Dividends to equity investors were estimated at $260 million, which seems like an inordinate amount of money considering the original hospital price was supposed to be $350 million in total. Add to the cost of higher interest rates and dividends management and consultant fees, and it doesn't take long to understand why the costs ballooned out of control. Even the municipal fund-raising requirement for the new facility jumped from $100 million to more than $230 million because the original cost estimates ended up being doubled. As part of the deal, support services are managed by the private sector for the entire twenty-five-year lease duration. A convoluted project agreement determines how the hospital would handle sub-standard care issues. In the Brampton case, the contract includes an arbitration and legal process that must be followed should quality issues arise. As executive director of the Ontario Health Coalition, Natalie Mehra explains, "… if the private companies lose a patient as they transport her around the hospital, the hospital's only recourse is set out in the project agreement… They can seek a fine from the private company… if the private sector refuses, everyone has to bring in their lawyers to fight it out… the hospital has to decide whether it spends its remaining money on doctors and nurses or on lawyers and arbitrators." The Brampton P3 facility will cost Ontario taxpayers $3.5 billion over twenty-five years, for a total gain of 130 new beds.[207] Future generations are now saddled with this burdensome boondoggle.

Thirteen years after its opening, the Brampton Civic Hospital remains in the news for its long wait times, allegations of substandard care, and severe overcrowding issues. It is only fair to point out that nearly all of Canada's hospitals (publicly funded as well as privately funded) are under excessive strain and experiencing long wait times. However, given the cost of the Brampton Civic and its relative newness as a facility, it seems odd for the hospital to have so many news stories pertaining to its failure in service delivery. Observers are left to wonder if the shoddy workmanship, cost overruns, contract delays, and private oversight of ancillary services are contributing to the list of growing concerns around this P3 venture.

In January 2020, the Brampton City Council voted overwhelmingly to declare a health care emergency related to overcrowding issues and prolonged wait times at the Brampton hospital. Quoting Mayor Patrick Brown, "Normally a community declares an emergency if there's a reasonable prospect of life is in endangered… We felt strongly in Brampton that we meet those conditions… the health care has deteriorated so gravely that our citizens are at risk. There is a reasonable prospect that lives are at risk."[208]

Unfortunately, the P3 hospital issues did not end with the Brampton experience. Whatever amount of money the taxpayers are out for the Brampton hospital and however many stories there are of how the facility has failed its constituents, none of it has helped ease the craze of the P3 hospital frenzy in Canada. Years after the Brampton debacle, the Stanton Territorial Hospital in Yellowknife was also contracted out as a P3 project. In 2015, the contract for this site was awarded to the Boreal Health Partnership. Although comprised of several companies, Boreal is led by the British company Carillion. It was Carillion who led the partnership in the Brampton P3 as well. In the original estimates, the territorial government was supposed to pay Boreal $300 million for construction of the new facility and an additional $18 million a year to operate it. At the time of the announcement in 2015, it was estimated that over the thirty-year term of the contract, the total hospital cost would be about $700 million.[209]

However, in a major transaction flub, that number did not include the property tax on the new building. The old hospital and lot were assessed for $48 million, placing the government's property tax at just under $1 million. The new building and lot were assessed much higher at $300 million, placing the government's property tax at $4.5 million—a figure left unaccounted for during the initial estimate. With the new tax adjustment adding $140 million, the total hospital cost ballooned closer to $900 million.[210]

The problems with Stanton Territorial did not end with the major tax error. Staff insisted the facility has been plagued with water and sewage leaks. Employees of the hospital's health authority raised concerns of grey-coloured water, possibly containing body fluids, leaking in the renal dialysis unit. The leak was reported the day after the hospital opened in May of 2019 and has led to concerns about mould. A few days later, an infection-control specialist put a stop to the repair work, citing concerns over construction dust near the dialysis unit where "… some of the hospital's most significantly immuno-compromised patients" were located. Staff emails assert that the contractor had not completed any hospital construction prior to this job nor had the contractor had any CSA-standards training. The hospital also encountered another problem. The project contractor, Carillion Canada, filed for creditor protection after its British parent company collapsed in 2018. Carillion was originally responsible for maintaining decades of support services that span the contract. Eventually a company called Dexterra took over Carillion. Shortly after the water leaks around the dialysis unit were discovered, more leaks and mould appeared. Health Emergency Planner Carolyn Ridgley described a leak in the staff change room/bathroom in an internal document dated July 26, 2019. This leak had led to mould infestation. Ridgley also documents concern around work areas where work sites were "wide open for dust and debris to enter the elevator and continue to the patient areas."[211]

The new 248-bed psychiatric hospital in North Battleford Saskatchewan was also a P3 project plagued with delays. The province spent $407 million to have the hospital constructed and to have the facility maintained for the length of the thirty-year contract. The hospital had a scheduled opening date for the spring of 2018, but that date was delayed until March of 2019, after faulty insulation was discovered in the walls. Unfortunately, the problem with the insulation wasn't found until the exterior cladding had been applied and the cladding now had to be removed. Then in 2018, the UK-based Carillion collapsed, leaving Carillion Canada to find another facility manager. SNC Lavalin was eventually awarded the project. In March of 2018, another delay was encountered when a sub-contractor was unable to deliver on schedule.[212] Seventy-four days after opening, the North Battleford facility required a new roof. During the spring melt, the modular roofing panels shrank, leaving the roof with multiple gaps. A *CTV News* report revealed there were "twenty different roof leaks with snow melting." In addition to the all the delays and roof issues, water discolouration was noticed by contractors in October of 2019. This prompted the province to place signs around the facility advising the staff and patients not to drink the water. Testing indicated high levels of lead and copper.[213]

Throughout the country, politicians seem more interested in deferring hospital costs than saving money and providing safe, quality-built facilities. The Canadian landscape is now dotted with P3 hospitals. The P3 North Bay hospital built in 2011, cost at least $160 million more as a P3. The Royal Ottawa Mental Health Centre in Ontario was assessed at costing about $88 million more because it was a P3. It also had a cost overrun of $46 million and opened with fewer beds than originally planned. In 2014, former Quebec auditor general Renaud Lachance released information outlining that the cost of Montreal's University Health Centres, another P3 project, had capital costs that were more than $1.8 billion over the original estimates.[214]

In 2018, the outgoing Liberal government of Stephen McNeil in Nova Scotia announced a much-needed redevelopment of the QEII Health Sciences Centre. The government announced that the $2 billion project would be a P3 venture with a thirty-year contract. It would appear Canada's methodical march to P3 madness shows no sign of abating any time soon.

Once governments have sufficiently defunded, defrauded, and deregulated the system, collapse becomes inevitable. It is really a perfect plan. Deplete the system, throw it into chaos, and convince the public there is simply not enough money that can save it. Drill that message home by inundating the narrative with doomsday budget scenarios. Make taxpayers feel overwhelmingly guilty about cost. Attempt to form a parallel between the depletion of public finances and taxpayers' own personal finances. Once the system starts to disintegrate, people will clamour for relief. As disintegration progresses, people become desperate. They will eventually pay out of pocket for services their taxes are supposed to cover. There are endless examples of Canadians doing this across the country. Disintegration of health care services has a way of blinding folks. It's the cruellest of the four horsemen because it preys upon the vulnerabilities of the sick and elderly. Once disintegration has been completed, the stage has been set. Create a problem—offer the solution.

Deliberate Disintegration

The deliberate disintegration of Canada's health care system is well upon us. Why is Medicare such a target? Public health care systems cost money. They remain a soft target for profiteers because investment is required to sustain them. Profiteers see a glorious opportunity to intervene. Capitalists see profits being forfeited for a system they don't need. Why should collective tax dollars support a system when there is another option that is more profitable? For capitalists, the better option will always be commodification. For them, the market is the great equalizer, so much so that even the blood in our veins has now been fully commodified. It is important that readers understand this fourth horseman completely. Disintegration is deliberate. It's conscious and calculated. It's intended to upset the funders to the point that they are forced to concede that the public system cannot function. This type of strategic disintegration becomes incendiary. Taxpayers know they are paying vital tax dollars to support a system that suddenly can't seem to deliver. The waitlists are too long, human resources are drained, hospitals are dirty, technology is outdated, and emergency departments are crashing. Panic and anger set in. There is a lot of panic and anger in the system at this moment. In frustration, funders abandon their principles of communitarianism and egalitarianism. When they do, a lifeline is thrown out. That line is secured to privatization, profit, and further public-system demise. Deliberate disintegration encompasses the final stages of a bigger plan. It's designed to not only tell funders public health care cannot work, but to show them, repeatedly. It systematically creates a slow ossification of public services. With the constant spinning of this roulette wheel, Canadians are selected randomly... many of them fatally.

Deliberate public health care disintegration is incremental. The deleterious effects of defunding, defrauding, and deregulation create a *measured form* of disintegration. Anything more acute or more abrupt, especially in Canada, would not be politically tolerated. Sudden dismantling of the public health care system would lead to increased activism. Activism is neoliberalism's *bête noir*. To avoid that, the funders need to come to their own conclusions. What better way to do so than to dismantle a system they cherish, stone by stone? As it falters, a new, improved alternative is offered. The new alternative doesn't triage according to acuity, it triages according to the ability to pay. Just like the old fable about the boiling frog, the temperature of disintegration starts out tepid and is gradually increased. Funders don't perceive the graveness of the situation until the end. This prevents them from jumping too quickly. But just like the frog in the story, the public health care system is eventually cooked to death.

The stories about the disintegration of Canada's iconic public health care system are now ubiquitous. If you listen to the news or follow social media, the stories are persistent. Those of us who have worked in the system since the 1970s are reminded of just how far and how fast we have fallen. Sadly, for the new generation of health care workers that reference does not exist. This makes the disintegration of Canada's Medicare system even more ominous. For the new crop of physicians, nurses, technicians, and administrators, the current level of system dysfunction is all they know. Older experienced staff are exiting the system. This exodus is contributing to system disintegration. Intergenerational intersectionality is fading. It's costing us not only a wealth of system experience, but a wealth of resistance to the system collapse. In other words, you can't miss what you never had, and you can't defend what you don't miss. In this environment, opposition to system disintegration is subtly stamped out. Activism acquiesces to attrition.

Brian Sinclair could never have guessed when he was a young boy growing up near Sagkeeng First Nation northeast of Winnipeg, that he would eventually become the face of the disintegration of the Canadian public health care system. Brian's mother was a residential school survivor and his father was of mixed First Nations and European descent. His family remember Brian as brave, as a young man who once ran into a burning building to help rescue people caught in a fire. He also volunteered at the Siloam Mission in his community. Shelter staff remember him as "quiet, humble and kind." His older sister reaffirmed that sentiment remembering him as "a kind and helpful little boy, a smart student." Life was not always easy for Brian Sinclair. He was placed in foster care at the age of twelve and was involved in sniffing solvents with a group of local kids. His parents eventually separated, and Brian and his siblings went to live with their father about a year after being released from foster care. When Brian was in his early twenties, his father passed away. Later in life, Brian would end up losing both his legs to frostbite.[215]

The real tragedy around Brian Sinclair's life occurred on September 19, 2008, when he was advised to visit the Winnipeg Health Sciences Centre's emergency department after visiting a community physician. The physician felt the forty-five-year-old double amputee might be experiencing a bladder infection, and so she wrote a note explaining her concerns. She advised Brian to give the note to the front desk staff in the ER. She also arranged a ride for him in a taxi van. But once in the ER, a lack of treatment and lack of attention turned deadly for Brian Sinclair. After thirty-four hours of waiting, he was eventually pronounced dead at 12:51 on September 21, 2008, slumped in his wheelchair, face ashen, with rigour mortis setting in. He was estimated to be deceased somewhere between two and seven hours before a security guard found him. During an inquest into Brian Sinclair's tragic death, thirty-four hours of security footage and witness testimonies were reviewed. A man had chatted with Sinclair at around the ten-hour mark of his stay. This man told a nurse about Brian's long wait, but he was informed she was attending to sicker patients first. A health care aide saw Brian on both his first and second night. She told a nurse Brian had waited twenty-four hours, but the nurse shrugged it off. The aide also told a security guard, who responded by saying, "I think he's here to watch TV." When Brian started to vomit, another couple also alerted security. He was given a bowl, but medical staff never came to see him.[216]

The inquest would hear that Brian Sinclair died as the result of a treatable bladder infection related to a blocked catheter. Staff also testified Brian was a regular at the ER, and when pressed by the Sinclair family lawyer, staff admitted they assumed he was "… sleeping it off."[217]

Many factors come into play in assessing the death of Brian Sinclair. A complete system breakdown of the emergency room process in tandem with overt racism were two major contributing factors. Both are characteristics of a constant and unrelenting form of system disintegration.

In a convoluted way, the ER cannot be held solely responsible. As previously outlined, the ER is a seismograph for the greater system functionality. When the greater system turns into a non-system, ERs around the country enter a state of dysfunctionality. ERs are meant to function within a collaborative, supportive community structure. They were never meant to function as the sole alternative to an entire public health care system.

In the reporting that followed after Brian Sinclair's death, the country heard about the working conditions in the Winnipeg ER at that time. ER nurse Susan Alcock said there was no reassessment nurse on duty for hours and that three nurses had called in sick. Reassessment nurses manage the waiting room and continuously reassess patients after they have been triaged. In an ironic twist of testimony, Susan Alcock confirmed the reassessment position had been created after another death in the Winnipeg emergency room in 2003. The ER nurse also asserted the waiting room was "A sea of people" the night Brian Sinclair was there and she described her shifts as "horrific and incredibly busy." The hospital also had a twenty-percent staff vacancy rate. Beds for admitted patients were hard to find. The nurse also commented on the layout of the ER, citing it was difficult to see patients in the waiting area from behind the triage location. Nurse Alcock said she had written a letter to management, months before Brian Sinclair's death, complaining about "overcrowding and staff shortages." She added she was eventually reprimanded for writing the letter of complaint and was accused of jumping the chain of command. No changes were made.[218]

At the time of Brian Sinclair's story, I was managing a community ER on the other side of the country in Dartmouth, Nova Scotia. The story of this patient's experience and his tragic death sent shock waves through Canadian emergency departments everywhere. Those of us working in emergency rooms lived with the stark realization that the Brian Sinclair tragedy could be our reality at any point in time. All of us, like the Winnipeg ER, were trying to cope with crushing workloads, circuitous vacancy rates, significant overflow issues, ambulance backlogs, and the proliferation of an in-patient cohort occupying emergency room beds with absolutely nowhere to go.

The inquest into Brian Sinclair's death ended six years after his untimely death, in 2014. It concluded that Brian's death had been preventable. The provincial government also announced it would be moving forward with sixty-three recommendations from the inquest.[219] The Health Minister also warned many of those recommendations could take months or even years to implement.

The inquest's findings were criticized by Dr. Jill McEwen, former president of the Canadian Association of Emergency Physicians. Dr. McEwen later told CBC, she believed the findings were flawed and that her organization's input was ignored. She was also disheartened to hear some of the recommendations would take years to implement saying, "hospital officials need to step up to deal with an overflow of patients, not just the emergency departments… we need to implement a solution right now, not years from now… because a similar thing could happen."[220]

The inquest also became a contentious event. The Sinclair family, along with advocacy group members, walked out of the proceedings. Vilko Zbogar, the Sinclair's lawyer, advocated for a special inquiry into the role that racism and stereotyping played in Brian's death. The inquest eventually rejected that request, placing more emphasis on structural changes within the ER and procedures around how patients were triaged. Dr. Barry Lavallee, an Indigenous family physician, who later became a member of the Brian Sinclair Working Group, didn't mix his words when referring to the inherent racism within the Canadian health care system that Indigenous people face every day: "Brian Sinclair died because he was Indigenous, full stop." Dr. Janet Smylie agreed, "… surveys have made it quite clear that Indigenous people cannot expect equal treatment when they go to the ERs." As soon as the inquest focused primarily on the Health Sciences

Centre and reduced the contribution racism played into Brian's death, Indigenous organizations walked away. Out of the sixty-three recommendations, only five hinted at the racist elements of Brian Sinclair's treatment.[221]

This leads us to one of the most unsettling aspects of health care disintegration. When superimposed upon marginalized groups, the effects are more heavy-handed. In addition, disintegrating systems may utilize racism as a means to an end, to justify the rationing of dwindling health care services. Brian Sinclair was revictimized, by another layer, a cultural triage if you will. A cultural triage works in tandem within disintegration, creating a deadly coalescence. Upon marginalized populations, this intersection of system disintegration and cultural triage creates a double-damage scenario. The system wants absolution from racism. It's easier to change the layout of a triage area or change a waiting room policy. It's much more work and requires more dedication to alter the pervasiveness of inherent racism within a dysfunctional health care system. Ultimately, disintegration and racism become moored to each other. Together they create a set of circumstances that leads to an entirely different level of sub-standard care. In a system disintegration, the social determinants of health are elevated to a new status. When they are lacking, the damage is more profound. Would the floundering system on the night of September 21, 2008, have resulted in the death of a white middle-class man? It could have. But in reviewing the testimonies and the security footage of that fateful evening, one thing appears certain: the double-damage effects of disintegration and systemic racism most definitely delivered a fatal blow to Brian Sinclair. As is the case in so many circumstances, when systems fail, it's often the people who need them the most who suffer the greatest.

The grainy security footage of Brian Sinclair slumped in his wheelchair in the Winnipeg Health Sciences Centre emergency room has long since faded into the archives. Every painful hour of the last part of his life had been captured on video. His name, like his image, is indelibly written into posterity as one of the most tragic reminders of what health care disintegration looks like. It represents the true pathology of neoliberal capitalism.

Dr. Robin McGee knows a thing or two about system disintegration. A clinical psychologist from Annapolis Valley in Nova Scotia, Robin was diagnosed with advanced colorectal cancer on May 6, 2010. Her harrowing experience is painstakingly chronicled in a book she authored, *The Cancer Olympics*.

A fit, non-smoking professional in her forties, on June 26, 2008, Robin began to experience rectal bleeding, a hallmark of colorectal cancer. She also had a strong family history of the disease. She wasn't able to get an appointment to see her family doctor until July 14. On that day, Robin didn't see her regular family doctor because another physician was covering. This doctor did not order any bloodwork, mention a colonoscopy, or book a follow up appointment.

For a while, Robin's symptoms improved. In October 2008, they returned, except this time, she was experiencing what she described as passing "bloody sheets of skin."[222] She went back to see her regular family doctor, who agreed to send a surgical consult, examined her, and ordered bloodwork. The doctor recorded serious signs of bowel pathology and was aware that Robin had a direct family history of the disease but did not include any of that information in her referral letter to the surgeon. The bloodwork had revealed an elevated inflammatory marker. This result meant Robin could possibly have cancer, but this information was also not mentioned in the referral letter.

Another piece of crucial information was left out of the referral as well—Robin's family doctor was dissolving her practice.[223]

By November 2008, Robin was searching for a new family doctor and eventually managed to find one. She also managed to have a fecal occult blood test (FOBT) done after advocating for this herself by speaking directly with the hospital's lab physician. The FOBT is a colorectal-cancer screening test. Robin called to make an appointment with her new family doctor and was told that she couldn't get an appointment until January 2009. In the meantime, the test for fecal occult blood came back positive.

In 2009, Robin visited doctor number three. He seemed sympathetic and agreed that she needed a colonoscopy. Meanwhile, Robin continued to pass "bloody epithelial tissue."[224] The third doctor agreed having a positive FOBT was a concern, particularly around timeliness. He said he would follow up with the surgeon's office regarding this. That follow-up never occurred because doctor number three forgot. His receptionist checked off that a call had been made to the consulting surgeon's office regarding the wait time for the colonoscopy. No such call was ever made, and the positive FOBT result was never sent to the specialist.

In July 2009, Robin's bleeding increased. She called her doctor's office attempting to find out where her referral was in the queue and to report worsening symptoms. The doctor's receptionist told Robin that the referral had been sent and received and for her to call the specialist's office. What Robin did not know was that the surgeon had abdicated the triage of consults to her administrative assistant. Upon calling the specialist's office, the receptionist told Robin that there was an eighteen-month wait for a colonoscopy. When asked if she should try and go to Halifax, the receptionist replied that the wait in Halifax and elsewhere in the province was worse. Robin McGee later discovered this information was not true. This particular specialist had an eighteen-month waitlist. So, with hallmark signs of colorectal cancer progressing, Robin McGee waited. Neither receptionist had conveyed Robin's message about worsening symptoms to their respective physicians.

By Christmas 2009, Robin's symptoms expanded to include pain and constipation. She called the specialist's office again and insisted upon being seen. She was given an appointment date of February 2010.

When Robin finally saw the specialist, she tried to articulate her constellation of symptoms that included "… copious bleeding… constipation and undue frequency, the bloody discharge mixed with mucus."[225] The specialist seemed indifferent. After the doctor's digital rectal exam, there was "dark red blood on her examining glove" and the doctor quipped, "There is a hemorrhoid there… nothing to write home about."[226] Ultimately, the specialist agreed that a colonoscopy was warranted to "… be sure of what we are looking at."[227] The colonoscopy did not occur until May of 2010, two years after Robin had first sought help. Eight days later, the specialist met with Robin and her husband to inform them of the results. "You have colorectal cancer… you will need radiation, chemotherapy, and surgery… You will need a permanent colostomy."[228] It is difficult to comprehend the web of system disintegration that entangled Robin McGee. As a result of it, her life is forever changed.

Since 2010, Robin has had five major surgeries, twenty-eight days of radiation, and over forty chemotherapy treatments. Diagnosed with metastatic colon cancer, she became a face of heroism and determination within a disintegrating health care system. She also became a tireless patient advocate and a voice for patients affected by medical error across the country. In the end, three of the physicians Robin encountered on her diagnostic pathway were disciplined by their professional college. All four were successfully sued in a malpractice action.

I first spoke with Robin McGee by telephone from her room at the Princess Margaret Cancer Centre Lodge in Toronto on April 15, 2019. She sounded amazingly bright and cheerful and exuded helpfulness and confidence. We discussed her journey through the health care system and what could be done to improve the glaring inadequacies. About a year later, I had the privilege of meeting her in person at her book signing. Her calm and cheery voice matched her kind and welcoming demeanour. She maintained an unambiguous air of serenity despite her experience with health care disintegration. That serenity didn't mean that she had stopped fighting.

Robin experienced medical error a second time in 2016. A radiologist missed a two-centimetre tumour in her pelvis on a CT scan. When the malignancy was discovered six months later another scan, the tumour had grown to ten centimetres. The lesion had progressed into an inoperable location in her pelvic sidewall. Sadly, her cancer surgeon reported this error had cost her the only chance she had of cure. Her first recurrence was in 2017.

In March 2020, just as Covid-19 emerged, Robin McGee's cancer progressed again. After numerous Covid-related resource delays, she accessed more cancer treatment. She must remain on chemotherapy for the rest of her life.

This is the thing governments and politicians do not understand about the face of health care disintegration. If it doesn't kill you as it did Brian Sinclair, it changes the trajectory of your entire life. It creates suffering and destroys families. It robs all of us of what could have been. It creates unimaginable anxiety and forces patients to stare down death every waking minute of their lives. Robin McGee once reflected that she was "... stunned at the prospect of losing my life and forfeiting forever the beauty of this world."[229] These are the harsh realities of cutting funding and not making health care a priority. This is what a disintegrating public health care system produces.

Health care disintegration knows no age limits. Ninety-four-year-old Rita Bedford from Chilliwack, BC, was blind. She lived in a Cascades senior care home, owned by Sienna Senior Living. In 2018, Rita's apartment became engulfed with bedbugs. Staff asserted they were ordered not to tell the ninety-four-year-old what was happening. They also allege they were told to keep the senior confined to her room.

In December of 2018, Rita's daughter, Anne-Marie Burgon, was contacted by the facility's head nurse. She was told another resident had brought bedbugs into the facility and one bug had been found on her mother's bed. Ms. Burgon assumed the facility would handle the issue. A timeline later sent to the health authority outlined a conflicting story. In it, staff allege on December 19, 2018, the day before the nurse called Rita's daughter, that they had found "10 small bite marks ... blood spots on her bed and five possible bedbugs on her floor." By January 2, 2019, an employee complained to the Ministry of Health. The employee asserted management had instructed them to lie to Rita about why she couldn't have Christmas dinner or visit with her friends. Staff were told to tell her she was sick. Staff also allege they were warned not to speak out about the infestation, or they would risk getting fired. The employee, distraught about the situation, said, "I just can't do it any longer... this woman is 94 and blind. Locked in a room, being chewed up while management hides it." Staff took photos and made a video. They sent the video of bugs hurrying across the resident's mattress, blood stains on her bedding, and dead bedbugs on her floor to Rita's daughter in Ottawa.

Anne-Marie Burgon played the video multiple times, in disbelief. According to the timeline, pest control did visit the facility but never treated Rita Bedford's apartment. An ant trap was placed under her mattress. Anne-Marie Burgon also heard from staff how upset her mother was, crying and asking, "Are these bugs crawling on my skin?"

Staff complaints, in conjunction with a complaint from Anne-Marie Burgon, ultimately led to an investigation, and in the spring of 2019, two reports were filed. Cascades was found to have insufficient levels of staffing and found guilty of not protecting residents and not providing a safe and clean environment. The Ministry of Health became involved. Sienna Senior Living apologized to Rita and her family, saying, "We recognized that there were actions that should have been better." No one from the company could say why Rita Bedford had not been allowed to leave her bedbug-infested room for weeks, nor would they comment on the threats of employee termination whistleblowers alleged. As for Anne-Marie Burgon, she, like the rest of Canadians who read this story, could never have imagined this substandard level of care could have occurred within the Canadian system. In 2018, Sienna Senior Living was worth $1.2 billion.[230]

Jim Patten's family knows a thing or two about Canada's disintegrating health care system. Several years ago, Jim was diagnosed with lupus and ended up on renal dialysis. He was living in British Columbia at the time and decided the proactive thing to do was to get on the kidney transplant waitlist. He went through the requisite testing and was told he was number one on the list for patients within his age group. Tested and confirmed to be a match, his daughter was going to be her father's donor. Things seemed to be going well. The family was hopeful. But in 2012, Jim had to move back home to Newfoundland. That's when things started to unravel. Once home, Jim spoke to the transplant coordinator for his region. Initially, the coordinator told him he could be on the transplant list within six months, but he would have to redo all the necessary testing. Jim started the re-testing process. The screening process ended up taking two years, not six months. Ongoing delays prevented him from getting on the transplant list. Every time he attempted to get placed on the list, another test was a year older or expired and he kept needing to repeat testing. When he went to see the specialist (with a letter from another specialist), he was told the letter was insufficient. He'd have to go back and get another letter. When the testing had finally finished, Jim met with the nephrologist. He was told he'd passed a physical examination. Despite this, he was turned down for a spot on the transplant list. Jim requested his file be reconsidered for a second opinion. The transplant coordinator told him the file would go to Halifax. Eight months later, when he called to check on the status of his file, the transplant coordinator confirmed the file had not left her desk. She asserted he would not be considered because of his lupus.

With ongoing dialysis, Jim Patten started to develop vascular issues. In 2017, an infected hip replacement led to a right-leg amputation. The sixty-nine-year-old started to develop the myriad of complications longstanding dialysis patients often encounter, one of the main reasons a transplant procedure is so vital. By the spring of 2019, Jim was staring down another operation—to have his left leg amputated.

In a statement to CBC, the Nova Scotia Health Authority said pre-transplant testing depends on the health status of the individual. Depending on age and pre-existing conditions, more or less testing is required. Once the chart is completed, it's then sent to a committee for review at the NSHA in Halifax. The review by the committee can take "several months."

By 2019, Jim Patten believed his chances of getting a new kidney were gone. The seven-year wait, coupled with ongoing dialysis treatments, had wreaked havoc on his body. For a man who had been at the top of a transplant list with a matched donor waiting, Jim Patten's trajectory within the health care system had taken a downward spiral. He became an amputee on regular dialysis and believed the health care systems of Nova Scotia and Newfoundland and Labrador were to blame. He also believed the transplant coordinator for his region bore some responsibility as well. His daughter told *CBC News,* she was "disgusted" by the health care system in the province of Newfoundland and Labrador. She also confirmed it was now too late for her dad to receive a new kidney because over the course of waiting, his health had deteriorated too much. In a heartbreaking 2019 admission, Raquel Patten told CBC, "We get to watch him die, because nobody would allow [the transplant] to happen."[231] On May 19, 2020, Jim Patten passed away.

The stories of Brian Sinclair, Robin McGee, Rita Bedford, and Jim Patten represent the thousands of patients caught in the final stages of the breakdown of our health care system. None of them could have imagined the unrelenting effects that disintegration would impose on their lives.

Disintegration cost Brian Sinclair his life. Disintegration cost Robin McGee a significant portion of her young life and years of increasing physical and mental anguish. Disintegration cost Rita

Bedford weeks of living in isolation, fear, and loss of personal dignity. Disintegration cost Jim Patten years of watching his body deteriorate and forced him to live his last years tied to a dialysis machine.

These are the real-life stories, the real people, the real families that health care disintegration affects across the country, every single day. Medicare was never designed to inflict this level of suffering or despair. It is the result of an unyielding agenda in which all levels of government are complicit. Proponents of defunding public health care assert their loyalty to the market. They have their arguments and the means to communicate them. Those arguments are as lightweight as their empathy towards the sick and vulnerable.

Chapter 5

THE REWARD PUPPETS

*When capital has more freedom than people,
serious democratic deficits are guaranteed.*

—Patrick Iber

Neoliberal proponents believe pretty much everything should be left to the free market. They also believe in protecting the rights of capital at all costs, even if it means sacrificing democratic systems. Neoliberal thinkers do not believe in reciprocity. They believe they should be free to influence government policy, but government policy should not be free to influence them. In other words, democratically elected institutions need to step aside. Left to their own free-market devices and allowed to disengage from regulation, fair taxation, and public services, capitalists offer the perfect solution for those who do not possess the same privileges. Let them freely build capital through private investment and they, in turn, will build businesses, hire people, and drive the economy. If only it were that straight forward.

As author Yuval Harari points out, "… in its extreme form, belief in the free market is as naive as belief in Santa Claus. There simply is no such thing as a market free of all political bias." Harari explains, "Markets by themselves offer no protection against fraud, theft, and violence."[232] Political systems are required to ensure trust in the system. When markets are not regulated appropriately, this leads to distrust, which can result in economic calamity. Harari reminds us, "That was the lesson taught by the Mississippi bubble of 1719 and... by the US housing bubble of 2007, and the ensuing credit crunch and recession."[233]

In a section of the book *Sapiens* entitled "The Capitalist Hell," Harari draws attention to two arguments capitalists rely on to promote profit accumulation.[234] The first is that they will always use their profits to expand production, hire employees, and drive the economy. This is not always true. In recent decades, we have seen the exact opposite scenario occurring. Corporations are not using surpluses or profits to reinvest in the economy. Rather, they are stock-piling their unprecedented profits to bolster executive salaries, hoarding profits in foreign tax-sheltered jurisdictions, and engaging in open-market repurchases (stock buybacks). William Lazonick, professor of economics at the University of Massachusetts, Lowell tells us, "From 2004 to 2013, 454 companies in the S&P 500 Index, expended fifty-one percent of their profits, or $3.4 trillion on repurchases, on top of thirty-five percent of profits on dividends... Of profits not distributed to shareholders, a big chunk was parked overseas, under a tax loophole that encourages US companies not to invest at home... the real bottom line: Corporate profits are high, but corporate investment is low."[235]

A similar observation prompted former Bank of Canada governor Mark Carney to take an unusual swing at Canadian corporations back in 2012. As previously mentioned, he advised them to stop sitting on "dead money" and to reinvest in productivity.

At the end of the first quarter of 2012, non-financial corporations had a cash hoard of $526 billion. David MacDonald, CEO of Toronto technology corporation Softchoice, said, "Part of the problem… is that many Canadian institutional investors are very conservative, and encourage companies to pay dividends or buy back shares rather than investing in growth."[236]

The second argument capitalists employ is that if they use their profits indiscriminately to build larger surpluses by mistreating employees or abusing labour, the unsupervised market will always protect workers. This is based on a premise that when this occurs and workers find themselves underpaid or overworked, they can simply leave and work for a competitor. Left without workers, profits will decline and the business will be lost. There is more fiction than truth in this argument. As Harari points out, "In a completely free market… avaricious capitalists can establish monopolies or collude against their workforces."[237] Harari reminds readers that "the rise of European capitalism went hand in hand with the rise of the Atlantic slave trade"[238] and "the slave trade was not controlled by any state or government. It was purely an economic enterprise, organized and financed by the free market according to the laws of supply and demand."[239] Harari cites both the American slave trade and the Great Bengal Famine as two examples of how atrocities were committed within burgeoning economies and points out that "capitalism has killed millions out of cold indifference coupled with greed."[240]

Both these neoliberal arguments, coupled with Harari's chilling reminders, bring us to this question: What happens when public health care systems are abandoned by the political institutions designed to protect them? We don't have to look any further than the United States health care plutocracy for answers.

While the American health insurance industry, big pharma, and other health care conglomerates continue to amass huge profit margins, approximately 45,000 Americans die every year because of lack of access to the system—more "cold indifference." This solidifies Harari's theory. If profits and surpluses remain supreme goods, people will continue to be sacrificed on the altar of greed. This remains the "sticky wicket" of the free-market argument. When applied specifically to the provision of health care services, it cannot be guaranteed that profits are either attained or distributed fairly. For services involving health, this becomes a crucial point. Health care systems do not deal with regular commodities. Instead, they deal with services that are required to sustain life and mitigate pain and suffering.

However dismal their performance in the allocation of health care services, proponents of the free-market system will always have what they feel are their shatter-proof arguments. Here are a few:

We cannot afford a public health care system. There isn't enough money.

Health care systems are expensive to operate and maintain. Health care is paid for via collective taxation systems; out of pocket (privately), which includes insurance-purchasing; or a combination of both public and private payments. In Canada, maintenance of health care systems costs provincial and territorial ministries of health anywhere from forty to fifty percent of their entire budgets. As shocking as this statistic seems, we must learn to counter the force-fed narrative that this is an expense Canadians cannot afford. Much like our own mortgage and rent payments that disproportionately whittle away regular paychecks, health care, like shelter, must be considered as a basic human necessity. The argument cannot be solely premised upon affordability. It must be shifted to one of prioritization. That is not to say that funds for health care services are infinite and should not be appropriately managed. They absolutely should be. Those of us involved in health care know there is waste occurring in the system every day. As chapter four recounts, it remains difficult to enter a discussion around affordability. Billions of dollars are continuously wasted by all levels of government and billions more foregone in tax loopholes, offshore tax havens, and laws that help corporations defer and dodge taxes. Before we accept the rhetoric of unaffordability, we must evaluate who is funding that narrative and who stands to gain by diverting valuable tax dollars away from the public health care system. Until Canadians insist that this "bleeding of revenue" ends, the affordability argument surrounding health care cannot be accurately assessed.

My home province of Nova Scotia offers perfect examples of "wasted tax dollars anywhere but let's rein in spending on health." Nova Scotia is a poor, tax-burdened jurisdiction with the highest child poverty rates in the country. It also has serious access-to-health care issues and at the time of this writing currently 105,187 residents are without a family doctor.[241] Waitlists are long and health care horror stories abound. Despite this, in February of 2018, the provincial Liberal government was busy renovating the back seven stairs to Province House. The $130,000 spent on the renovation (which included a consultant's report saying the renovations should cost $85,000) went to repair the seven stairs the premier used to get to his office. At the time, the deputy infrastructure minister, Paul LeFleche, said about the cost overrun, "We wanted the work commensurate with the prestigious nature of the building."[242]

In keeping with those prestigious spending models, the next year, the same Liberal government spent another $1.1 million on the south garden update at Province House. But just as the provincial government was writing its $1 million cheque for gardening services, Nova Scotians were becoming familiar with the beautiful face of thirty-three-year-old Inez Rudderham. In 2019, Ms. Rudderham was diagnosed with stage three anal cancer. In her frustration with the health care system, she made an emotional plea on social media daring Premier McNeil to meet with her. With no family doctor and several unsuccessful ER visits, Rudderham's two-year delay in getting treatment meant her cancer had likely become more advanced. She had to undergo rounds of treatment and, like Robin McGee before her, wishes the system had been different. The premier acknowledged that there were challenges in the health care system with respect to access, saying, "… we've always acknowledged that… but we've continued to make adjustments."[243] This left taxpayers wondering, if you've always acknowledged that, why would you spend $1.1 million to update a garden at Province House or pay $137,000 to refurbish seven stairs? Why wouldn't health care be prioritized and positions for family doctors be funded to help people like Inez Rudderham?

In February 2020, the premier of Nova Scotia told the Halifax Chamber of Commerce he was cutting the provincial corporate tax rate by two full points, dropping it to fourteen percent. Claiming the cuts were an investment in business the premier said, "… I *hope* it's an investment you turn around and reinvest in Nova Scotians."[244] The keyword in the premier's sentence was "hope." After all, once the rate was dropped, there was absolutely nothing binding the business community to reinvest the windfall back into the province or its citizens. What was binding for the province, though, was the precipitous loss of $70 million in badly-needed revenue from the tax drop. No small amount of change for a poor province. At the time of the corporate tax-cut announcement, the province had yet to release its 2020–2021 budget. When pressed about how the lost revenue would affect spending, the premier wasn't offering any specifics. But he did say, "Our budget will also reflect a real understanding that there are some people in the province that are not feeling the same growth that we are."[245] He also told reporters after his speech the budget would be "targeted towards organizations and communities… who haven't felt the success of this economy."[246]

That brings us to another point. The premier repeatedly referred to Nova Scotia's economic picture as a success story. As early as June of 2019, he was touting his government's economic success within Nova Scotia. After all, since 2018 there had been a two-percent increase in the provincial population and Halifax, as a capital city, was growing. Halifax Index chief economist, Ian Munro, seemed to endorse the premier's sentiments when he said, "The consistent population growth has helped foster an all-time high in business confidence."[247] Not only that, but young people seem to be heading back to the province in record numbers, and Stephen Moore, vice president of MQO Research, said, "Young people are increasingly looking at Halifax and Nova Scotia as a place where they can establish a career and raise a family."[248] The labour force also saw a jump with about 8,000 more workers employed in 2018, which Ian Munro says, "… is a sign of a healthy and thriving economy."[249] Although you'd be hard-pressed to find children living in poverty, seniors, students, young families, or Nova Scotians looking for a doctor like Inez Rudderham saying they felt like they were in the midst of an economic boom, the point is this: Long before the premier dropped the corporate tax rate, the government's assertion was the economy is booming. Munro used words like "healthy and thriving ... Strong population growth... our labour force is expanding... 8000 more workers employed."[250] The Halifax Partnership tweeted, "The Halifax Index tells our city's story—the strength of our economy."[251]

Despite the boom, the provincial Liberals saw the need to forgo $70 million in revenue the following year, not to stimulate a sluggish economy or prop-up a flailing economy but to give additional support to an already robust economy. It's a picture we see again and again across the country. While lack of money always seems to be an issue when funding health care, governments like the McNeil government of Nova Scotia continue to reduce vital revenue streams by dropping corporate tax rates, even when it's not required. They aren't even apologetic about it. The Nova Scotia example reminds us that even when business is thriving, more corporate profit is always better. The problem with that logic is those same governments are the ones voicing the loudest concerns about the affordability of public health care. They continue to reduce revenue with "the hope" that the corporate excesses will somehow find their way back to the Inez Rudderhams of the world. Most often, they do not.

Of course, there are endless examples of how dropping corporate tax rates and losing revenue don't translate into reinvestment. What does happen when revenue is lost is that there must be an adjustment. Most often that adjustment comes in the form of reducing funding to public services like health care. Corporate profits are paid for by cutting public health care systems. Alberta is a prime example.

In April 2019, Jason Kenney announced he wanted to drop Alberta's corporate tax rate to eight percent over a four-year period, a move that would cost the Alberta government about $1.76 billion annually. Kenney touted the approach as a game changer with respect to job creation. He asserted the massive corporate tax cuts would create 55,000 jobs and boost the Alberta economy by nearly $13 billion. The tax cut only applied to large and general corporations. Interestingly enough, small businesses, which make up the majority of businesses in Alberta, remained exempt from the cut.[252] If we look at the figures around Kenney's corporate tax cuts, it would appear he may have been dreaming.

In Alberta, large corporate entities such as Suncor, Huskey Energy, and Imperial Oil are substantially owned by foreign shareholders. This means the profits obtained by cutting the corporate tax rate flow to foreign ownership outside the province. In the past, revenue gained by dropping the corporate tax rate has not fallen back into the hands of labour. As a matter of fact, while corporate tax rates continued to fall, wages of workers when adjusted for inflation, stagnated. As corporate profits continue to surge, households continue to go deeper and deeper into debt. During the twenty-year period between 1998 and 2018, Canada's combined federal-provincial corporate tax rate fell by thirty-eight percent. In contrast, the rate of investment fell by forty-five percent over the same time period.[253]

So, what about Kenney's claim of 55,000 new jobs as a result of the tax cut? According to Statistics Canada and Finance Canada's economic impact numbers, the $1.76 billion dollars in annual tax cuts may lead to about 5,300 jobs over a two-year period, a far cry from Kenney's claim of 55,000. Of course, the way Kenney planned to cover the lost revenue was to cut provincial spending by $7 billion. Economist Hugh Mackenzie estimates that strategy would lead to "a net loss of 58,300 jobs over four years,"[254] proving again that revenues lost on corporate welfare are being paid for by cuts to public services.

There is another side of the affordability argument. In 2013–14, West Africa became engulfed in one of the worse Ebola epidemics in history. Canadians watched in horror as over 11,000 people of all ages died. Health care systems in Africa became overwhelmed and ran out of supplies. Canadian researchers had long been conducting Ebola research at the Public Health Agency of Canada (PHAC) National Microbiology Laboratory in Winnipeg. They had created an experimental vaccine that had yet to be tested on humans. The Canadian Institutes of Health Research (CIHR) quickly partnered with PHAC and the Canadian Immunization Research Network (CIRN) in Halifax to start phase one of the clinical trials. The study involved forty participants from the Halifax community and was a success. Soon afterwards, phases two and three were conducted in Guinea with the help of Canadian researchers. The results were tracked and it was concluded that the Canadian vaccine had proven to be very effective against the disease. Dr. Alain Beaudet from CIHR said, "The vaccine has proven itself to be effective, and holds the promise of saving many lives in the future… as Canadians we can all take pride in the major role Canadian science is playing in the global struggle against this deadly disease."[255]

In 2021, thirty-seven-year-old Candice Cruise was told her inability to breathe was related to a condition called pulmonary hypertension. Cruise's condition was further complicated by the fact she was twenty-one weeks pregnant. Doctors at the Toronto General Hospital decided to place the young mother on a form of life support called extracorporeal membrane oxygenation (ECMO), in effort to keep both her and her baby alive until the baby was big enough to deliver. Until now the treatment had been used for significantly compromised Covid-19 patients. Tubes inserted into Candice's chest delivered oxygen and pumped blood from one side of her heart to the other. For seven long weeks, she remained in ICU connected to the machine, trying to buy her baby time. What was so incredibly amazing was that the treatment had never been used before on a pregnant woman suffering from pulmonary hypertension. On June 10, 2021, a team of specialists from the pulmonary unit at Toronto General, the high-risk obstetrical unit from Mount Sinai Hospital, and neonatal teams from Toronto's Sick Children's Hospital delivered a one-pound baby boy via C-section as his mother lay connected to life support. Three months later, Candice Cruise underwent a successful double lung transplant and eventually went home to her family, including her new baby boy. The story is one for the Canadian medical history books. Not only because it had never been done before, but because it saved two lives and helped blaze the trail for other women suffering from this life-threatening disease.[256]

These two examples and hundreds more like them, offer another side to the health care affordability equation. While the system may be expensive and costly to maintain, we have to ask what do we get for our money and what are we buying? Capitalists want us to be preoccupied with the cost side of the equation. Seldom do we concentrate on the benefit side. The stories surrounding the Ebola vaccine and Candice Cruise and her baby tell us that even at the height of defunding, the Canadian Medicare system continues to do ground-breaking work all across the country. Imagine what we could do if reinvestment was poured back into the public health care system.

So, what exactly are we buying when we fund public health care systems? We are buying health and vitality for all citizens. We are reducing pain and suffering, improving lives, researching ways to combat chronic disease patterns, inventing life-saving vaccines, and saving lives. Our technologies and treatments are getting people back to work and helping them live more productive lives. They are flying organs across city limits via drones, expediting their arrival to anxiously awaiting recipients. They are engineering gene therapies that are helping the immune systems of cancer patients to recognize and destroy cancerous cells, sending patients into remission. They are keeping one-pound babies alive in neonatal units and helping seniors stay in their homes longer. What dollar value should one assign to such triumphs?

In the fiscal year 2016–17, the federal government spent $311 billion. The largest expenditure ($48.1 billion) went to cover elderly benefits such as OAS and GIS payments. Canada Health Transfers accounted for $36 billion and Canada Social Transfers came in at $13.3 billion. The budget was also crystal clear on where most of the revenue comes from. It comes from taxpayers. Personal income tax accounted for forty-nine percent of revenue while GST accounted for almost twelve percent. Corporate income tax paid for the 2016–17 fiscal year was a little over fourteen percent. Although there are always detailed discussions and explanations around costs, economist Armine Yalnizyan reminds us all that "… we don't talk about how those expenditures benefit us."[257] If we are caring for the sick and elderly, sending cancer patients into remission, and saving babies, that speaks to who we are as a country.

No health care system is the world is free. Health care costs should be managed and evaluated in a responsible and ethical manner. No discussion around health care affordability can be had while billions of dollars are squandered by government at all levels, and tax laws continue to allow the siphoning of funds from valuable revenue streams. Cuts to public health care should not be funding corporate profits.

Capitalists inundate Canadians with the cost narrative only. Money spent on saving the lives of baby Cruise and his young mother was not money lost. Just as the money spent on developing the Ebola vaccine that saved thousands of men, women, and children from dying was not money that disappeared down some dark hole. For the people who become the beneficiaries of such care, it is a reminder that as humans, we all have a responsibility to help each other. Public health care systems reduce health care disparities between the rich and the poor. They speak to what we value as a nation. They are investments in national solidarity and our interconnectedness as people. Caring for people is very much a Canadian characteristic. Medicare ensures that when our turn comes to access care, Canadians will have our back. Our turn could always be just around the corner. The affordability argument brings us full circle to asking, can we afford to have a public health care system? The response to that question is best answered by asking—can we afford not to have a public health care system?

Allowing the rich to buy their own health care will free up services and spaces in the public system.

In February of 2010, Newfoundland's premier Danny Williams caused quite a stir. Williams had been diagnosed with a faulty mitral valve, and in February, he decided to have his valve repaired—in Florida. Almost immediately after the news hit the presses, public opinion lined up on opposing sides of the topic. Medicare supporters saw William's decision to seek medical treatment in the US as a betrayal of the Canadian public health care system. Ardent free-market supporters saw William's decision as his individual right to seek treatment wherever he wanted. Whatever way opinions divided, the debate reignited the question, if you have the means, why can't you have the freedom to buy your own health care? For-profit health care supporters will tell you doing so allows the rich to jump the queue. This will free up space in public systems and reduce wait times. If this seems like an oversimplification, that's because it is.

There is a finite number of health care resources including skilled professionals. Nurses, doctors, technicians, or therapists cannot be massed produced. It takes time and money to educate health care professionals. People continually exit the system for a litany of reasons and matching supply with demand is a complicated process. Health care professionals can only work in one system at a time. Within the duality of a private/public parallel system, a competition for human resources emerges. If a jurisdiction with one public hospital is compelled to share its nurses with a private facility, the public facility will have fewer nurses. The same holds true for family practitioners, surgeons, physiotherapists, and technicians. Given current wait times, where there is no competition for resources, it stands to reason that wait times will increase if a percentage of health care professionals are removed from the public system. The argument that the coexistence of private/public systems reduces wait times and frees up spaces in the public system is not supported by evidence. The people who can afford to jump the queue are in the minority. Once the private/public/parallel system is created, it leaves many Canadians on public waitlists, with significantly fewer human resources.

Doctors have traditionally made more money in the private sector. This is because long public waitlists have been used as incentives for doctors to promote their private clinics. Keeping the public waitlist long sends frustrated patients towards private care, even if they have to borrow to pay for it. As previously mentioned, there are numerous examples of Canadian physicians suggesting frustrated patients visit their private clinics as an alternative to public waitlists. By dividing their time between public and private facilities, these physicians are reducing their ability to work in the public system—contributing to increased public wait times. This creates a cyclical pattern of depletion.

Evidence supports the finding that in jurisdictions where there is more private care, wait times in public hospitals have risen. Take Manitoba, for example. Until 1999, patients who had cataract surgery done in private clinics had to pay an additional cost listed as a "tray fee." In 1998–99, researchers found that the wait time for patients whose surgeons worked only in the public system had a median wait time of ten weeks. Patients whose physicians worked in both the public and private settings had median wait times of twenty-six weeks. The same holds true for countries that have embraced parallel/private/public hospital systems such as New Zealand and England. In these countries the waitlists are larger and the wait times longer for patients in the public system when compared to countries like Canada that have a single-payer, universal system.[258]

MRI waitlists in Saskatchewan also point to longer public wait times as private clinics move in. Between 2015–2019, the number of patients waiting for an MRI scan in the province doubled despite the government allowing patients to pay privately for MRIs. The plan was for the government to allow the private operators in as long as they promised to provide a free scan to someone on the public waitlist every time a private scan was done. The free scan had to be done within fourteen days of the private scan, creating a one-for-one arrangement. As waitlists mounted, the provincial auditor general was eventually called in to investigate the backlog issue. It appeared the one-for-one process was not always being done, at least not in a timely fashion.[259] As of June 2019, there were 10,018 patients on the waitlist, up from 5005 in April of 2015.[260]

Australia has a combination of a tax-supported public system that coexists with a privately insured option. Proponents of a hybrid system often refer to Australia as a shining example of duality. A closer look at the data suggests a more cautionary tale is unfolding.

In an article by Dr. Bob Bell and Stefan Superina, the authors explain the impact the two-tier system has had on Australia's public hospitals and public bed spaces. The hybrid system was initiated in Australia in 1997. Currently forty-five percent of the population have some form of health insurance. About two-thirds of hospitals are publicly funded, and the remaining one-third are privately funded. Out of the 630 private hospitals, only thirty-six (as of 2015) had ERs. Trauma services are only available in publicly funded facilities.

When it comes to hospital bed access, the impact that privately insured patients have had on publicly funded beds makes for an interesting story. The proportion of privately insured patients in publicly funded beds continues to increase. According to the authors, "… The proportion of private patients in public hospitals has more than doubled over the past thirteen years and some public hospitals will admit up to forty percent of patients under private insurance."[261] Privately insured older patients are more likely to end up in publicly funded beds. This may be related to the co-morbidities associated with age and/or the lack of ER availability within the private settings. This also means publicly funded hospitals receive a revenue boost from insurers, in addition to their global budgets funded by the state. This further incentivizes hospitals to place privately insured patients in publicly funded beds.

Access to beds is not the only issue. Wait times for procedures for public paying patients in public beds are more than twice as long as privately paying patients in public beds. Bell and Superina point out, "A longer wait for public patients might be acceptable if the extra revenue achieved with private pay patients improved public access... looking at wait times for four high volume services—cataract extraction, coronary bypass, hip replacement, and knee replacement—average wait times for public patients in Australia are longer than in Canada."[262]

There is one last cautionary word for Canadians who feel that a privately insured option might be worth trying. Insurance costs continue to rise faster than the rate of inflation. As Bell and Superina remind us, "Tiering of private insurance (bronze, silver, gold) is currently underway in Australia, getting insurance for cataract or total joint surgery now will require the most expensive gold coverage."[263]

Allowing a minority of rich patients to circumvent public health care systems does not free up or reduce wait times in those systems. Evidence demonstrates that the opposite is true. Canada adopting a private insurance system for medically necessary treatments and physicians' services would create a two-tier system that would adversely affect public bed spaces and waitlists. If this system existed, public facilities would receive additional private funding for housing private-paying patients. This would increase public hospital bed utilization rates, as public hospitals are incentivized to house more private patients. The Australian system is an exemplar of this. The waitlists for private patients will decline as the waitlists for public patients will increase. Should Canadians embrace the world of health care duality? Based on the evidence, Canadians would be wise to avoid the tiering of health care. Building a world-class health care system where everyone has access based on need is cheaper and more efficient.

Health care is not a right but a commodity. As such, it should be allocated to the free-market system.

Proponents of the free-market system in the United States insist the free market distributes health care services better than state-run systems. The hype around this discourse centres on the argument that health care is like other market commodities and should be relegated to market forces. A closer look at the economics surrounding this rationale tells another story.

Core tenets of the free-market system cannot be applied to health care services. Take supply and demand, for example. When a company sells a regular commodity like watches, price is adjusted based on the principles of supply and demand. If demand for watches continues to rise, one of the first things that happens is that prices of watches will increase. As long as demand exceeds supply, sellers can raise their prices. The more prices rise, the more watches will be offered to buyers because doing so will increase the seller's profits. Eventually prices even out at the new higher level of demand and an equilibrium is set. These principles of supply and demand don't work the same in a health care market. Higher prices rising from increased demand has not always brought forth more supply. It takes years to graduate nurses and doctors and develop new drugs. Rarely does health care supply overshoot demand. Unlike watch prices, health care prices rise quickly when demand picks up and they remain high. Defying regular supply and demand dynamics has caused health care costs within the free-market system to continue to soar.

The supply and demand model has notable features. The main parties are buyers and sellers. Buyers are good judges of what they get from sellers. Market prices are the primary drivers for coordinating the decisions of buyers and sellers and left to its own devices, the market leads to an efficient allocation of resources. For regular goods and services, this is how the market works. The commodification of health care services complicates the above laws of supply and demand. Unlike in a traditional market, third-party insurers exist and have a financial interest in health care outcomes. Because these insurers, instead of patients, are paying the providers directly, they set the rules surrounding the allocation of health care services. Their insertion into this equation, more than market prices, determines how resources will be allocated. Unlike buyers being good judges of what they get from sellers, patients are less able to be good judges of what they need. This is because they often do not have the expertise of health professionals. This also limits their ability to evaluate the treatment they are getting. The laws of supply and demand do not apply when commodifying health care resulting in a highly inefficient allocation of resources.[264]

The unpredictability in health care is another key feature that distinguishes it from regular market dynamics. If you go shopping for a car, chances are you've crunched the numbers and feel you can afford to buy. You select a car that best suits your needs and your budget and begin to shop. Buying a car, like buying a house, is usually a planned event. Suffering a heart attack or having a stroke is not. If, after crunching the numbers and talking to salespeople, you decide the car or house purchase isn't going to work for you, it can be cancelled. Not buying either of these commodities doesn't mean your diabetes or high blood pressure will get worse; your stage-two cancer might proceed to stage four; or you'll lose your vision, a limb, or possibly your life. No matter how much money you try to save, requiring a sudden quadruple bypass in a market system could financially break you. Impending uncertainty and cost relegate health care services to an insurance model. Unlike buying a car, the health care insurance industry operates on risk mitigation. It complicates the buyer-seller relationship by adding multiple layers of transaction and brokering multiple stakeholders. With private health insurance, someone other than the patient decides what must be purchased. This decision is profit driven. Unlike regular commodities, consumer choice is restricted.

Paying for your health care is something your insurer does not want to do. When compelled to do so, they attempt to select the most economical choice. If you're going to be a successful health insurer, you are going to try and deny as many claims as possible. That is different than trying to be a successful car salesman, where selling the most cars is your ultimate goal. A successful health insurer will always try and avoid high-risk clients. Insurers exist because of illness. They accumulate profit based on wellness. Their end game is to sell insurance to the people who need it the least and try and deny it to the people who need it the most. The people who often need the most comprehensive care are the people insurers try to avoid. Insurers utilize an enormous number of resources to try to deny claims. When compared to a single-payer system like Canada's, private insurance systems have much higher administrative costs. These high maintenance costs are eventually downshifted to patients, further inflating prices. Health insurers are also subjected to rigorous transactions of complexity in their relationships with other insurers, employers, care providers, patients, and hospital conglomerates. As University of Toronto professor, Joseph Heath points out, "Markets for private health insurers are also subject to extremely severe adverse selection problems. This generates enormous transaction costs at best, complete market failure at worst... The Canadian "single-payer" system eliminates these inefficiencies in one fell swoop... not that there is something intrinsically wrong with buying and selling insurance, it is that markets fail to do so effectively."[265]

There are other unique features of health care services that make market allocation highly inefficient. The previously mentioned dissymmetry of information between patient and provider is crucial. In other sectors of the economy, consumers are usually informed about the products they want to consume and about their prices. In a health care market, patients consume service based on what their providers suggest. For the most part, patients rely on the services suggested by doctors because doctors have so much more information about the service than the buyer (patient). This asymmetry has the propensity to create an induced demand situation where patients consume large quantities of health care services that are not always necessary for them. Doctors may overshoot treatments for fear of litigation or, in private pay scenarios, may do so as an incentive to increase their profits.

Authors Christos Iliadis et al. also list the "monopolistic structure of the health care market," as another feature that distinguishes it from the rest of the economy. The authors assert providers like physicians have amassed enormous power over patients that is monopolistic. This power, in return, allows them to determine the prices of health care services.

The authors also point to the existence of a large number of "exteriors" in the health care market that do not exist in regular markets. People's behaviour towards the consumption of health care services can significantly affect entire communities. Vaccination is offered as an example of a health care service that not only affects the individual being vaccinated but can also protect other community members by reducing the spread of disease. All these features and their unique interactions distinguish the health care sector from other sectors in the economy, and as Iliadis et al. conclude, they also "… explain why demand and supply mechanisms cannot work."[266]

The free market doesn't work in the drug industry either. Take the cancer drug Gleevec as an example. When it was launched in 2001, it cost $24,000 a year, and in 2016, it cost $90,000. This happens partly because of competition. As new drugs enter the market at higher prices, the manufacturers of Gleevec kept raising their prices. This phenomenon defies the law of supply and demand and in examples surrounding the price of pharmaceuticals, the law of supply and demand actually works in reverse.[267]

One last point about health care services relegated to the free market: Unlike regular commodities where markets produce important innovations, health care services often receive billions of public dollars. In the United States, pro-market advocates like to point out that the US is a world leader when it comes to health care research and innovation. They attribute this leadership to their free-market health care system. But is that entirely true? One of the reasons the US is a leader in medical innovation is because, each year, via the National Institutes of Health, the government pumps billions of dollars into research. As assistant professor of epidemiology at Columbia University, Abdulrahman

El-Sayed explains, "In fact many of the drugs, medical devices, and clinical tests that ultimately get marketed and sold by the private sector medical companies originated in the NIH-funded labs across the country."[268]

Where privatization has creeped into Canadian health care, the story is much the same. Private, long-term care facilities in Canada are often run by billionaire investors. If you recall, in February of 2020, British Columbia seniors' advocate, Isobel Mackenzie, released a report on the relationship between for-profit care homes and public funds. In BC, the long-term care sector receives about $1.3 billion annually, with funds averaging about the same for non-profit and private facilities. As the report points out, non-profits spend more on direct resident care and more on staffing. Mackenzie reported that private homes were paying employees about $13,000 a year below standard. Private homes did outspend their non-profit counterparts on construction. Twenty percent of their revenue went towards construction while only nine percent of non-profit revenue went towards construction. In short, BC taxpayers were helping private home operators subsidize building costs and accrue profits. As Mackenzie points out, "For-profit operators are getting paid for the use of their building through capital building costs, and they're making the profits... we are paying mortgages for buildings we don't own and the people who own those buildings can sell those buildings, leverage those buildings—whatever way they want."[269] While the numbers may differ from province to province, this arrangement between public funding and private care homes across Canada is much the same as the BC experience.

Covid-19 also made the case for how private, long-term care facilities failed seniors, even after they were infused with billions of public dollars. In Alberta, seventy-three percent of long-term care facilities had outbreaks. This meant 1000 residents from long-term care institutions died of Covid-19 and 8627 health care workers were infected. Across the country, the statistics are the same. Private facilities fared the worse. Eighty-three percent of long-term care deaths in Eastern Ontario occurred in private facilities.[270]

Health care is not a competitive market commodity. It is a societal good with distinct characteristics and a unique complexity. Its many moving parts, hidden operations, and distinctive characteristics set it aside from regular commodities. For all these reasons and more, it continues to defy economic laws of supply and demand. Health care cannot be marketed like iPads or television sets. Continuing to insist that free-market competition is the answer will continue to cause health care prices to soar and exclude the most vulnerable. When it comes to the provision of health care services, the free market is not a stand-alone concept. Everywhere it is being propped up by public funds. The only true freedom it has is freedom from transparency.

People should be free to buy health care. Mandating a public health care system stifles autonomy and individuality.

Proponents of private health care are skilled at using the autonomy argument to support the rich buying their own care. They assert restricting the well-heeled from buying private care stifles individuality and personal choice. After all, why should you be forced into a public system if you have the money? Isn't that socialism at its worse when "the government" decides how you spend your money? This is a common criticism that many free-market supporters within the United States have about universal, single-payer health care. This narrative is supported by free-market proponents and capitalists who often stand to lose large amounts of profit if private health care services are abandoned.

Neoliberalism is the driving force behind this narrative. With its free-market obsession, it peddles the theory that government systems should not stand in the way of the rich buying their own services because it's an infringement upon personal liberty. Where health care services are concerned, does the individuality argument hold any weight?

One of the first observations that comes to mind is that health care is a communal entity. Our communities consist of networks of shared connections. Where health is concerned, what individuals do affects our interconnectedness as people. This is certainly the case surrounding public health vaccination programs and the concept of herd immunity. Being vaccinated not only protects the immunized individual, it also protects entire communities and has the ability to eradicate deadly diseases globally. This is the rationale behind wanting health care workers in long-term care to be immunized against influenza, to protect the vulnerable populations they care for.

The same can be said for diseases like measles or mumps in a daycare or school setting. While you may make the individual decision to immunize your own child (or not), this choice has consequences for the children that your child may encounter. The well-being of the collective is related to individual choices. The same can be said for alcoholism and drug addiction, which affect individuals, entire families, workplaces, and communities. Successful treatment of addiction ultimately restores individual, family, and community well-being. This is a crucial concept where health care services are concerned. So, if the rich have the money to jump the queue and buy any health care service they want, that choice will, by default, have some effect on the health and well-being of others. It means a finite number of resources is accessed by people who can get to it first simply because they have the money. Where buying health care services based on wealth is concerned, acuity (need) takes a back seat to capital. It's not the same as buying a yacht. Buying all the yachts doesn't mean someone else may suffer a heart attack or die because they can't have a yacht. Precluding someone else from a health care service does.

Covid-19 demonstrates this. As the virus continues to ravage communities around the world, there has never been a clearer indication of how individual behaviour affects all of us. Outbreaks can only be managed when all of us follow public health guidelines. Battling Covid-19 means individual rights cannot override the collective needs of society. As long as people discredit the use of masks, vaccines, and social distancing guidelines, everyone remains at risk. This also allows time for the virus to mutate and become more infectious or vaccine resistant. Society's ability to thrive has always depended on restricting individual choices where health and safety is concerned. Legislation around speed limits, seatbelts, firearms, noise, and the use of pesticides are all designed to limit activities that have the potential to harm society. Therefore, it is illegal (persons do not have the freedom) to drive a vehicle while intoxicated. Individual choices concerning health, like driving under the influence, can adversely affect others. Our collective safety depends on looking beyond individual choices towards the greater good of society.

When entire populations are triaged based on need rather than ability to pay within publicly funded systems we all benefit. Allocating health services to public systems makes sense because health care services are both communal and infrastructural in nature.

Imagine a society where public services like fire and police were allocated to people who could afford to pay for them. In this society, many people would have the remaining police and fire services. With the wealthy covered for any police or fire need, the rest of us would have to share the remaining resources, even though we may need those services more than the people who have them on retainer. This may sound absurd. It is just as absurd to allow the rich to reserve a portion of essential health care services, while leaving the majority to share what is left in a depleted public system. This is because health care services, like police and fire services, are infrastructural in nature. Having a public fire or police service benefits all of us even if we never have to use it. Living in a community where there are police services keeps crime rates low, prevents looting, reduces impaired driving, and accomplishes things that benefit society. While I may not currently need dialysis or neonatal ICU services, having them in my community benefits my friends, neighbours, their children, and families. The same holds true for other health care services. Having all those services means I get to benefit from living in a jurisdiction with a robust medical infrastructure. That infrastructure may keep disease rates low, have an acute stroke protocol, and provide robust emergency services—all of which helps everyone. Universal access to health care improves our standard of living, gives us reassurance, and collectively makes us healthier and safer. It saves lives. The notion that a rich minority isn't "free" because they can't buy their way to the front of the line negates the communal and infrastructural nature of health care services. Moreover, it highlights how those actions adversely affect persons in greater need and confuses demand.

The American health insurance industry boasts that it is built on the notion of autonomy. Health insurers spend millions of dollars getting behind the argument that private health insurance enables people to freely chose the type of coverage they need. The autonomy argument is an "easy sell" in a cultural climate that champions individuality. If you examine how health insurers structure their business, you'll learn that the young and healthy customers subsidize the sick. If low risk patients couldn't subsidize high risk patients, health insurers could not stay in business. This shared risk, which is the soul of the American health insurance industry, is closer to a communal endeavour than any sort of individual freedom model. As health insurance conglomerates embrace "the freedom to buy your own health care" message, they neglect to acknowledge that their own industry only exists because the people who need insurance the least, cover the costs of the people who need it the most. This makes the health insurance industry more of an inter-dependant communal business model than any type of free-style service.

In the free-market American system, consumers of health insurance are less free than patients within universal, single-payer systems. This is because when health services are allocated to the free-market system where insurers are required, a cascade of events restricts patient autonomy. If your health insurance is tied to your employment, losing your job also means losing your coverage. This means you may never be free to search for your ideal job. Similarly, you may not be free to leave an ill-suited or stressful job for the same reason. The same holds true if you're interested in being an entrepreneur. Your freedom is greatly limited. Being tethered to a health insurance plan acts as a disincentive to starting a new business where coverage may not be available. The restrictions do not stop there. Escalating premiums, deductions, changes in coverage, soaring drug prices, and limits on tests and treatments all restrict individual choice. They are restricted by decisions made by insurance executives, drug companies, employers, and a litany of other private interests. These interests are bound together by suffocating administrative bureaucracy. Special interest groups, not individuals, decide what treatments will be covered, how comprehensive plans will be, what doctors will treat, and what those treatments will cost.

Similarly, for the millions of people who are uninsured there are no choices. They do not get to have access to the system like the people who can pay even if they need it more. That choice has already been made for them. For the under-insured, restrictions on freedom of choice are also commonplace. After paying escalating premiums and deductibles, the cost of one major health catastrophe can financially ruin patients and their families. If patients are not able to cover the rising deductibles, their insurance plans are rendered inert. This results in a restriction or suspension of treatment, leaving limited choices or none at all.

We can all agree that bankruptcy places a limit on what many people and families can do. Yet every year in the US free-market health care system, close to 530,000 bankruptcies are filed because of the debt associated with medical bills. This includes people who are insured. Suzanne LeClair of is one of them. She had employer-based insurance and paid her co-payments. Diagnosed with cancer, LeClair started to receive stacks of invoices after surgery. Her insurance only covered her hospital bed because she was told her hospital was out of network. Hundreds of thousands of dollars later, she was forced to file for bankruptcy. The nightmare didn't end there. LeClair might have to declare bankruptcy a second time as more surgeries, treatments, and drugs necessary for her recovery have added more to her existing medical debt—all of this despite having medical insurance. LeClair has piled debt on credit cards and applied for consolidation loans to pay off other credit cards. She is not the only American battling insurmountable debt and bankruptcy while fighting a life-threatening illness. Professor David Himmelstein, at City University of New York's Hunter College, explains, "Health insurance that we have today is a defective product… medical debt is incredibly common… it's the main cause of calls from collection agencies, and the vast majority of people with it have insurance." In Georgia, a thirty-five-year-old diabetic man found himself homeless and jobless after he required hospitalization for a toe amputation followed by a leg amputation. He also tried to file for bankruptcy to release the medical debt he was carrying. In October of 2019, he lost his house. Jobless and homeless with $400,000 in medical bills after two amputations represents a clear picture of how health care service in a free-market system can destroy all sorts of personal freedoms.[271]

There is another argument for why allowing the rich to buy health care services cannot be justified using the autonomy argument. Health care services belong to all of us. In their book *The Trouble With Billionaires,* authors Linda McQuaig and Neil Brooks remind us that we owe much of our wealth and productivity to the accumulation of the knowledge from our past. The authors cite a 1957 ground-breaking study by Nobel prize-winner Robert Solow, whose findings support the idea that much of the exponential growth in productivity between 1909 and 1949 was due to "technical change." Upwards of eighty-eight percent of all growth in this era was attributable to technical change, not from the contributions of capital or labour as previously thought. Another Nobel-winning economist, Herbert A Simon, refers to this huge store of knowledge from the past as our "social capital." Simon asserts that, "access to it was our main source of wealth responsible for 90 percent of national income." The authors assert that it is this cumulative technological inheritance, not our isolated, present-day technologies, that propel us forward. A third Nobel laureate, George Akerlof, reinforces this concept by saying, "Our marginal products are not ours alone… but are due almost entirely to the cumulative process of learning that has taken us from stone age poverty to twenty-first century affluence." This of course raises the question who should the beneficiaries of this inherited wealth be? If it is true as Alperovitz and Daley note, "… the overwhelming source of all modern wealth comes to us today through no effort of our own. It is the generous and unearned gift of the past," then it stands to reason that the benefits of that inheritance should be spread equally among all of us, not just the wealthy few.[272]

The same holds true for health care services and treatments. The cumulative work, knowledge, discoveries, and innovations of the people who came before us have built the foundation of today's "health care inheritance." It is difficult to imagine any current drug manufacturer, skilled clinician, or medical-device engineer who has not mastered a skill or created a treatment or a product that hasn't evolved from this collective inheritance. Health care is rife with examples of pioneers who have laid the foundations for others to expand upon, including people like Canadian engineer John Hopps, whose work led to the development of the first implantable cardiac pacemaker. Marie Curie's work on isolating radioactive isotopes and creating mobile X-ray services to field hospitals during WWI laid the foundation for all modern-day radiography advances. Banting and Best's discovery of insulin revolutionized diabetes treatment. This also includes those who performed the first heart transplant, lung transplant, and successful skin graft. It encompasses those who discovered the first successful link between sanitation and disease prevention, the first antibiotics, the first vaccines. All of it is built upon a cumulative legacy willed to each successive generation from pioneering predecessors. This legacy from the past is directly responsible for modern innovation, advances in medicine, current treatment algorithms, and newly organized health care service-delivery models. The pacemaker work done by Hopps, Dr. Bigelow, and Dr. Callaghan was publicly funded through institutions like the National Research Council. In this regard, quality public health care is something society has rightfully inherited. The fruits of these past labours belong not just to a minority of rich people—they belong to all of us.

Banting and Best understood this concept fully. On January 23, 1923, Banting, Best, and Collip were awarded the patents for the drug insulin. They promptly sold the patent to the University of Toronto for one dollar. In giving away the patent, the researchers were reaffirming their contributions to our health care inheritance. An unfortunate side of this revolutionary discovery has evolved. Ninety-seven years later, in places like the United States, young, type-one diabetics are dying because profiteers have made insulin unaffordable.

The reward puppets in a privatized health care system have demonstrated a unique ability to pit various segments of society against each other while stacking up enormous profits along the way. In the beginning, reward puppets like the American Medical Association (AMA) were determined to keep government-sponsored health care out of the American system. Christy Ford Chapin, professor of political economy at the University of Maryland Baltimore County, and Physicians for a National

THE REWARD PUPPETS

Health Program insist the AMA did so by "deploying class hostilities, red baiting, deceptive appeals to frontier individualism and by associating public programs with charity and personal failure."[273] These tactics have been deployed for decades within the United States by the groups who stand to gain the most by ensuring the system remains privatized. These are the same narratives that are creeping into policy discussions around the re-design of Canadian Medicare. Their arguments pit the rich against the poor, the unionized against the non-unionized, the employed against the unemployed, and insured against the uninsured. This divisive dialogue persists because the reward puppets stand to lose the fortunes they continue to amass by imposing greater burdens on society's most vulnerable.

In 2019, the top health insurers in the United States saw their revenues skyrocket to almost $1 trillion. As they continue to amass huge profits and surpluses, another alarming trend solidifies their power even more—mergers. Merger activity boosted the profits of Cigna, netting them an overall profit of $5 billion dollars for 2019. After Cigna completed its merger with Express Scripts, its fourth-quarter revenue in 2018 went from $14.3 billion to $38.2 billion in 2019. UnitedHealth made $14.2 billion in profits for 2019.[274] Kaiser Permanente also saw its bottomline triple for 2019, with a net income of $7.4 billion dollars, up from $2.5 billion in 2018. Kaiser also has plans to construct a new $900 million headquarters in Oakland, consisting of 1.2 million square feet.[275] As insurance company profits soar, the number of people uninsured in the US continues to rise. In 2018, 27.5 million people had no health insurance of any type. That figure is up from 2017, which saw 25.6 million people uninsured. Most alarmingly, from 2017 to 2018, the number of uninsured children rose by 0.6 percentage points, to 5.5 percent.[276]

Reward puppets continue to do amazingly well. In the first quarter of 2019, the three pharmaceutical giants of Pfizer, Merck, and Eli Lilly continued to rake in billions of dollars in revenue, as the cost of vital drugs for almost every chronic condition continued to escalate. Pfizer reported a revenue of $13.12 billion dollars. Merck reported a revenue at $10.81 billion. Both these topped company estimates. Eli Lilly recorded a revenue of $5.09 billion. Trulicity, Lilly's top selling diabetes drug, was up thirty percent in the first quarter of 2019 when compared to the first quarter of 2018, raking in $879.7 million for that quarter.[277]

Universal, single-payer health care systems pool risk and allow patients greater, not lesser, liberty than privatized systems. A single government entity regulates the administration of services, greatly reducing bureaucracy, and cutting out the middle profiteers such as health insurers. If Americans value their freedom as much as they proclaim, they need to shake off the chains of private health care and end their bondage to wealthy conglomerates.

The task ahead for Canadians is great, but it's not impossible. If we are to rescue Medicare from the clutches of our current political economy, it will mean countering the reward puppets who currently control the lion's share of the wealth, resources, narrative, and most of the political influence that currently shape our health care policy.

Chapter 6

COVID-19 MAKES THE CASE

At some point, a person must decide whether they belong to the people who loved them, or whether they belong to the emperors.

—Madeline Thien

The vertigo known as Covid-19 is currently creating a world of dizzying unsteadiness. On December 31, 2019, the WHO was alerted to cases of a viral pneumonia circulating in Wuhan, China. At this time, the etiology of the illness was unknown. On January 7, 2020, what initially started as a cluster of viral pneumonia cases emerged as a health care crisis. On January 13, 2020, the first case was detected in Thailand as the virus spread beyond Chinese borders. The first case was detected in Canada on January 25, 2020. By the end of January 2020, the WHO announced the virus as "a public health emergency of international concern."[278] Between February and March of 2020, the world started down a dark corridor.

The Canadian government began to repatriate Canadians abroad and set up posts where they could be screened and/or quarantined. In March of 2020, Prime Minister Trudeau set up a cabinet committee as the federal response to the Covid-19 virus. A few days later, the federal government offered $27 million to help research groups and universities devise strategies to manage the outbreak. On March 11, 2020, the WHO officially declared Covid-19 a global pandemic.[279] On March 13, 2020, the Canadian parliament unanimously agreed to shut its doors. By the end of March, the Canadian economy had shed one million jobs and the unemployment rate had risen to 7.8 percent.[280] Between March 11 and May 30, 2020, the virus ravaged countries worldwide. Governments scrambled to close borders, ground air traffic, close schools and universities, and shut down entire sectors of their economies. The federal government set up stimulus packages to assist flailing businesses and individuals who had lost income. Canadians became familiar with the prime minister's daily Covid-19 news briefings outside his Ottawa home. Casualties from the virus continued to mount as countries like Italy, Brazil, and the US became rapidly overwhelmed. In Canada, hospitals cancelled elective surgeries and re-prioritized medical procedures. Thousands of booked tests and treatments, including cancer surveillance procedures, were cancelled. Emergency rooms emptied out as Canadians, fearful of contracting the virus, stayed away. With businesses closed and the unemployment rate rising, the Canadian parliamentary budget office announced that the federal deficit for the fiscal year of 2020, could balloon beyond $250 billion. By June 2020, Canada had reached 100,000 Covid cases and 8,348 deaths.[281]

The unemployment rate in Canada skyrocketed to 13.7 percent in May of 2020.[282] As countries practised social distancing, hand washing, fourteen-day quarantines, contact tracing, and wearing face masks, governments began the long trek towards opening their economies. Amidst this frenzy, one group of individuals was disproportionately sacrificed and ravaged by the virus. In a world where the frail elderly should have been protected, they, like no other demographic, bore the brunt of the virus's brutality. Exacerbated by failing systems and government indifference, Canadian seniors in long-term care facilities died at twice the average rate of those in other developed countries. By May 2020, Canada had the highest proportion of deaths in long-term care with these accounting for eighty-one percent of all reported deaths from Covid-19. In comparison, the average in other OECD countries was thirty-eight percent.[283]

The Covid-19 story reinforces the necessity of this work. The arrival of Covid-19 in Canada demonstrated the depth of long-term care disintegration within our borders. It also demonstrated how government priorities were misdirected. The concerns and the predictions of front-line health care workers came to fruition. The virus would also lay bare the ravages that decades of neoliberal policy produced. It demonstrated how the most vulnerable members of our society and people devoted to their care were lost along the way. This would become a jaw-dropping revelation.

By July 2020, 7,050 deaths (out of 8,700 total deaths) were of residents and caregivers in long-term care.[284] Despite Canada's history of the "just society,"[285] years of defunding and system neglect had taken their toll.

From the onset, long-term residential care was not a priority for Medicare. Back in the 1950s and '60s, the frail elderly were largely taken care of by extended families. Advanced dementia was less common as life spans were notably shorter than they are today. With the inception of Medicare, Douglas and his followers focused on eliminating user fees and convincing Canadian doctors that Medicare would not financially ruin them. In subsequent decades, long-term care was left out of health policy debates within Canada. It was missing in the 2002 *Romanow Report* and was excluded from the Canada Health Act in 1984.

The year before the Canada Health Act was enacted (1983), a task force was created by the Canadian Medical Association (CMA) to study the earmarking of Canadian health care resources. In their final report, the CMA commented on the lack of standards in many Canadian nursing homes, saying, "The standard of care provided in many nursing homes is grossly inadequate. They provide a life of immobility and tedium, and lack any guarantee of adequate basic care." Even after the release of the CMA's report, long-term care was never incorporated into the 1984 Canada Health Act as an insured service.[286] As a result of not being included in the Canada Health Act, national standards for the sector were never established. As neoliberal policies of conservatism and defunding of social programs raged throughout the 1980s and 1990s, billions of federal transfer dollars were cut to the provinces. This meant the provinces had to find creative ways to overcome their funding challenges. Partnering with the private sector was a way to usurp these fiscal difficulties. Private operators soon discovered the profitability of housing older Canadians. With the introduction of debt-financing for private operators and the entry of real estate investment trusts into long-term care, the financialization of the sector was complete. The dual trends of privatization and financialization steadily increased across the Canadian long-term care landscape.[287] As a result, improving the deplorable conditions for both seniors and staff within Canada's care facilities was never a priority. As past researchers noted, "... most of our efforts as a nation and much of that as individuals are focused on keeping ourselves and others out of long-term care facilities rather than on the work and care within them."[288]

On the heels of the 1983 CMA report, decades of families, staff, and seniors' advocates sounded alarm bells about the deteriorating conditions within Canadian long-term care facilities. These concerns centred around disintegrating systems, outdated infrastructure, defunding policies, staffing shortages, and most notably—increased privatization. The sector was operating so dangerously close to the line that a small gust could collapse it. When the gale-force winds of Covid-19 arrived, the Canadian long-term care sector was in no position to weather the slightest storm. It would take a world-wide pandemic with much suffering and many deaths for the country to finally realize just how much the four horsemen of destruction ravaged the Canadian system. Leaving long-term care out of Medicare proved, as author Aaron Wherry described, "Medicare's original sin."[289] Horror stories about the care of Canada's seniors would send shock waves around the world.

Residence Herron in Montreal is a private home for seniors owned by a Quebec real estate company. The facility was already in deep trouble prior to the arrival of Covid-19. Two months before Covid, the residence had to be staffed by a placement agency and the director of nursing care left and had to be replaced in 2020. By the end of the first wave of the pandemic, forty-seven deaths occurred here. A coroner's inquest was convened to investigate the deaths at the facility. Although Covid-19 was repeatedly cited as the cause of death of most of these residents, a nurse reported that most of the staff abandoned their posts when the pandemic hit. The nurse also testified that there were discussions about triaging residents so that those who were dying didn't have to be fed.

The nurse also recalled how a deceased woman's body had been left in the room she shared with her husband for an entire day. Other testimony included the inhumane conditions residents and their families endured, such as misleading information to families about residents' conditions. One resident appeared to have died from dehydration after being forgotten in his room. Another resident, Leon Barrette, passed away but was not found until hours later. Mr. Barrette was admitted in need of oxygen. The staff testified that they never saw oxygen in his room, nor were there any notes on his chart between the time of his admission and his death. Family members were convinced that staff forgot about him.

There were also discussions with the owner about whether to feed the healthy residents and just hydrate the rest. As the nurse reported, "With such a skeleton crew... some of them were not getting fed." Another resident who died was left covered in their own vomit.[290]

After it was determined that Hamilton's Rosslyn Retirement Residence was not meeting safety standards, all fifty-two residents were moved out of the facility. But an elderly man with Covid was inadvertently left in the empty building after staff moved everyone else out. Staff at receiving facilities were told that he was in the hospital. The man was alone for eighteen hours and not found until the next night when his family began to raise questions about his whereabouts.[291]

The situation became so dire in Ontario and Quebec that eventually the police and military were called in. This led to a shocking report chronicled by Canadian military staff. Reporting on the appalling conditions within five Ontario nursing homes, the military found "a dozen patients with bleeding fungal infections from poor catheter care... staff were aggressive and abusive... residents were given food and water by force, causing 'audible choking'... infestations of ants and cockroaches... patients left in soiled diapers instead of being moved to toilets... inappropriate use of PPE... staff reported that they'd given out medication when they had not... and in one case a worker left food in a patient's mouth while they were sleeping." Residents were also not being fed regularly and had pressure sores from not being moved.[292]

Despite being subjected to provincial inspections, pre-Covid conditions in long-term care were so precarious that they rendered any additional strain intolerable. Canada's most frail and elderly citizens had always been a public-health emergency away from complete disaster. That disaster arrived.

By July 2020, the first wave of Covid-19 seemed to be flattening, but the Canadian numbers that emerged were shocking. In Canada, there were five care-facilities where more than forty percent of the residents died from the virus. Another nineteen facilities lost between thirty and forty percent of residents between March 1 and May 31, 2020.[293] Bobcaygeon's Pinecrest for-profit nursing home had a fatality rate of forty-three percent. Out of sixty-five beds, twenty-nine residents died from the virus.[294] Eastern Ontario and places like Laval had a higher incidence of deaths from Covid-19 among for-profit homes.[295]

Northwood is the largest long-term care facility in Atlantic Canada. Located in central Halifax, Northwood is a high-rise, not-for-profit senior's complex run by a community board. Built in 1962, the facility has outdated infrastructure and is overcrowded. Many of its 485 residents share small, older bathrooms. Dining areas in Northwood Centre are in the middle of a ward-like setting. Small, kitchen-like areas for food servers are also located behind the residents' dining section, making the areas very congested during mealtimes. Occupants reside in rooms that house two to three residents at a time. There is little privacy, and many residents congregate in common areas. The common areas on these specific units are small and space is limited.

I worked at Northwood Halifax years ago as a night nursing supervisor. The facility was not air conditioned. Kitchen staff told me that during the summer temperatures in the main kitchen could soar upwards to forty degrees Celsius. As of recent days, Northwood still lacks a central air-conditioning system. Although listed as a not-for-profit, two and three people cohabiting a room serves an economic purpose. It creates long-term care capacity without spending money on infrastructure. As the Covid-19 outbreak at Northwood demonstrated, that type of capacity-building would prove deadly. In June 2020, fifty-three of Nova Scotia's sixty-three deaths from the virus would occur at the Northwood Halifax campus. Its size, outdated infrastructure, and overcrowding made Northwood a Covid-19 epicentre.

For years staff and their unions called upon provincial governments to listen to their concerns about the issues at Northwood. Many of those concerns were never addressed. Personal care workers and continuing-care assistants are lower paid workers, who survive by stringing several casual jobs together and working an abundance of overtime. Like other long-term care sites across the country, Northwood staff frequently worked several casual jobs to make ends meet, darting from one workplace to another. Staff often worked extraordinarily long shifts at several different facilities.

Staffing shortages and burnout pre-Covid-19 are well documented within the entire long-term care sector. As staff became infected at Northwood, pre-existing staffing shortages were compounded by staff who fell ill or were required to self-quarantine. Staff from the health authority had to be deployed to help, further underscoring the dysfunctional staffing levels within the sector. It wasn't until Covid-19 arrived, that policy makers began to think about the transient nature of how staff, within places like Northwood, are forced to work. Working at multiple places predisposed staff to become vectors of infection. As of April 23, 2020, Nova Scotia was one of the last jurisdictions to discourage care staff from working in multiple locations.[296]

Prior to Covid-19, Stephen McNeil's Liberal government cut the budgets of long-term care and residential facilities. Grants to long-term care were reduced by $8.1 million between 2015–2017. Hounded by the opposition and public criticism, the McNeil government eventually reinstated funding to the long-term care sector. By 2020, McNeil reinstated $6 million of the $8,764,120 million he had cut. Not allowing for inflation, this still resulted in a net loss of $2,764,120.[297]

As Covid-19 ravaged nursing homes within Ontario and Quebec, there were lingering questions for homes like Northwood that fell prey to the virus later than their central Canadian counterparts. Front-line staff from Ontario and Quebec, with their faces covered during interviews for fear of employer reprisal, insisted on the need for personal protective equipment (PPE) for staff before the virus entered facilities. Grim statistics mounted about insufficient staffing levels in long-term care and residents dying en masse.

On April 2, 2020, the medical director at Northwood and the facility's executive director penned a rambling letter to residents and their substitute decision makers about what to expect regarding the care of residents with Covid-19. In that letter, the two asserted, "Covid-19 is a viral illness that spreads like the flu and is hard to contain, despite everyone's best efforts."[298] The statement acknowledges that the organization was aware of the infectious nature of the virus and the difficulty containing it. Yet it wasn't until days later, after the first staff member tested positive (April 5), that the leadership mandated the masking of employees.[299] By that time, the virus had already entered the building. Dr. Samir Sinha, head of the National Institute on Aging, believes Nova Scotia could have done what other provinces did and acted sooner based on the precautionary principle established after the 2003 SARS outbreak.[300] The principle asserts that we should "always take the safest approach in an outbreak and not wait for all the scientific evidence before acting."[301] Mario Possamai, a senior advisor on the 2007 SARS Commission, agrees not adhering to the precautionary principle put Canadians at risk. Citing Justice Archie Campbell, who headed the 2007 SARS Commission, Possamai said, "What Justice Campbell said was that when there is scientific uncertainty, err on the side of caution and protect health care workers and protect Canadians." As Possamai added, "… we didn't do that."[302] Dr. Sinha also maintains, "By the end of March the evidence was clear from the CDC in Atlanta that asymptomatic transmission was a thing, for example, [as was] the importance of universal masking… The CDC was warning about asymptomatic cases on March 18." By March 27, it reported that fifty to seventy-five percent of people testing positive were asymptomatic… Northwood began testing on 'atypical symptoms' on April 11… and testing all residents including those who were asymptomatic, only on April 22, 2020.[303]

As far back as March 13, 2020, four health care unions who represented front-line workers wrote a joint statement urging government to ensure workers had enough PPE. The March 13 statement makes it clear that PPE was being withheld at the nursing home for fear of impending shortages.[304] Staff readily told stories about how the PPE was kept under lock and key. There are many questions that now haunt the families of those who died at Northwood. Could the use of face masks have been initiated sooner? Could staff moving among multiple workplaces have been prohibited sooner? Was separating infected residents from non-infected residents done appropriately? Why wasn't the precautionary principle instituted? The province of Nova Scotia conducted a review into the Northwood tragedy. It stopped short of a public inquiry.

By the fall of 2020, results from the Northwood review were out. It highlighted critical staff shortages, problems with separating Covid-19 infected residents from non-infected residents, and the difficulty accessing infection-control specialists as some of the primary factors contributing to the Northwood deaths. Other factors included, "… inconsistent cleaning, shared rooms and bathrooms, and limited control of temperature, humidity and ventilation… because of a breach in Northwood's online system before the pandemic, officials were tracking staff levels using pen and paper." The review emphasized the need for transparent communication, even though the province would not release the full review details and denied requests for a full public inquiry. Remarking on this issue, the opposition leader at the time, Tim Houston, said, "The format of the review seems designed to protect the province from embarrassing revelations on issues such as whether sufficient protective gear was available to staff."[305]

Family members launched a class-action lawsuit against the facility, alleging it failed its legal obligations to residents by not taking the necessary steps to prevent the spread of the virus. Prior to Covid-19, Northwood Halifax, like many other long-term care facilities across the country that failed seniors, was accredited with an exemplary standing.

As shocked as governments were after the military's fifteen-page exposé on the conditions within some of Canada's long-term care facilities, much of the information could hardly be categorized as novel. As mentioned, in 2017, the federal government gave the green light to a Chinese insurance company to purchase one of the biggest senior-care providers in the province of British Columbia. By 2019, the local health authorities had to take over a string of those homes after provincial inspections revealed a litany of serious ongoing licencing infractions. Complaints included "neglect, emotional abuse, staffing shortages, health and hygiene issues and dangerous facilities."[306]

A litany of reports clearly articulated the dire circumstances within long-term care across the country. In a 2015 report published by the Nova Scotia Nurses Union, entitled *Broken Homes,* nurses spoke out on the state of long-term care in Nova Scotia. While the report cited fifteen recommendations that needed to occur, the number-one priority centred around staffing shortages within the sector. The quality of resident care, occupational health and safety issues, staff education, work-life balance, and staff retention and recruitment were also issues of major concern. The report also suggested the province should call in the auditor-general to review the issues raised within the report.[307]

The New Brunswick nurses' union published a report in 2020, entitled *The Forgotten Generation: An Urgent Call for Reform in New Brunswick's Long-Term Care Sector.* The nearly 200-page report outlined issues around the rapidly disintegrating sector and called upon the Higgs government to launch an independent inquiry. The nurse's union described the system as "in desperate need of reform." Other sections of the report outlined that "… in some cases, one registered nurse (RN) took care of as many as

200 residents. In other cases, not even one RN was on duty for more than a month." Citing a survey done by 505 unionized RNs who worked in the province's homes, sixty-three percent said the job of toileting residents is being left undone—sometimes (thirty-two percent of the time), often (twenty-two percent of the time) and always (nine percent of the time).

The report also cited accepted workplace violence claims by employees doubled between the years 2013 and 2018. The report called for the immediate cessation of privatization of the sector, saying, "The introduction of for-profit nursing homes in New Brunswick has not solved the problems it was meant to address." Deborah Van den Hoonaard, gerontologist and St. Thomas University professor, said the persistent lowering of hours of care by government reflect "a custodial attitude, as if the people who live in nursing homes just need to be fed and watered and kept clean... it does not see them as full human beings."[308]

In a 2009 report by the Canadian Department of Justice, staff burnout, work associated stress, and inadequate staff training were all cited as contributing factors in the abuse of residents within long-term care facilities. The report *Crime and Abuse Against Seniors: A Review of the Research Literature With Special Reference to the Canadian Situation* cited an Ontario study where over 1600 nurses were surveyed. Researchers found that a third of respondents had witnessed the rough handling of residents in nursing homes and staff being verbally abusive and swearing, as well as making embarrassing comments to residents. Ten percent had witnessed staff members shoving or hitting residents. The study also indicated that there was a gap, both in the research of victimization against seniors and in "our understanding of the extent, patterns, and types of abuse as well as risk factors in Canadian institutions."[309]

While long-term care facilities remained overcrowded and understaffed, there were more problems that emerged from warehousing seniors in crowded facilities. Levels of aggression within homes were high. A 2013 W5 investigation revealed that homicides within Canada's care homes were a national crisis. One of the stories in the report centred around a veteran named Frank Alexander. Mr. Alexander was placed in care in Winnipeg because he had developed Alzheimer's disease. From the beginning, the family had concerns about their father's care at Parkview Place. They alleged that the place was overcrowded and staff couldn't control resident outbursts. Family members described the home as a place where there were "fights and arguments and people upset with each other… the place was bursting with people." On March 24, 2011, the Alexander family was called to the hospital where their father was restrained and bleeding from his left ear. He had sustained a skull fracture. Four days later, Frank Alexander died, succumbing to the head injury that had occurred within the care home. Police at the hospital told the family that Mr. Alexander was attacked by another resident who violently shoved him, causing him to fall backwards and crack his skull on a tile floor. The resident who had shoved him had nine previous incidents on record. This included one incident where he punched a nurse in the face. The W5 investigation revealed there were approximately five homicides per year inside Canadian long-term care facilities. Previous data also revealed over 10,000 other incidents of resident-to-resident abuse within Canadian care homes.[310]

In 2019, the Ontario Health Coalition reported that there were at least twenty-nine homicides in long-term care homes within six years. In 2014, the province's chief coroner described homicides within long-term care an "urgent and persistent issue." Five years later, Natalie Mehra, executive director of the OHC, claimed reports coming in related to the level of violence within Ontario's long-term sector were "intolerable and unacceptable."[311] With crowded units of dementia patients and low staffing levels, acts of resident-to-resident aggression continue to escalate.

In 2016, seventy-nine-year-old Keith Wood died of blunt force trauma after being assaulted by another resident in a hallway in a Mississauga care home. The same holds true for eighty-four-year-old Meyer Sadoway of Toronto. He also died four days after he was pushed by another resident in his care home. Provincial data for Ontario shows that resident-on-resident abuse has more than doubled between the years 2011 and 2016.[312]

Covid-19 not only makes the case for the dismal state of care within nursing homes. It also demonstrates that when it came to being pandemic prepared, Canada's hospital system was lacking. Canada's acute-care system was also depleted by years of defunding—in terms of pandemic planning, personal protective equipment, ventilator capacity, and staffing levels. It also was operating so close to the edge that when the virus arrived, many clinical decisions would ultimately become fatal Faustian bargains.

When Covid-19 hit, PPE supplies within the country were neither sufficient nor updated. N-95 masks require regular fit testing to protect staff efficiently. Across the country those fittings had not occurred. As the pandemic progressed, provincial and federal governments struggled to protect Canadian health care workers. At times, this meant allowing them to wear masks that had expired. By March 2020, the federal government passed an interim order allowing PPE supplies to be imported and sold within Canada even if they did not meet pre-Covid-19 Health

Canada standards. The order was prompted by the demand the pandemic generated, which had created a critical supply issue. Much of the Canadian PPE supply comes from China, and China has had problems with quality PPE products. At one point, China's own government admitted it had seized about eighty-nine million pieces of substandard products. Since the pandemic started, Canada has received at least one million masks from China that did not meet Canadian standards. In Saskatchewan, the health authority allowed health care workers to wear expired N95 masks, which had been purchased for the 2009–10 H1N1 outbreak. Those masks had been expired for five years. In May of 2019, Ottawa tossed into a Regina landfill two million N95 masks that also had expired since the H1N1 outbreak. Dr. Sandy Buchman, president of the CMA, said that he's heard from physicians across the country "who are concerned about a lack of quantity and quality of PPE." Dr. Buchman attributed the supply issue to a failure of government planning. Wesley Wark, a national security expert from the University of Ottawa, also agreed that the national stockpile of equipment was not what it should have been, saying that "the pandemic has exposed a gaping hole in Canada's supply chain." Patty Hajdu, former federal health minister, also conceded that Canada, "likely did not have enough PPE."[313]

Early in the pandemic, long-term care workers were voicing their concerns about the quality and the rationing of PPE. As residents fell sick and died, staff insisted they went without face masks as management seemed worried about scarce supplies and had PPE under lock and key. In Ontario, directives were issued to staff to only wear PPE once a case had been confirmed within a facility. Whistleblowers assert PPE was in facilities but locked away in storage rooms or basements, where administrators claimed they were saving it because there were such short supplies.[314] Staff in other nursing homes were under similar directives. Later, studies surrounding the transmission of the virus altered that line of thinking, but only after the virus had raged through long-term care. In April of 2020, a group of nurses who volunteered to help staff in a private, long-term care facility, said there was, "shockingly little" PPE for staff. At the CHSLD Vigi Mont-Royal Home, nurses told stories of how their fellow health care cohort were wearing the same PPE for hours, unable to change gloves or masks because there weren't enough. Staff were not changing gloves between residents. At one point, Vigi Mont-Royal had fifty-six percent of residents testing positive for the virus. One nurse relayed a story of a worker who improvised by wearing a blanket as an isolation gown. Hospital staff helping said they would bring in extra PPE, but it was never enough.[315]

In Nova Scotia, a community residential care home mandated staff to log their own temperatures and those of their clients as part of a plan to monitor early signs of the virus. Supplies were so limited, their pandemic plan included instructions for staff to wash a single oral thermometer, wipe it with alcohol, and share it amongst staff and residents. Whoever approved this plan was unaware that certain viruses, like Norovirus, are not destroyed using soap, water, or alcohol. It wasn't until staff complained to their union that this practice ceased.

In some Halifax nursing homes, staff were using tympanic thermometers to check their staff and resident's temperatures. To conserve supplies, they were asked to wash the disposable ear covers between uses. Washing the thin ear shields for repeated use is against manufacturer's recommended guidelines. There were harrowing stories across the country about how staff were being treated and supplies distributed.

- In Stoneridge Manor, Ontario, nurses wrote to the Ministry of Health outlining their concerns about a "very dangerous situation" related to a lack of appropriate measures used to respond to the Covid-19 outbreak. Fifty-three out of sixty residents had tested positive for the virus and sixteen had died. Workers complained about lack of access to PPE including N-95 masks.

- At Carling Manor in Ottawa, a Ministry of Labour health and safety inspector indicated that the fear inside the building was "unbelievable" and "cleaners and kitchen staff are wearing garbage bags as gowns."

- Two employees at Madonna Care Community in Orleans, Ontario, died in the spring of 2020 after contracting Covid-19. The staff reported, "We had equipment, but we weren't given it… We didn't have the staffing needed." Reports from Madonna Care showed that on April 15, 2020, there had been an anonymous complaint made to the Ministry of Labour citing a lack of PPE, including N-95 masks that were being locked up. On April 21, 2020, the first staff member died. The second worker died in May.[316]

- In Dalhousie, New Brunswick, staff at Villa Renaissance lived in campers in the Villa's parking lot for three weeks, fearful of bringing Covid-19 home to their friends and family. While self-isolating, Nurse Natalie Poirier was unable to see her children and missed the birth of a granddaughter during the outbreak. Forty-eight-year-old Reno Maltais, who worked at the Villa for twenty-five years, died after he contracted Covid-19. His death instilled more fear among the already beleaguered staff.[317]

COVID-19 MAKES THE CASE

As Covid-19 spread from jurisdiction to jurisdiction, it became apparent that pandemic planning and PPE supplies had not been a priority for either level of government for a very long time.

Supplies were not the only problem for Canada pre-Covid. Canada's hospitals were operating far beyond their maximum capacity before the virus arrived. In 2018, Canada ranked near the bottom of all OECD countries when it came to the availability of acute-care beds and ICU beds. In 2018, Canada had 1.95 acute care beds for every 1,000 people. According to OECD data, there has been a steady decline in the number of beds since the 1980s.[318]

Concerns about pre-Covid infrastructure within Canada's hospitals was highlighted by the arrival of the pandemic. During the early stages of the pandemic, hospital administrators were left with very difficult decisions to make. They scrambled to make surge capacity within an already overcrowded system. In March of 2020, Paul-Émile Cloutier, who heads up a group that represents hospitals and health-care organizations, voiced concerns about Canada's existing infrastructure and care provider resources. With hospitals in the country operating at about 110 percent capacity, there would be little room to handle a surge of acutely ill patients.[319] There were also jurisdictions where capacity had exceeded Cloutier's 110 percent statistic. *CBC News* reported that some Ontario hospitals ran beyond a hundred percent capacity nearly every day in the first half of 2019. The CBC's findings for 169 acute-care facilities in Ontario from January to June 2019 revealed: Eighty-three hospitals were beyond a hundred percent capacity for over thirty days. Thirty-nine hospitals hit an astonishing 120 percent or higher for at least one day. Forty hospitals averaged a hundred percent capacity or higher. Donald Redelmeier, a physician and professor of medicine at the University of Toronto, stated, "… it means when there's a surge of new patients, there's nowhere to relieve the congestion… you ought not strive for 100 percent capacity because it doesn't leave you any reserve when things get tough."[320]

Stories of overcrowding prior to the arrival of Covid-19 bear an eerie similarity across the country. The Campbellton Hospital in New Brunswick took the unprecedented step of closing in the fall of 2019 due to overcrowding. As part of a mitigation strategy, the medical management team said they would be diverting patients to other hospitals in the region. But as Dr. Natalie Cauchon, a doctor at the neighbouring Chaleur Hospital in Bathurst, pointed out, their hospital was also full. Their own obstetrics unit was forced to close in 2018 and again in 2019.[321]

With several hospitals in Canada running at 110 percent capacity, it is unsurprising that pandemic planning included a plan to quickly empty hospitals. With hospitals at the risk of an acute-care surge related to Covid-19 patients, policy makers quickly started to cancel surgeries and procedures. These cancellations superimposed on already lengthy waitlists added further congestion to an already congested system. As of July 2020, there were 25,000 Nova Scotians waiting for surgical procedures. Of those, 1,075 were cancer patients. In Nova Scotia, it may take two additional years for wait times to return to pre-Covid levels. By 2020, Dr. Greg Hirsch, from Nova Scotia Health, said that about 3,600 surgeries were cancelled.[322]

In March of 2020, the Nova Scotia Health Authority also stopped mailing out home screening kits for colon cancer, because their system was only at fifty percent capacity for colonoscopies. Testing also dropped because of Covid-19. It is estimated that 8000 polyps have been detected because of the colon-cancer screening program—polyps that may have led to colon cancer if the prevention initiative wasn't in place. Additionally, the program detected 1000 cases of early-stage colon cancer. This type of early detection makes treatment easier, prognosis better, and saves valuable health care dollars in the long run. As of August 2020, the health authority was experiencing a backlog of roughly 700 colonoscopies.[323] With pre-Covid access to vital colonoscopies already an issue, this reduction in procedures and temporary halting of provincial cancer surveillance, surely puts patients at greater risk.

In Ontario, the news about cancellations and cut-backs related to Covid-19 was equally grim. A hospital network in the province estimated that thirty-five people may have died because heart surgeries were cancelled. Saying she really didn't want to call it "collateral damage," Christine Elliott, former minister of health, said, "... we were required to make decisions... space was made to make sure we had enough acute care and critical care beds and ventilators available for people with Covid-19... thousands of lives were saved." Small consolation to the thirty-five families who lost loved ones related to the delays. Between March 15 and April 22, up to 52,700 procedures in Ontario alone were cancelled or delayed. Most of the cancelled procedures were medically required, leaving Ontario hospitals to cope with significant backlogs.[324]

Jerry Dunham's loved ones lost a son and husband in one of those Canadian hospitals that were planning for a surge of patients that never came. Dunham's story is one that Canadians need to know. On April 16, 2020, he was told at his Alberta doctor's office that his defibrillator insertion was cancelled because of the pandemic. After waiting almost an hour to see his doctor, the forty-six-year-old was told that his doctor was "too busy" to see him, even though Mr. Dunham had booked an appointment. He wrote an impassioned plea on Facebook, saying, "Let me say that again… my government told me they're willing to let me die, which according to them is for my own safety…" That is exactly what happened. Two months later, the father of two young daughters died on June 7, 2020, at the Medicine Hat Regional Hospital. About a year and a half earlier, the young, fit, construction worker had started to feel short of breath and was diagnosed with heart failure. Told at the time he may eventually need a heart transplant, the treatment plan was to do more testing, place him on medications, and fit him with a defibrillator. Writing on his Facebook page, the young hockey player wrote, "Heart surgery, apparently considered nonessential. Now I know some say that's non-essential, but it's pretty goddam essential to me. Now I'm told today possibly could be a year or two?" The mother of his two girls said, "I vowed to him on his death-bed with our daughters sobbing for their daddy to wake up, that his death would not be in vain." Dunham suffered a heart attack and spent far more time in ICU on a ventilator than he ever would having a defibrillator inserted.[325]

In British Columbia, fifty-year-old Chris Walcroft also died waiting for a fistula insertion procedure. The surgery was cancelled exactly one day before the operation was due to take place. With seventeen-percent kidney function left, the father of two required the fistula to receive dialysis in order to stay alive. He had a follow up doctor's appointment on April 15, 2020. That was the day he died. As of April 15, 2020, 13,900 surgeries in the province of BC were cancelled.[326]

By the end of 2021, the evidence was undeniable. A report published by the Canadian Medical Association (CMA), in collaboration with Deloitte, detailed the impact Covid-19 had on regular operational procedures. The report estimates that about 4,000 people died between August and December 2020 because of delayed or cancelled care directly related to the fallout from the pandemic. In August 2020, Alberta cancelled or postponed more than 15,000 surgeries as a result of the pandemic. Looking at eight different types of surgeries across the country between April 2020 and June 2021, researchers concluded "on average, there was a forty-six day wait period for breast cancer surgeries... MRI scans came with an average sixty-nine day wait... hip replacements involved an average delay of 118 days... It also noted an increase in opioid-related deaths—up to twenty per day in the first three months of 2021."[327] Covid-19 exposed the results that years of defunding, defrauding, deregulation, and deliberate disintegration produced. What front-line staff had predicted for decades became the country's stark reality.

Serious pandemic planning requires preparing the system for a surge of sick patients. Canada's pandemic preparation was limited by the total lack of flex within the pre-Covid-19 system. It also created a serious ethical dilemma. Seniors should have been transferred from overwhelmed hospitals into care homes in a coordinated and timely fashion prior to Covid-19. Instead, transfers were fraught with bureaucracy, procrastination, and glaring inefficiencies. As hospital systems collapsed under the weight of overcrowding, moving seniors out of acute-care beds was sluggish at best. Despite the pleas from emergency rooms and families of seniors trapped in acute care facilities, the pre-Covid-19 transfer process seemed impermeable to change. Covid-19 also provided hope that the transfer process employed across the country was amenable to change. Acute-care facilities operating at a hundred percent capacity (or greater) suddenly found themselves with a short window of time to shore up beds. Erratically, emptying beds became a desperate strategy. Surgeries and procedures were cancelled to reduce hospital congestion, and seniors were frantically moved out of hospital beds at unprecedented rates. This accelerated movement came at a very high cost.

A hundred and fifty-two beds were occupied by non-medical patients within the Nova Scotia Health Authority in February of 2020. By March, forty-two patients were transferred out of hospital beds into long-term care facilities. This movement included transfers to Northwood in Halifax where fifty-three residents died from Covid-19. Transfers were expedited within a three-week period. By the end of March 2020, Nova Scotia Health CEO, Brendan Carr, announced that hospitals across Nova Scotia were at seventy percent capacity, significantly down from their usual hundred percent.[328]

The same holds true for jurisdictions across the country. In the beleaguered Campbellton Hospital in New Brunswick, fifty seniors were moved less than a week after the province announced it needed to free up hospital beds to prepare for Covid-19. In the weeks that followed, fifteen more moves were also expedited. Victor Shea, CEO of the Kenneth E. Spencer Memorial Home in Moncton, said, "We are trying to get people out of the hospital." Spencer said the moves were expedited because the province was allowing moves to occur within a larger radius and patients were being moved to the first available bed rather than to beds of their choice.[329]

In Laval Quebec, a health authority was so desperate to move elderly patients out of Cité-de-la-Santé Hospital that they moved 130 palliative and mental-health patients into a hotel.[330] When the first Covid-19 cases hit in January 2020, 3000 patients (who were medically discharged, waiting for beds elsewhere) occupied one-in-five Ontario hospital beds. About one-third were waiting for long-term care, others were waiting for rehabilitation, and some for other services. By May 2020, 2116 of these patients were moved out of hospital beds to various destinations—some with health care supports and some without. In British Columbia, 1,000 patients were moved. In Quebec, 6,000 beds needed to be cleared. Between March and early April of 2020, Alberta transferred 901 patients out of hospitals into long-term care or other community facilities. According to Alberta Health Services, the transfers in March were the highest number recorded in history.[331]

Frantic to create space for potential Covid-19 patients, Canadian health authorities expedited the movement of seniors everywhere. They did so because hesitating could cost lives. Health authorities found themselves making these difficult choices partly because funded beds in Canada had not kept pace with population growth. Provinces like Alberta, Ontario, and British Columbia that saw greater population growth had fewer beds per capita than areas like the Atlantic Provinces, where there were more beds per capita because of lower growth rates. Covid-19 raised the curtain on Canada's shortcomings on creating a robust health care system that could better manage a public health care crisis. As journalist Frances Wooley remarked, "A system that constrains costs by limiting the supply of essential services is a system that cannot cope with a pandemic."[332] The Covid-19 crisis readily highlighted the fragility of our health care system. Decades of not dealing with overcrowded hospitals placed the Canadian health care system in this precarious situation. The Covid-19 pandemic worsened the situation for seniors unfairly blamed for blocking Canada's hospital beds. Older Canadians became national scapegoats.

Many of the seniors who moved in record numbers died. For most, it meant being sent to nursing homes that were ill-prepared to accommodate an influx of frail, elderly people. Years of ignoring the pitfalls of long-term care privatization and defunding ailing infrastructure left Canada's nursing homes unable to cope with the sudden inward migration of seniors. In Ontario, Natalie Mehra, executive director of the Ontario Health Coalition, voiced concerns about patients landing in institutions where there might be inadequate care. Mehra was concerned about "the offloading of patients to assisted living or retirement facilities… most are for non-profit and self-regulating under Ontario's Retirement Homes Act, which is not a medical act."[333] In many instances, transfers were uncoordinated and non-negotiable. Despite not having either the staff or the appropriate infrastructure to deal with a pandemic, many nursing homes were compelled to accept the hospital transfers. Health departments across Canada frenetically directed the moves.

During March of 2020, Quebec hospitals were mandated to do something called "load shedding." This was the term given to the process of rapidly moving patients out of acute-care beds to create capacity. While the term also applied to patients whose surgeries and procedures were cancelled or postponed, it predominately related to the movement of seniors out of hospitals. In some jurisdictions, health authorities were so desperate to move seniors out that they resorted to paying private facilities to take their patients. In Montreal North, the health board paid $133,800 to three such private facilities to take twelve people because as their procurement contracts outlined it was necessary to "apply our load-shedding plan because of Covid-19…"[334]

Once the virus entered nursing homes, it became a perfect storm for the crisis that ensued. Seniors were subjected to a highly transmissible virus threatening their overcrowded and understaffed environments. Due to quarantines, families also were locked out. This restricted family advocacy for residents, especially those with significant cognitive impairment. The entire situation placed insurmountable stress on devoted staff, many of whom worked relentlessly, around the clock, for weeks on end. Canadian seniors and the staff who cared for them bore the burden of years of non-investment in a system that was supposed to protect them. Many died. Others were sent to destinations without nursing supports or languished in Covid-infested environments subjected to isolation, abandonment, sub-standard care, and various levels of abuse.

In Woodstock, New Brunswick, the family of Glen Thornton had less than twenty-four hours to prepare for his arrival home from hospital, while he waited for a long-term care bed. He required the highest level of nursing care. But that didn't seem to matter when the province called his wife. They said he had to go home the next day because "… they were moving anybody who could be moved, because of the pandemic." With Mr. Thornton's multiple health problems, a broken hip, and cognition issues, his family were wondering how they were going to cope on such short notice. They also had concerns about what this meant for Mr. Thornton's admission into a nursing home bed.[335]

Frantic with a fear of being overwhelmed by sick Covid-19 patients, and a possible ventilator shortage, an Oshawa hospital also expedited the transfer of seniors to nearby long-term care facilities. Nina Watt was one of those seniors moved out of the hospital to Orchard Villa. Ms. Watt's son said his mother had told him she didn't want to go there but was told she had no other option. On March 23, 2020, Nina Watt reluctantly agreed to the transfer. Orchard Villa was a long-term care facility that eventually became one of the deadliest nursing homes in the country. Seventy-seven residents at the home succumbed to Covid-19. Three weeks after her move, on April 15, 2020, eighty-six-year-old Nina Watt also died. Her death—another nursing home Covid-19 statistic.[336] The shoring up of hospitals by emptying beds irresponsibly sacrificed the country's seniors.

While seniors were being moved to nursing homes, another disturbing phenomenon happened. Families started to receive letters from care homes explaining that sick seniors would not be transferred to hospitals. Some letters explained the futility of sending seniors to hospitals where they were not likely to survive mechanical ventilation or heroic measures to save them. Rather, they would be better served remaining inside care homes where staff could administer comfort care. Policymakers decided that hospital beds were best left empty for more appropriate Covid-infected patients, that is those more likely to survive. Officials created a concerning ethical dilemma. Seniors in hospitals awaiting placement were pushed out to unprepared nursing homes at a frantic pace. Care homes harboured the perfect conditions for the proliferation of Covid-19. This was because of overcrowding, staff shortages, and the frailty of the residents. Infected residents were not to be treated in the empty hospital beds their own transfers had created. This strategy was a deadly trifecta: rapid transfers, high-risk communal environments, and acute-care denial.

Protecting scarce hospital beds in anticipation of a Covid-19 surge may have been well intentioned. In places like Belleville, Ontario, long-term care facility administrators were asked by Quinte Health Care to speak to families about not sending their Covid-19-infected loved ones to hospital. A March 23, 2020, letter to families from Quinte's chief of staff and chief of emergency medicine said that emergency departments would still accept Covid-19 patients if families insisted. But the letter also said, "Our critical-care colleagues are of the strong opinion that ventilator treatment will not make a survival difference to patients who are frail and ventilator support is very unlikely to be offered." In Bobcaygeon, Ontario, the medical director of Pinecrest Nursing Home sent a letter urging families to think twice before sending their loved ones infected with Covid-19 to the hospital. Twenty-eight of Pinecrest's sixty-five residents died of Covid-19. All twenty-eight died outside of hospital. Long-term care residents infected with Covid-19 were not supposed to be denied hospital care according to Ontario's health department.[337]

When a nurse at Orchard Villa called and asked Linda Cottrell where she wanted her father, Manuel Marques, treated when he spiked a fever and was awaiting coronavirus test results, Ms. Cottrell said that she wanted him taken to the emergency department. A doctor at the Villa angrily chastised her for trying to send her ninety-three-year-old father to the hospital, even though it was a step she had decided to take. The hospital sent her father back, and he died of Covid-19 at Orchard Villa.[338]

On April 2, 2020, Northwood in Halifax also sent families a letter. The letter outlined how "all doctors are working remotely" and asserted that "the safest place and most comfortable place for your loved one to be cared for is in Northwood." The letter continued, "… hospital interventions are very likely to be physically and emotionally traumatic… we have put in extra safeguards to avoid transfers to the ER… many residents in the long-term care population… will not likely meet the criteria for transfers to Covid-19 units or intensive care because they would not likely survive… although there is no treatment for Covid-19… Covid-19 infected residents will be provided with fluids and nourishment as needed for their ongoing comfort... and some residents might develop a rapid and severe pneumonia that can only be managed palliatively." Northwood had already charted a clear course for the treatment of Covid-19-infected seniors before the first resident tested positive. Families that weren't allowed into the facility or could not reach staff by phone were left to wonder about the treatments being administered to residents. One daughter remarked, "My mother had a do-not-resuscitate order. But that didn't mean, 'Don't save me from Covid.'" The letter affirmed to families, "We are prepared to care for any of our residents who become sick, with Covid-19... on special units equipped to manage this illness..." Families later testified about the ephemerality of that promise, remarking that not all infected residents were moved because the designated Covid-19 units filled so quickly.[339] Journalist Stephanie Nolen did an investigative piece on the Northwood crisis. After reviewing mountains of documents and conducting forty interviews, she concluded that the sequence of events "... tell[s] a story of a confluence of historic choices that left the facility perilously vulnerable to this virus, and a chaotic response where leadership collided with a cold calculus about who would be prioritized for saving."[340]

On March 23, 2020, the Quebec government issued guidelines saying residents in long-term care who contracted Covid-19 should only be sent to hospitals "on an exceptional basis after consultation with the doctor on duty." Jean Pierre Menard, a lawyer who specializes in patients' rights, said he was so concerned about the guidelines that he wrote the health minister arguing that it was hard for elderly patients to give proper consent as they were locked in care homes without access to family members.[341] Many substitute decision makers didn't have easy access to their loved ones or decision-making input at such a critical time.

As families received warnings about sending their sick loved ones to hospitals, long-term care casualties continued to mount. With most nursing homes unequipped to effectively manage large numbers of acutely ill seniors, most of the sick residents were deemed palliative and died under the auspices of comfort care. By the end of the first wave, most of the Covid-19-prepared hospital beds remained empty. Meanwhile, seniors died without advanced care hospital treatment/management. It was later reported that many of these older persons had died without the most basic of needs, such as food and water. A generation of people that had paid decades of taxes continued to die at an accelerated pace as hospital vacancy rates fell. By April of 2020, officials understood the predicament they had created. On April 10, 2020, the Quebec government halted the transfers of seniors from hospitals to long-term homes. On April 15, 2020, Ontario's health department took similar action. They requested that hospitals stop transferring seniors into long-term care homes because only sixty-four percent of acute care beds in Ontario were in use. National data revealing how many seniors died in long-term care homes remains scarce. Toronto Public Health found that as of April 17, 2020, only twenty-two of 899 residents diagnosed with Covid-19 were being treated in hospitals. That is roughly 2.5 percent. By May 1, 2020, that percentage rose to 5.6. percent.

The same holds true for other Canadian jurisdictions. In Alberta, data from May of 2020 confirmed that only twenty-four of 364 residents with confirmed Covid-19 cases were in hospital. It also remains unclear how many of those hospitalizations occurred at the insistence of families. By the time it was discovered that seniors were dying at expedited rates in long-term care, many facilities began sending them to vacant hospital beds to create more private spaces and reduce the spread of the virus.[342]

As the first wave flattened, family-initiated class-action lawsuits emerged. In Quebec, the son of an elderly woman who had died from Covid-19 in a government-run facility filed a class action against CHSLD-Ste-Dorothee. A Toronto law firm filed a class-action suit on behalf of all Ontarians within long-term care.[343] In Halifax, where fifty-three residents died from the virus at Northwood, families also launched a class-action lawsuit. They later expanded the suit to include the provincial government. Court documents indicate that the Nova Scotia government repeatedly rejected funding requests to create private rooms before Covid-19 arrived. The documents also indicate that the government cut funding to Northwood "without apparent justification and notwithstanding ongoing need."[344]

In Ontario, a $40 million class-action lawsuit was filed against Southbridge Care Homes and Orchard Villa, one of its long-term care homes. At one point, the facility had ninety-six staff and 225 residents infected with Covid-19. Orchard Villa was one of the hardest hit homes in the country, with seventy-seven deaths related to the virus. The lawsuit lists the Villa's history of violations. Complaints around care included severe staffing shortages and shortage of supplies such as linen and incontinence products. The families of residents at the Villa claim the home failed to supply adequate PPE to protect residents and staff, failed to institute reasonable measures to prevent the spread of Covid-19, failed to train staff, and failed to practise appropriate isolation and social distancing measures. The claim also asserts the home did not follow provincial guidelines to keep residents safe. While the outbreak was first declared inside the home on

April 9, 2020, the suit alleges that residents were not isolated until April 14. Orchard Villa receives over $11 million in funding each year from the Ontario government.[345]

Covid-19 demonstrated to Canadians everywhere just how fragile and defunded the Canadian health care system was prior to the arrival of Covid-19. Staff had been desperately trying to convey this message to government for decades. Clinicians and front-line staff had attempted to relay the fragility of the health care system and its inability to cope with any additional strain. The devastation that the virus inflicted on the long-term care sector clearly demonstrates that it was in a state of ignored crisis for an extended period. Personal protective equipment, infection control education, protocols, pandemic planning, and adequate staffing levels were lacking in facilities across the entire country. Residences were overcrowded and infrastructure was outdated. There were no national long-term care standards. Pleas to government were largely ignored and many of these precipitating issues remain unresolved. Despite this, these facilities continued to be licenced and accredited year after year.

In acute care, the story was similar. Pandemic preparedness, equipment, and adequate staffing were all in short supply as well.

This led to gruelling workplace scenarios with many staff exiting the system all together. In Quebec, thirty-five-year-old emergency room physician Karine Dion died by suicide. Her family asserted that it was stress-related to the pandemic that caused Dr. Dion to end her life. She was on the front lines in an emergency department, working relentlessly to help patients. When she took a mental health break from the Quebec hospital where she worked, it only left her "guilt ridden." Disheartened and drained from the stress of Covid-19, Dr. Dion was unable to cope any longer.[346]

Twenty-five-year-old Stephanie Van Nguyen also died by suicide. Stephanie was a nurse at Humber River Regional Hospital, who worked consistently throughout the pandemic. Her suicide sent shockwaves across the country. Doris Grinspun, the CEO of the Registered Nurses Association of Ontario, said, "The death of Van Nguyen is devastating and highlights the need of more mental health support for frontline workers."[347]

The Canadian Institute for Health Information (CIHI) reported that Covid-19 infections for health care workers reached 94,873. As of June 15, 2021, forty-three Canadian health care workers also died from Covid-19.[348]

Covid-19 demonstrated what happens to public health care systems when they are left unfunded and not made a priority. People died who should still be alive. This includes the brave people who care for all patients. We now have a stronger moral obligation to repair the system that decades of neoliberal policy have destroyed.

The virus also demonstrates the inextricable link between a robust economy and a healthy society. Previous policies implemented to save money and keep front-line workers subjugated, exacerbated economic woes: Policies like zero sick days forced people to choose between working while sick or losing income. Policies that froze salaries of low-paid workers forcing them to work multiple jobs to survive also forced them to spread Covid-19.

We cannot lose sight of how decades of living so close to the line within the health care system failed so many people. Having a robust public health system makes us more productive as a society. All human potential emanates from good health. If we do not change how health care is delivered, we will continue to lose more Canadians.

There is a golden opportunity to learn from the Covid-19

experience. A well-funded public health care system is essential to the future of Canada. As funders, we have the power to insist that governments develop policies that will grow and modernize Medicare. Collectively, in communities across the country, we must stand up and demand that change. There must be a complete revival surrounding how we deliver health care services in Canada. It begins with re-establishing what we value as a country—as a people.

Chapter 7
―――――

THE ROAD FORWARD

The only counterforce is you.

—Noam Chomsky, *Requiem for the American Dream*

An incredible demonstration of situational irony unfolded on September 18, 2020, as various news outlets convened to speak with Canadian premiers. The second wave of Covid-19 was surging across the country as four of the country's premiers met in the Chateau Laurier in Ottawa. The goal of premiers Doug Ford, Francois Legault, Brian Pallister, and Jason Kenney was to convince Prime Minister Trudeau to increase funding for health care. Ford, the Conservative premier of Ontario, stared into a television camera and soberly declared, "Nothing is more important than health care."[349] Looking at the solemn-faced Ford, no one could have guessed that just months before Covid-19 ravaged his province, his Conservative government was on track to consolidate thirty-five public health units into ten, merge ambulance services, and cut provincial public health funding, leaving municipalities to cover thirty percent of costs.[350] After Covid-19 killed thousands of Ontario seniors, the provincial government was now pleading with the federal government for help. By Ford's side was United Conservative Party Premier Jason Kenney, who, one year earlier, had extolled the virtues of health care privatization. Kenney's government was in talks with lobbyists about creating a $200-million private orthopedic surgical facility to be run by non-unionized staff.[351] Premier Brian Pallister, famous for his deep cuts to health care in Manitoba, including money earmarked for the expansion of Cancer Care Manitoba, was also present.[352] Even Premier Legault, an ardent supporter of private-pay health care systems, joined the chorus.

Back in 2018, Ottawa had threatened to cut health care transfer payments to Quebec because of their tolerance of private clinics and queue jumping. At that time, Legault responded by saying, "We will not be dictated to by the federal government."[353] It is discouraging to think that it took a global pandemic to convince conservative politicians that health care should be the country's priority. Without it, their market economies are unsustainable. Could it be possible that after all the lost revenue, soaring unemployment, and untimely deaths related to Covid-19 that these conservative premiers had finally come to their senses? As businesses collapsed and employees vanished, were these four premiers beginning to understand the crucial interrelatedness between health and productivity? Tommy Douglas articulated and thoroughly understood it many decades before the arrival of Covid-19. Perhaps the premiers have seen the light—fifty years later.

The group made one salient point. Salvaging Medicare must be a collaborative effort between the provinces, territories, and the federal government—with the federal government taking the lead. Ottawa must become a serious funding partner and set the trajectory for the direction of health care in the country. The federal government must end its reinforcement of standards while consistently reducing funding designed to sustain those standards. Provinces and territories must commit to serious health care reorganization and fiscal responsibility of health care dollars. The taxpayers, as the system funders, must send a clear message that restoring a strong universal health care system is a priority for Canadians.

The purple saxifrage is the territorial flower of Nunavut. It is a hardy, low-growing flower that can grow in the most austere conditions. It commonly flowers in areas where the snow melts late in the year. Its delicate, purple-lilac flowers grow in short stalks. Being one of the hardiest flowers in the world, it can survive even on the Arctic tundra. Author Matt Haig wrote an article outlining reasons why humanity should remain hopeful for the future by making a compelling analogy between the purple saxifrage and humankind. Haig described the flower's petals by saying they look so delicate, as if "... they could fly away in the wind."[354] Yet the flowers survive by clustering together, sheltering each other from their severe surroundings. Haig went on to say that he believes "humans, too, can be saved by one another."[355]

These past two years have given us countless examples of how people sheltered each other during a global crisis. In his analogy, Haig captured the essence of what Tommy Douglas believed: people can be saved if they are frail or elderly, have limited resources—or are living under the harshest of conditions. This is accomplished by pulling together and pooling our collective resources. That belief ignited the spark of Medicare, and it is that belief that will rescue Medicare. The federal government, provincial and territorial governments, and we, as funders, must conjointly reinvest in our public health care system. We must follow the example of Nunavut's purple saxifrage. Leadership must begin with Ottawa, whose job it will be to set a new national direction on health care by creating a cultural shift in how health care services are delivered throughout Canada.

Federal Government Action Required

1. The Government of Canada needs to join the Wellbeing Economies Governments Group.

According to SCOREGolf magazine's Rick Young, people are clamouring to get to my home province of Nova Scotia. That affirmation was also made in a 2017 CBC news article. It was a comment that really perked my interest since Nova Scotia has seen its fair share of difficult economic times.

Far from the harsh economic realities of everyday Nova Scotians, SCOREGolf magazine panelists do two things—play golf and rate Canadian golf courses. In 2017, sixty percent of their top-rated golf courses were in Nova Scotia. David Campbell, the executive director of the Nova Scotia Golf Association, seemed to agree, saying, "I think it's a good indication of what we already know in Nova Scotia—that Nova Scotia is a wonderful and amazing golf destination."[356] SCOREGolf's claim must have also captured the interest of some well-heeled golfers and politicians. Two years later, a group composed of several former premiers and business figures made a pitch to build a new airport in Inverness, Nova Scotia. The airport would facilitate connecting golfers to two of those famous golf courses. The eco-district of Inverness runs along Lake Ainslie, which is the largest natural freshwater lake in the province. The area also includes the Margaree Valley, with its designated Canadian Heritage River. The current airport in Port Hawksbury is about one hour away from the courses.

THE ROAD FORWARD

The group felt having direct, scheduled, commercial air access to the prestigious golf courses would be a tourism and business deal breaker. The new airport could possibly create millions of dollars in revenue and entice more golfers to visit the province.[357] I hold no personal animosity for golfers or their sport, but let's be frank. If you're affluent enough to golf or to travel to the prestigious Cabot Links course, you're probably not worried about putting food on the table or paying rent. It struck me as odd that a multi-million-dollar proposal to bring golfers closer to their golf destinations would even be considered. Nova Scotia was the only Canadian province that saw a spike in child poverty rates from fourteen percent in 2016 to seventeen percent in 2017.[358] It also has the highest undergraduate tuition rates in the country[359] and the dubious distinction of having the lowest median after-tax income in Canada in 2019.[360] One of its hospitals, the Cape Breton Regional, also had the highest mortality rate in the country for a few years in a row.

Hard-working Nova Scotians must have also found it odd because by the fall of 2019, plans to fund the massive infrastructure project in Western Cape Breton were scrapped. The discussion around ferrying golfers closer to majestic seaside golf courses made me think about what we value and what we measure as a community—as a country. Revenue aside, what would be the real long-term costs of building an airport in the pristine countryside of Inverness County? How would things like the increased air pollution, noise pollution, increased health risks, environmental damage, and diverting of millions of infrastructure dollars away from badly needed roads and hospitals ultimately affect everyday Nova Scotians and their families? Would the economic benefits trickle down to children living in poverty? Would anyone even bother to measure any of the adverse side effects of such a project?

Research on the Inverness airport project led me to a lecture given by Scotland's Nicola Sturgeon, which raises these exact questions in a broader sense—about world economies. She reminds us what a country measures really does matter because it "drives political focus and public activity." Her argument is that although GDP is a valuable measurement of all the output of a nation's work, it doesn't measure the effect on nature through the work done to obtain that GDP. It also does not measure the long-term effects those GDP-generating activities have on our communities/planet. Growing socioeconomic inequality, environmental impacts, or the fairness of workplaces are not captured within the GDP measurement. GDP does not measure whether our work is worthwhile or fulfilling. Success, and what it means to be successful, must be more broadly defined.

Sturgeon argues that we must ask ourselves, what do we value in our communities and what kind of society do we want to be? While economic growth is obviously important, its sole focus is much too narrow. Sturgeon asserts that GDP should not be pursued "at any and all costs." Somewhere in determining a country's success, we must measure that country's collective well-being. In 2018, Scotland set out to form a coalition with other countries interested in running states that accentuate personal growth and environmental stewardship. The group, aptly labelled the Wellbeing Economies Governments (WEgo) Partnership, charted a course to measure a nation's success more inclusively and use those metrics to push a "well-being agenda." The group wants their economic policy objectives to include the collective well-being of citizens, including a measurement of how happy and healthy they are.[361]

In one of the first budgets ever to place mental health at its core, the New Zealand government poured investment dollars into improving its country's mental-health challenges. The 2019 well-being budget dedicated $1.9 billion to improving the country's mental-health issues by targeting factors such as health education, corrections, justice, and housing.[362] The budget aimed to integrate mental health services closer to communities that needed them. It also sought to address societal issues that influence mental illness such as poverty and homelessness.[363]

Canada needs to join the WEgo coalition as soon as possible. This will allow the federal government to confirm its dedication to several key issues associated with the health of the country. Canada can also acknowledge the narrowness of the GDP as a stand-alone metric. This will better equip the country to counter the deleterious effects produced by the unraveling of Medicare. Joining the coalition stands to shift the country's political ideology and policy focus. It will confirm the federal government's commitment to the concept that what we eat, where we live, where we work, the level of education we have, and the quality of the air we breathe all impact our national health.

GDP is a retrospective measurement that is calculated after the previous year's input occurred. GDP is, therefore, not a real-time quality indicator. By joining the WEgo partnership, Canada could assert itself as a progressive country on the global stage. This change in trajectory would move us from a solely economic focus towards a more integrated well-being focus. Issues like the country's escalating opioid epidemic or Nova Scotia's rising child poverty rates would edge to the policy forefront as "well-being" priorities. These pressing societal issues currently remain unresolved because they're eclipsed by the GDP as the nation's narrow priority metric.

The status quo is no longer a viable option. The emphasis on greater GDP growth at the expense of much else, including ongoing environmental damage, has led some experts to coin the term "degrowth." Degrowth aims to create an economy that focuses more on protecting the environment and less on stripping the planet of natural resources in pursuit of higher GDP numbers. It aims to curb the generation of infinite wealth and consumerism.

Professor Bengi Akbulut at Concordia University says degrowth "aims to reduce the amount of energy and resources taken from the biosphere in the production and consumption of goods and services, and to create an economy that is more oriented toward environmental stewardship, as well as wealth redistribution and social justice." When referencing economic growth, Akbulut indicates that it "smothers and… dominates other social goals that a society might deem preferable." Professor Peter Victor, at York University, asserts that Covid-19 has demonstrated to many of us what things really matter in life: "… I think there's a big question about… how many people are out there, who are saying, well, I'm not sure I want to carry on doing what we were doing before." Amanda Janoo, policy lead for the WEgo alliance, agrees: "We need to transform our notion of progress, because right now, our notion is defined by economic variables of wealth generation or GDP."[364]

Economic policy debates are ultimately about what kind of society we want. In a predominately neoliberal society, there is a contortion between means and ends. In the neoliberal world we live in, most citizens have become a means to an economic strategy. This approach leaves most people behind and creates a narrow minority of powerful, financial heavyweights. A well-being economic order is one where the economy switches its focus to achieving collective societal goals. In a well-being economic order, goals other than wealth accumulation prevail and include social policies that centre around a more humane and just society. This stands to effectively mitigate neoliberal doctrines of unbridled capitalism. Ensuring an allegiance to the well-being of its citizens is a necessary first step in Canada's race to save Medicare. Canada must recognize the limits of using the GDP as a stand-alone quality indicator and shift the country's trajectory towards a new view on what we measure, what we value, and what we urgently need to resolve.

2. Federal funding for health transfers must be restored and federal, provincial, and territorial relationships must be immediately renewed.

Health care in Canada remains the responsibility of the provinces and territories. The 1867 Canadian constitution contained no provisions for the central government to initiate a national public health care system. As a result, the constitution assigns the stewardship of health care to the provinces. However, its interconnectedness to federal government funding and, later, to the Canada Health Act cannot be understated. Much like our salaries dictate our own standard of living, you can't keep experiencing salary reductions or stagnation and maintain a consistent standard of living. This is particularly true in view of inflation/rising costs. Similarly, the federal government cannot continue to legislate the quality of health care via the Canada Health Act while continuing to decrease the funding designed to support the tenets of the 1984 legislation. In short, you can't continue to "make high-quality bricks with less and less straw."

In 1944, the CCF party campaigned for provincial health

insurance across Saskatchewan. By 1947, led by Tommy Douglas, the CCF implemented the Hospital Insurance Plan.[365] By 1962, Saskatchewan also pioneered a universal medical services insurance. Forced to "go it alone," it put strain on Saskatchewan's treasury. Saskatchewan was a poor jurisdiction. Tommy Douglas noted during his 1944 election win in Saskatchewan, "… we were a bankrupt province; we hadn't been able to borrow a dollar on the open market since 1932."[366] By the 1950s, other provinces were clamouring for medical insurance plans within their own jurisdictions. With pressure mounting from more provinces, the federal government passed the Hospital and Diagnostic Services Act in April of 1957, which offered funding to participating provinces at approximately fifty percent of the per capita costs of applicable services delivered at general hospitals. In 1966, as more provinces continued to sign on, the Government of Canada passed, The Medical Care Act, which promised to cover fifty percent of the national average per capita cost of all insured medical services. These two initiatives formed the fiscal groundwork for Medicare in Canada. The last year for which funding for these two acts is recorded is 1976–1977. For that year, federal coverage included forty-eight percent of hospital spending and forty-nine percent of physician spending, demonstrating that Ottawa lived up to its 50:50 cost sharing obligation.[367]

In 1970, Ottawa calculated how to reduce its share of health care funding by limiting spending to the rate of growth of the gross national product (GNP). In April of 1977, the provinces and territories signed onto Pierre Trudeau's Established Programs Financing Act (EPFA), which replaced the 50:50 cost sharing arrangement in favour of block grants. The grants would pay one-half of the payments for the three cost-shared programs of the Hospital Insurance and Diagnostic Services

Act, the Medical Care Act, and post-secondary education, as a block grant. That escalated yearly in accordance with a three-year average of nominal, per capita GNP growth. Within this block scheme, federal taxes were reduced, leaving the provinces and territories to utilize those revenues for health care.[368]

In 1995, the federal government unilaterally rolled all its cash transfers in the Canada Health and Social Transfer (CHST) to reduce its own deficit. The value of the transfer was cut dramatically, but the reduced federal tax portion (tax point transfers) remained.[369]

The federal budgets between 1985 and 1995 scaled back their automatic flexibility (escalator clause) on health and social transfers or froze the payments completely. Alistair Thomson calculated that the health transfer money was reduced by $30 billion between 1986/87–1995/96. Reductions between 1995/96 to 1998/99 cut another $11.2 billion, relative to the initial 1977 agreed terms.[370]

Between 1996 and the early 2000s, with health care services dramatically cut across the country and voter discontent growing, the *Romanow Report* called for Ottawa to reinvest in health care. In 2003, the CHST was split into the Canada Health Transfer (CHT) and the Canada Social Transfer (CST). Sixty-two percent of the of the CHST cash went into the new CHT along with an additional $16 billion as a Health Reform Transfer to the provinces. In 2004, Paul Martin agreed on a ten-year accord with new spending amounting to $41.3 billion. Growth in the CHT accounted for $35.3 billion over two years. Martin later applied a six-percent annual escalator, adding automatic flexibility to the wider base.[371]

These increases eventually allowed the provinces to "expand" health care spending, but by this time, the damage had already been done by the years of federal defunding (specifically during the late 1990s). This expansion of health care spending was a false economy. The earlier economic damage was so extensive that the provinces were really just playing a game of catch up.

Working in health care during this time, I experienced massive restructuring programs, staffing shortages, the defunding of long-term care, infrastructural collapse, increased wait times, and the demise of emergency services.

In 2006, Stephen Harper promised to negotiate a fourth health accord with the premiers. That never happened. Instead, in 2011 the federal Conservatives announced that when the 2004 health accord ended in 2014, that the CHT escalator would remain at six percent until 2017. Then it would grow for the next decade at the higher of three-percent per year or a three-year moving average of nominal GDP growth percentage. Experts estimated this move would reduce federal transfers for health by $36 billion overall (compared to leaving the six-percent escalator in place for the decade of 2014–2024).

In 2015, the premiers were still calling for Ottawa to increase health care funding to cover twenty-five percent of all health care spending. In October of 2015, after the Liberals won a federal majority, they reaffirmed the reduction in the CHT escalator as set out by the previous Harper government.[372].

This period coincided with the aging of the baby boomer generation and more people requiring long-term care.

If the federal government is serious about its commitment to Medicare, it must renegotiate a serious transfer funding program with the provinces and territories and tie that funding to specific performance indicators. Provinces must realize more federal cash has to come with the responsibility of transforming the system, meeting real targets, and acting fiscally responsible. More federal cash without transformative change means Canadian taxpayers will continue to lose. Despite Ottawa's extensive history of frustration with the provinces and territories, surrounding health care funding, it must step up to the plate. It must be prepared to restore desperately needed cash to the system—but not blindly. It must, in collaboration with the provinces and territories, come to a reasonable agreement on inter-jurisdictional funding tied to conditions that will help the provinces enact greatly needed health care reform. Federal money, leadership, and patience for such an initiative is long overdue.

3. Establish universal support for poverty.

Within all health care systems, there is one recurring observation that cannot be denied—poverty and poor health outcomes are inextricably linked. Poverty and poor health collide every day in emergency departments across the country. Patients who are economically disadvantaged suffer more stress, are more likely to hold down lower-paying jobs without benefits, work multiple jobs with longer hours, live in more contaminated/unsafe environments, eat less nutritiously, and are more exposed to infectious diseases. Once sick, this patient population is less likely to afford medications, physiotherapy, treatments, home care, and medical devices that assist with recovery. Being poor can have such a deleterious effect on health outcomes that the World Health Organization has called poverty "the single largest determinant of health."[373] Reasons for this are well documented and researched by experts around the world. In a 2020 letter addressed to Prime Minister Trudeau and members of his cabinet, several clinical practitioners and scholars explained that "… research that illuminates the consequences for human health… caused by poverty abounds. Shortened life expectancy, chronic diseases, infant mortality, addictions, and a myriad of other physical and mental health impairments are all similarly distributed across a wealth-health gradient with those among the lowest income quintiles getting sick and dying years before higher-earning Canadians."[374]

During the early years of Medicare, policy makers strongly believed that the best way to improve health status was to improve medical access. One of the ways to achieve this was to implement a strong, universal public health care system. Medicare sought to break down financial barriers that prevented people from accessing timely medical care and hospital services. By the 1970s, experts came to understand that other factors influenced health outcomes. The old policy prototype expanded the definition of health to include other "determinants of health." As Bolaria and Dickinson described, "This definition of health… gives rise to a need to develop multidimensional measures of health… "[375] Since the 1970s, ongoing research has demonstrated the effects that inequality and poverty exert on the health status of individuals. Although access to medical care and hospital services are still crucial to health outcomes, they remain inadequate when other determinants of health are left unaddressed. Poverty leads the list as the most vital predictor of health outcomes. As a result of being at the top of the social determinant hierarchy, poverty has often been referred to as a social determinant leader regarding health. Tom Boyce, chief of the University of California San Francisco's Division of Developmental Medicine, captured the significance of poverty as it relates to health by saying, "Socioeconomic status is the most powerful predictor of disease, disorder, injury and mortality we have."[376]

Compared to non-Indigenous persons, Indigenous Canadians

have unemployment and poverty rates that are three times higher.[377] The abject poverty endured by many Indigenous persons in Canada is among the worst in the country. It is also no coincidence that health outcomes among Indigenous persons in Canada are also among the worst.

Health statistics speak for themselves. When compared to non-Indigenous populations, life-expectancy rates for Indigenous persons are less. Indigenous persons die younger; live with more disabilities; have three to five times the infant mortality rates and babies born with birth defects and debilitating conditions; have three times the rate of diabetes and four times the rate of traumatic injuries; have suicide rates that are six times higher than non-Indigenous populations; suffer heart disease at a younger age; and are more likely to experience motor vehicle crashes, poisonings, and fire-arm related injuries.[378] It is not just a matter of individuals suffering from poverty. Entire families and communities become trapped within a cycle of colonialism and poverty over time. Impoverishment becomes transgenerational in this regard and breeds what journalist André Picard calls "… the perfect storm of conditions to destroy health," where "misery has bred ill health, and ill health more misery."[379]

Modern science backs up what clinicians see in emergency departments and doctor's offices every day. New evidence suggests "stresses associated with poverty have the potential to change our biology in ways we hadn't imagined. It can reduce the surface area of your brain, shorten your telomeres and lifespan, increase your chances of obesity, and make you more likely to take outsized risks."[380] Poverty-associated stress is more far-reaching than previously thought. Scientists studying epigenetics (how our genes work) are producing new data demonstrating the effects of poverty-related stress on fetuses in utero. Although the science of the biological effects of the stresses of poverty is still evolving, it has laid out multiple possibilities through which effects can happen including an inheritable component. As science author Christian Cooper explains, "If a pregnant woman, for example, is exposed to the stresses of poverty, her fetus and that fetus' gametes can both be affected, extending the effects of poverty to at least her grandchildren."[381]

Breaking cycles of poverty resonates into the health care of nations. Directly addressing this social determinant leader would improve the lives of citizens caught in the poverty cycle and it could save millions of dollars in the long term by reducing chronic disease rates, hospitalizations, treatments, and disabilities. The health care system needs to focus on preventing illness before it occurs instead of trying to keep pace with it after it happens—and continues to evolve. Study after study demonstrates that Canadians who live in more affluent areas have lower disease rates, better health care screening opportunities, and lower mortality rates than those who live in poor neighbourhoods or are homeless. An Ontario report recently found that only fifty-four percent of women living in the poorest neighbourhoods got screening for cervical cancer. In comparison, sixty-seven percent of women living in more affluent, urban neighbourhoods received full screening. Similar disparities also exist for colorectal cancer screening.[382]

Canadian social programs have changed little over the years compared to the substantive socioeconomic changes that have occurred within the country. In a recent *Canadian Medical Association Journal* (CMAJ) article, authors cite increased migration and diversity, transformation of family structures and gender roles, globalization, changes to the economy, and the growing threats of climate change as reasons why the federal government needs to do more to address the country's growing inequities.[383] The decline of Medicare will continue unless we incorporate the reduction and eradication of poverty into the concept of health.

What can the federal government do to thrust Canada's social mobility forward? A recent CMAJ paper advocates for a "Health in All Policies" (HiAP) federal action plan. The authors argue that although Canada has always had an ambitious and egalitarian history of using progressive policy to promote health and equity, recently "Canadian leadership in broad health policy has stalled."[384] This puts the sustainability of Medicare and the health of Canadians at risk. "Health in All Policies," as defined by the authors, is "an approach that systematically considers the health and social implications of policies contemplated by all sectors of government—aiming for synergistic benefits and to minimize social and health-related harms."

The authors maintain such a program is a crucial policy lever because "… many of the drivers for health outcomes… are beyond the reach of the health sector… a fundamental aspect of HiAP is careful attention to root causes of poor health…"[385] The authors believe that implementing such a federal program would be a major step towards health promotion and health equity for Canadians.

Whether it's implementing a HiAP program or expanding existing programs, improving health outcomes via health equity is a complex undertaking. There is certainly no "one size fits all" approach. Other experts have advocated for poverty reduction to increase health status by expanding existing social programs, establishing national standards for the long-term care sector, providing a universal childcare program and a universal pharmacare program, expanding dental services, restoring federal involvement and funding to provincial and territorial jurisdictions for health, and implementing a universal basic income. The federal government must make a firm commitment to reduce poverty levels in Canada to rescue Medicare and improve health outcomes.

During the Covid-19 pandemic, the Canadian government brought in emergency programs to support unemployed, sick, or quarantined Canadians, and to assist struggling business owners. The benefits renewed the conversation surrounding the notion of a Universal Basic Income (UBI). Implementing a UBI has been floated by policy makers for years. It seeks to guarantee a basic income that would keep all Canadians above the poverty line. Many front-line health care clinicians support the idea, although many of the details of such a plan remain obscure.

Guy Caron is an economist who has studied the notion of guaranteed minimum income. He calculates the cost of implementing such a program at about $30 billion per year.[386] While the price may sound cost prohibitive, the overall savings and increased revenue generated by such a plan would have to be included in any cost equation. Proponents believe it has the potential to substantially reduce poverty-associated health care costs, recirculate money into local communities, increase tax revenues, lead to better jobs for youth, and improve health outcomes overall by raising the standard of living. In a 2020 open letter to the prime minister, 167 health professionals called for Ottawa to implement a UBI for Canadians. The group counters the affordability argument by asserting progressive tax reform could cover the cost. The group also maintains implementing a UBI would reduce health care costs and decrease hospitalization rates by 8.5 percent. Toronto's Dr. Danielle Martin is a proponent of a UBI plan and has pointed out, "If we discovered a drug that reduced hospitalizations by 8.5 %, we'd put it in the water."[387]

The Canadian landscape has changed enormously since the inception of Medicare. The federal government must make a clear statement surrounding a plan to reduce poverty in the country if it is serious about protecting Medicare. Since the days of the Lalonde Report, we have come to understand that health outcomes are affected by variables beyond health care access. One of those leading determinants is poverty. Health care equity in Canada is declining. Until the federal government understands the interrelatedness between health and poverty, the cost of health care will increase, and outcomes will not improve. Dr. Nancy Adler, from the University of California's San Francisco Center for Health and Community, likes to explain the health and poverty relationship this way: "If you are hit by a truck, you are going to want to be treated... But, in the end, your health is going to be more affected by the fact that you were hit by the truck than by how the health care system managed your care. Poverty is that truck."[388]

4. The federal government must launch a national pharmacare strategy.

Bill was one of my most memorable patients. He was a truck driver who had fallen on some difficult times. Because of these difficulties, Bill was forced to ration and eventually stop taking his high-blood-pressure medications. Persistent high blood pressure, a sedentary lifestyle, and the stress of ongoing financial insecurity left him to choose whether he paid the rent or purchased necessary medications. This ultimately landed Bill in the ICU where I worked. He had sustained a heart attack and significant renal damage as a result of untreated high blood pressure. The ICU team worked diligently to mitigate the damage done to Bill's organs and a five-day stay in ICU greatly stabilized his condition. A social worker assisted Bill in securing funding for his medications in preparation for his discharge. The details surrounding the discharge planning wouldn't be addressed until after the New Year holiday passed. Bill and two other patients were my companions as we celebrated New Year's Eve inside the tiny ICU. We played music, toasted our water at midnight, and sang "Auld Lang Syne" as a group of two nurses and three patients.

Bill's transfer out of ICU was written for New Year's Day. He was excited to go to the medical unit and eventually from there to home. I had the next the next couple of days off and assured him I'd try and visit him on the medical unit when I came back.

I left home early on my first shift back from the holidays, anticipating visiting Bill before my shift began. But as I walked through the medical unit, he was nowhere to be found. I approached the nurses' station and asked if Bill had been discharged early. The small group of nurses looked solemn. The charge nurse stepped forward to tell me that Bill had suffered a second heart attack on New Year's night, just hours after being transferred out of the ICU. He'd gone into cardiac arrest and died.

The shock and sadness of the news was paralyzing as I walked up the hall to the ICU. Once in the unit, I stared at the vacant bed where Bill had been hopeful and happy a few short nights before. I thought about the harsh reality of how the cost of life-saving medications had competed with his food and shelter needs. This choice had cost Bill his life.

Bill's story is now decades old. Since that heartbreaking night, the lack of affordable medication has worsened and continues to claim patients across this country. I witnessed it repeatedly and consistently over the past forty years of my practice. In jurisdictions across the country stories of patients forced to choose between paying rent or buying medications continues to claim lives. Grace Fogarty is one such resident. She received a letter stating her rent would be increasing by $650 a month by April 2021. That increase would leave the sixty-three-year-old, full-time worker, with $625 a month to pay for just about everything else. Fogarty made it clear what that would mean, stating, "The choice would be no heart medication, no food."[389]

The same holds true for sixty-two-year-old Fabian Donovan. On a fixed disability pension, Donovan admitted there have been months where he has had to choose between medication, food, and rent. Although his recent rent increase of $30 a month is much less than that of other renters, Donovan admits he "dreads what's to come down the road"[390]

With every year that passes without an affordable national pharmacare plan, more Canadians keep slipping through the cracks. The Canadian Federation of Nurses Unions estimates that hundreds of Canadians continue to die every year because they cannot afford to buy medications. In a report by the organization, researchers estimate that between 370–640 premature deaths related to ischemic heart disease occur annually from lack of prescription drug coverage. They also estimate that between 270–420 premature deaths of working-age Canadians with diabetes occur, and that 550–670 premature deaths from all causes among working-age Canadians continue due to lack of prescription drug coverage.[391]

Those unable to afford medication are disproportionately the most vulnerable. According to Shikha Gupta and Mary Ann McColl, from Queen's University, close to one-third of disabled Canadians may be skipping medication doses or not getting their prescriptions filled at all because of cost. Gupta and McColl's research shed light on two misconceptions about people with disabilities and drug costs. Firstly, that most disabled Canadians are either seniors or are on welfare, and therefore, their drug costs are covered. This is not true. The Canadian Survey on Disability demonstrates that sixty percent of disabled Canadian adults are under the age of sixty-five. This excludes them from accessing senior's benefits. Another thirty to sixty percent are disabled adults who work, which excludes them from many government drug plans.

The second misconception asserts that drug insurance helps with lessening the burden of prescription medication. The study also demonstrated that although ninety-two percent of the sample participants had some form of drug insurance, they still suffered from hefty out-of-pocket prescription drug expenses—about five times the national average. Disabled Canadians usually require more prescription medications. The average number of medications taken by people with disabilities was five. Considering dispensing fees, drug costs, co-payment arrangements, and other out-of-pocket expenses, the costs of medication ranged from $197 per month to upwards of $3000 per month. Deductibles also must be maintained in order to preserve any existing coverage. Deductibles for some of these patients reached as high as twenty percent of their annual income.

Additionally, disabled individuals often have other medical supply costs the rest of us normally do not think about. Catheters, special equipment, maintenance of equipment, supplies, dressings, and gloves also contribute to the financial burden. Disability also imposes lower-level employment status, further reducing the ability to afford medication. According to the study, "... the average income for someone with a disability is $20,000 lower than for those without a disability... and twenty-eight percent of people with a severe disability live below the poverty line."[392]

A national pharmacare plan would ensure that these Canadians are protected from these burdensome costs.

Canada is the only developed country in the world with a universal public health care system that doesn't have a public system for providing prescription medicine. Currently there exists a patchwork of programs that cover prescription medications for Canadians. About half of Canadians have employer-based, private insurance that covers medication costs. These plans vary in coverage and cost. Most of them come with requisite copayments and deductibles. Other government plans cover Indigenous people, people receiving social assistance, or people over sixty-five. About one in five Canadians are forced to pay directly out of pocket for medications. The cost of those medications has escalated to four times what it was twenty years ago. With this inconsistent medley of drug coverage, thousands of Canadians are either unable or struggling to afford their medication.[393] The adverse outcomes related to inconsistent medication use continues to cost the Canadian health care system millions of unnecessary dollars.

This assortment of plan coverage also means Canada is paying some of the highest costs for drugs in the world. A study by the University of Ottawa and the Bruyère Research Institute maintains Canada is still paying more than other industrialized countries for its generic drugs. The study maintains that the cost of six drugs commonly used to treat high blood pressure and high cholesterol remain much higher in Canada than elsewhere. Canadian prices for some medications are double those of their peer countries.[394]

The real issues surrounding the patchwork of drug coverage in Canada are concerning. There are about 100,000 private drug insurance plans across the country. Other plans include about a hundred government-run drug insurance programs. The coverage these plans provide is far from uniform. Depending on where you live, medication coverage under these plans may vary. Jurisdictional variation means access to specific medications depends entirely on what part of the country you live in. This creates an exceptional unfairness and as André Picard points out, "The fact that a person with a $20,000 out-of-hospital drug cancer treatment will pay nothing out-of-pocket in Nunavut, $3000 in British Columbia and $20,000 in Prince Edward Island offends the principles of Medicare and Canadian values."[395]

These jurisdictional variations continue to wreak havoc on Canadian cancer patients. Some cancer drugs are funded in one province but not in others. Some provinces cover the cost of cancer drugs that are given intravenously but do not cover the oral version of the same drug. This means if one patient is prescribed one version, they may have no costs to incur, but another patient that is prescribed the second version will have to pay. As Sorin et al. point out, "Those scenarios outline the inequities that plague public cancer-drug coverage programs across Canada and support the need for a standardized national pharmacare program."[396]

Three million Canadians don't fill their prescriptions at all because of cost. Of these three million, thirty-eight percent have private insurance coverage and twenty-one percent have public coverage. However, it still isn't enough to cover their costs. About one in five Canadians continue to struggle to pay for their medications. Almost one million Canadians borrow money to pay for prescription drugs. Another one million cut back on food or home heating in order to pay for their medications. In 2018, Canadians spent $34 billion on prescription drugs, making drugs the second biggest expenditure of health care, surpassing what we pay our doctors.[397] Workers also exchanged drug coverage in lieu of increased wages when negotiating contracts with employers. This means they would lose their drug coverage if they retired or became unemployed—oftentimes when they need coverage most.

Covid-19 demonstrates the urgency for a national pharmacare plan. Over eight million Canadians applied for the federal government's emergency relief program (CERB) related to the pandemic. In a recent Angus Reid survey, forty-four percent of Canadian households say they lost work because of Covid-19. While we don't know how many have lost drug coverage because of those layoffs, it is safe to assume that this occurred. Dr. Eric Hoskins delivered a federal government-commissioned report calling on Ottawa to implement a national pharmacare program. Dr. Hoskins agrees that the coronavirus has demonstrated the need for a national pharmacare strategy, saying, "It really has underlined, or exposed even more, the vulnerability of Canadians and the challenges that they face to access prescribed medicines… there's an opportunity to respond now in a way which will protect access for these individuals and their families and also move us one step closer towards pharmacare."[398]

The Nova Scotia Senior's Pharmacare Program, with its penalties for not joining, makes it all but impossible for seniors over sixty-five to opt out. The annual premiums remain costly for many, but those premiums do not ensure all necessary medications are covered. The newest groups of anti-coagulants designed to treat non-valvular atrial fibrillation and other clotting disorders are a prime example of the program's inefficiency to cover medically necessary medications. Direct-acting oral anticoagulants (DOACs) have all but replaced Warfarin in the treatment of non-valvular atrial fibrillation. These drugs were approved by Health Canada after extensive research. They remain the first line of treatment in the prevention of atrial fibrillation-related strokes. In comparison to their predecessor, Warfarin, they have a much broader therapeutic window, a more controlled response, and limited drug interactions, and they eliminate ongoing bloodwork evaluation and dose monitoring. These drugs do not require patients to have bi-monthly bloodwork done like Warfarin. As a result, lab expenses related to requisitioning, collection, equipment use, and labour are eradicated. Physician oversight is greatly reduced, freeing up physician time and resources. Yet, in most provinces this group of anticoagulants are not covered under provincial plans.

Warfarin, with its excessive limitations, continues to be covered because it's cheaper. In Nova Scotia, a month's supply of the new DOACs runs approximately $122 a month. This cost remains out of reach for most seniors on a fixed income. The Heart and Stroke Foundation estimates about 200,000 Canadians have atrial fibrillation.[399] That number should continue to rise as the population ages. Even if half of these patients require anticoagulation therapy and cannot afford the newer DOACs, it means every day across the country, thousands of Canadians are inundating laboratories with lab work that may be unnecessary and costing the system millions of dollars. It also means patients may not be getting the best available treatment because it remains cost prohibitive. This leads us to ask, what is the purpose of research and innovation investment if the results cannot be delivered to the people who will benefit from the new therapies the most? As a result, Canadians are forced to continue to buy cheaper medication or less effective medication or go without treatment at all. A national pharmacare program would remedy this situation and save valuable health care dollars in the long run.

The debate surrounding how much a national pharmacare

plan would save is ongoing. A report released in 2017 by the parliamentary budget officer maintained a universal pharmacare system could save $4.2 billion a year, by conservative estimates.[400] Other estimates cite savings closer to $11 billion a year.[401] Bulk-buying medications and significantly reducing administration costs could lead to substantial savings. The health care system could also save by being able to treat patients comprehensively and preventatively based on clinical need, rather than affordability. A recent research study found that by removing drug-cost barriers for just three health problems—diabetes, cardiovascular disease, and chronic respiratory diseases, would reduce emergency room visits by 220,000 a year and result in 90,000 less hospital stays per year. Just covering drug costs for three diseases has the potential to save $1.2 billion per annum.[402]

Since 2018, numerous standing committees have also endorsed the implementation of a universal public pharmacare system. In June of 2019, the Advisory Council on the Implementation of National Pharmacare released its final draft, stating that Canada should adopt a universal public pharmacare system with definite timelines for covering essential medications for major conditions and developing a comprehensive medication formulary.[403] In November 2019, by signing a joint document entitled the Pharmacare Now Statement, over 175 national and provincial organizations called on the federal government to implement a universal public pharmacare system. In February 2020, a private members Bill C-213 presented by MP Peter Julian, also called upon the federal government to implement a public universal pharmacare system.[404] Nurses, physicians, pharmacists, and activist groups throughout Canada continue to lobby for a universal public pharmacare program. The desire for a public pharmacare system free of insurance sector involvement continues to grow.

5. Long-term care must be brought under the Canada Health Act (CHA) and national standards implemented for the sector.

Decades ago, Tommy Douglas saw where it would be necessary to bring long-term care within the scope of Medicare. As a New Democrat federal MP in 1976, he told Parliament, "A lot could be done in this country by the establishment of more nursing homes and the provision of homecare."[405] Douglas advocated for bringing long-term care in from the periphery of Medicare. That idea never gained any real traction during his lifetime.

While federal governments were involved in directing, shaping, and legislating the direction of care delivered in hospitals, the same cannot be said for their involvement with long-term care. Amy Twomey from Trent University breaks down the reluctance of the central government to address long-term care issues into three distinct historical perspectives:

<u>1945–1970:</u> Twomey described this period as the "long term care aversion" period. Problems in residential care were ignored as the emphasis remained on the hospital system and the medicine model. As Twomey explains, "Between 1945 and 1970, addressing problems in long-term care ranked low on the list of government priorities. As in Britain, geriatric issues were overshadowed by the ambitions of political actors committed to a national health system centered on hospital and curative measures." Parliamentary debates throughout the 1950s and '60s, including the 1966 Senate Committee on aging, saw a number of parliamentarians attempting to promote long-term care policy into political discussions, but as Twomey points out, there was an "unwillingness of the federal government to broaden the health care system beyond the walls of hospitals

and physician's offices." During this period several opposition MPs were critical of the federal government's lack of enthusiasm regarding these discussions. CCF MP Stanley Knowles pointed out the federal government was "not taking the necessary steps" to understand how seniors were doing on a national scale. Even the 1966 final report of the Senate Committee on Aging noted they were "reminded on all sides of the gaps and weaknesses in current facilities for meeting the health needs of older people" and of "the extreme shortage there is in Canada of facilities designated and equipped to meet the needs of long-term care patients." The committee also noted the lack of federal policy surrounding long-term care and made special mention of the emergence of for-profit homes stating, "... a profit-making ethos had come to dominate a field ignored by Ottawa." Twomey asserts during this period, "while Ottawa cost-shared hospital and physician care and ensured... strong public sector involvement, when it came to long term care, 'lethargy' characterized the federal government approach."[406]

1970–1980s: Twomey describes this period as the "long-term care ad hoc-ism" period. The demand for federal support for long-term care started to increase. Socio-economic changes like the rapid rise of working women, hospital costs, staff remuneration, and the deinstitutionalization of mental hospitals, highlighted the need to pay more attention to the long-term care sector. The 1974 Lalonde Report was crucial in outlining the shift from institutionalized medicine to a more preventative model. It served as an impetus to legitimize federal government spending on care other than hospital care.

The Extended Health Care Services Program (ECHS) was a small block of federal funding designated to support less-expensive care outside the hospital setting. Opposition MPs continued to press the federal government throughout the 1970s to help the provinces cost-share nursing home care. New Democrat David Orlikow argued that the federal government showed a "marked lack of will" when it came to treating the nursing-home sector with any sense of national priority. While the EHCS funding assisted with the development of more nursing homes, it didn't shift the reconsideration of funding long-term care like hospitals were funded. The funding program was short lived, and as former national health and welfare minister Monique Bégin pointed out, the program was never a comprehensive plan intended to address the long-term care situation. "Each province is at a different stage in the development of extended care service, and for that reason we could not impose upon all the provinces the minimum standards that were applicable under the hospital insurance and medical care programs." Clearly, long-term care was not a federal priority.[407]

1980s and beyond: Twomey describes this era as the "absent mandate" period. She claims, "After the 1970s a great silence loomed over residential care in Ottawa." This era included the exclusion of long-term care from the 1984 CHA and included the "marginalization in cost-sharing arrangements." Long-term care was not defined within the CHA and the five tenets of the act did not apply to the long-term care sector. The political will to expand Medicare to long-term care simply was not there. In 1984, the CMA was highly critical of the expansion of for-profit long-term care homes and commissioned a task force. It maintained "permitting nursing homes to be run for-profit under a lenient system of legislation and an impotent system of inspection is a measure of social negligence we can no longer allow to continue." The concerns of the country's doctors didn't seem to matter. By 1983, the federal Conservative government changed federal funding for health care and this trend continued under the Chrétien Liberals during the 1990s. The 2002 *Romanow Report* contained no suggestions on how to address the issues in long-term care. Twomey concludes that "the federal government's approach to facility-based long-term care in the 2000s, like in the 1960s, is characterized by an absent mandate."[408]

There are innumerable examples of government's complete indifference towards the long-term care sector. In 2005, the Alberta auditor-general released a report on the state of continuing care within his home province. Fred Dunn's findings established what staff and advocates had asserted for years. Alberta's long-term care facilities were not complying with standards with "one third of the audited facilities failing to meet basic care requirements." Staff at one facility were told to wash and dress residents who were awake by three am. Fifteen years later, Alberta Health Services has not revisited the deficiencies identified by Dunn in 2005.[409] Like Alberta, provinces across the country continued to turn a blind eye towards the needs of seniors.

Long-term care in Canada is currently offered via an assortment of private, public, and religious care facilities. With the exception of First Nations, Inuit communities, and long-term care for veterans, federal funding for all other long-term care models exists only as block funding within the CHST scheme. There has been an ongoing push to expand care of older Canadians within the community and away from institutional long-term care. This trend is increasing as provincial governments struggle with decreased federal transfer schemes and the cost of maintaining aging long-term care infrastructure.

Community care models also have downsides. Many of the home care models across Canada are not covered under

Medicare. Others have limited funding schemes based on income. This leaves many seniors and their families forced to pay out of pocket. The incessant push to deliver care at home and having that care remain outside the current Medicare system has led some experts to ask, have we pushed seniors into a privatization model? Seniors who can afford to pay may receive better-quality service at home. Those who cannot are left with minimal or no service at all. This creates another tiering of care within the sector. With a partiality towards community care, older Canadians are now entering long-term care later. With the push to keep older Canadians at home longer, those entering long-term care are doing so with greater needs and higher acuity. This cohort of residents with chronic, multi-system illnesses have health needs that are complex, placing additional pressure on staff workloads and educational requirements. Working to maintain the health and independence of older persons in community settings and keeping them out of institutionalized care is a noble and appropriate aspiration. It cannot be achieved without adequate funding models and necessary infrastructure. Home care must include a robust plan for the future and abandon the current patchwork of expensive, episodic care.

There are vast regional variations in long-term care throughout the country. Some provinces have more for-profit facilities than others. Others have more publicly funded homes, or a combination of both. Structures for long-term care are equally varied. Some facilities are high-rise towers like Northwood in Halifax or those in Ontario and Quebec. Others are smaller, one-level facilities. Any reference to long-term care in Canada is complicated by the myriad of structures and varied provincial histories of the facilities. This leads to confusing language when referring to the sector. As Dr. Albert Banerjee points out, "Speaking about long-term care in the Canadian context is further complicated by the lack of a common language ... thus across jurisdictions similarly named facilities do not necessarily provide similar services. The 2007 CIHI report examines, 'residential facility-based care,' by which they mean 'nursing homes.' Yet in Nova Scotia, 'residential care facilities' are not nursing homes at all. They are... more akin to the type of care provided in what Nova Scotians call 'community-based options' or what people in other provinces... might term 'supportive housing.' Such differences in terminology can lead to confusion."[410] Quoting the Federal/Provincial/Territorial Working Group On Home Care, Banerjee adds, "Review of available information revealed that there is hardly a statistic or description that would not be misleading or inaccurate without lengthy or complicated elaboration of its nuances, special circumstances or unique meaning in a provincial or territorial context."[411]

Discussions of the perils of long-term care in Canada would be incomplete without highlighting the situation in Canada's northern communities—where circumstances remain dire. For years, the government of Nunavut has been forced to transfer elders requiring long-term care to a home in Ottawa. Embassy West Senior Living is a transformed hotel that cares for dementia patients. Nunavut is compelled to transfer its residents because there aren't enough long-term care beds in their communities. There are no existing resources for special units for elders requiring dementia care. Approximately forty Nunavut elders currently reside in the Ottawa facility and many of them are unilingual, speaking only their Inuit languages. Natan Obed, president of the national Inuit organization Inuit Tapiriit Kanatami, says sending Nunavut seniors thousands of miles away from their families and communities continues to be "a huge failing."

Opening new long-term care spaces and maintaining existing beds remains problematic. Covid-19 has not helped. Today, Nunavut has one-third fewer operational beds for long-term care than it did six years ago. Political inertia, cost, and lack of available trained staff contribute to building long-term care facilities within the northern communities. Until a federal plan is designed to help elders remain within their own jurisdictions, this type of expulsion will only continue. While moving elders from their Indigenous communities is devastating, it is equally traumatic for their families. Many Inuit families cannot incur the costs of regularly flying to Ottawa to see their elders. Aluki Kotierk, president of Nunavut Tunngavik Inc., says this means that "because so many Inuit live under the poverty line... many of them will not see their elders again alive."[412] Until national standards for long-term care are established for all Canadian communities, northern families will be forced to try and manage their elders at home in crowded, under-resourced surroundings or send them away—in most cases forever.

Long-term care's stand-alone status, outside the CHA, has left it in a serious state of neglect. Superimposed upon these chronic incongruences, years of underfunding, understaffing, and privatization, and a clear lack of standards leaves older persons in a position of enhanced vulnerability. The Covid-19 crisis has more than highlighted the gaps within the sector. From coast to coast, the stories surrounding the deficits within long-term care are tragically similar.

By May of 2020, CIHI stats reinforced that Canada's inability to protect its seniors during Covid-19 was indeed real. Canada had the highest proportion of deaths occurring in long-term care, where residents in the sector accounted for eighty-one percent of all Covid-related cases.[413] In my home province of

Nova Scotia, the long-term care facility of Northwood was the province's epicentre. As Dr. Andrew Boozary, executive director of health and social policy for Toronto's University Health Network, summarized, "If we were going to be judged by how we protected our most susceptible and people who are structurally vulnerable—we failed them."[414]

Much of what occurred in long-term care during the Covid-19 outbreak didn't need to happen. As the virus raged through nursing homes everywhere, health authorities, the military, and even the police were forced to step in. In areas where health authorities and the military intervened, the findings were similar. There was shock and dismay surrounding the deplorable state of these facilities, the workload expectations of staff, the lack of education and PPE supplies, and, in some cases, the complete absence of standards. The patchwork known as long-term care in Canada must be united under the Canada Health Act if we are serious about protecting older persons and preventing another long-term care crisis.

The federal government must legislate national long-term care standards using the tenets of comprehensiveness, public not-for-profit, accessibility, universality, and portability. In their 2020 report *The Pandemic Experience in the Long-Term Care Sector*, CIHI also point out, "OECD countries have different models of funding and regulation for LTC… countries with centralized regulation and organization of LTC (e.g., Australia, Austria, Hungary, Slovenia) generally had lower numbers of Covid-19 cases and deaths."[415] Medicare must be expanded to include the long-term care sector as Tommy Douglas envisioned. High-rise, aged infrastructure must be replaced with expansive uni-level or bi-level structures. Private rooms with private bathrooms must be a priority except where two-person families wish to reside in a double room. Infection-control nurses must be hired to manage all facility outbreaks. Collaborative connections to health authorities and public-health services must be enhanced. Policy must be data-driven. Standards around regular deep cleaning of rooms and beds must also be developed. Facilities should reflect a neighbourhood setting with access to communities designed to combat social isolation. Crowded high-rise structures must be closed as they age. Otherwise, we run the risk of repeating "… one of the most damning failures that's taken place through the pandemic.[416]

6. Establish a federal council designed to deal with wasteful spending with the objective of redirecting reclaimed dollars towards Medicare and to other departments that underpin social determinants of health.

The federal government must set up a council dedicated to financial accountability regarding expenditures (FARE council) that would come under the auspices of the federal auditor general's office. It should seek ways to prevent the waste of millions of tax dollars and divert the savings towards the advancement of health care objectives. The council must include representatives from the Canadian Health Coalition, the Auditor General's Office, front-line clinicians, and anti-poverty advocates. The council would set the example and the blueprint for similar provincial and territorial FARE councils that would regularly collaborate with the federal government. The council must be available to front-line government employees and health care workers, who would be able to anonymously contact members (with full whistle-blower protection) about concerns of wasteful spending within their respective departments. There must be an available forum for health care and other government staff to make presentations to the council based on real alternatives on how to save health care or other government department dollars.

This forum could be set up like the Nova Scotia Standing Committee on Law Amendments, which allows the committee to hear representations from any interested party or organization during the second reading of bills. In cases where wasteful spending has already occurred, the council would be responsible for mitigating similar occurrences in the future, with full powers given to the Auditor General's Office to carry out corrective, fiscal action. The FARE council cannot be another bureaucratic mechanism for rewarding retired politicians or lobbyists. The council must be added to the duties of existing working members and must create actionable goals with real timelines. The council's work must consist of a transparent annual report available to taxpayers. This could create an opportunity to incorporate the Canadian Medical Association's program of "Health in All Policies" (HiAP) into the Council's mandate. The program should be defined by "an approach that systematically considers the health and social implications of policies contemplated by all sectors of government—aiming for synergistic benefits and to minimize social and health-related harms."[417] A FARE council can help save tax dollars, redirect money back into Medicare, and influence spending for other departments that support the social determinants of health.

The ongoing feud between Ottawa and the provinces and territories must end. The federal government must take the lead and set the trajectory for change. It must divert the narrative from "no money for public health care" to "here is how we are rearranging our fiscal management to revitalize health care." Ending the inordinate, wasteful spending at the federal level and working with the provinces collaboratively must become a priority for Ottawa.

The provinces and territories cannot expect Ottawa to advance the preceding agenda and indiscriminately hand over funds. If the federal government demonstrates it is serious about reinvesting in Medicare, the provinces and territories must prove they are committed to meeting fiscal and health-policy objectives within definable timelines. Otherwise, nothing will change.

Provincial Government Action

1. Establish provincial/territorial health care councils to deal with financial accountability regarding expenditures (FARE) associated with health care.

FARE councils should be established to interface with the aforementioned federal counterpart. The councils should operate under the auspices of the provincial and territorial offices of the auditor general. They should include at least one member from provincial/territorial health coalitions, front-line clinicians, and anti-poverty advocates. Their mandate should align with that of the federal council and the council's mandate should be used to help reassure Ottawa that there is enhanced fiscal oversight of federal transfer money for health and new stewardship over the misappropriation of tax dollars. Councils should also include a means of incorporating the Health in All Policies Program. Local councils must report to their federal counterpart at least once every fiscal year and have the same ability to hear from front-line clinical staff and government employees about cost-saving strategies without fear of reprisal.

In the fall of 2020, the Alberta government gave the National Hockey League Enterprises Canada $4 million to flash a thirty-second clip of Jason Kenney promoting the province. The deal also included a second clip of Alberta wheat fields flashing on a screen during an NHL game. The sole-source contract used a loophole in the Procurement and Sole Sourcing Policy that had been used only once since the policy came into place.[418] The same summer, the Kenney government dropped the province's corporate tax rate to eight percent, a move critics say will result in a $2.36 billion loss over four years.[419] The NHL pay-out and the lowest drop in corporate tax rates in the country occurred as Albertans were battling the Covid-19 crisis.

The following year, exhausted front-line staff, desperately trying to hold the health care system in Alberta together, saw Covid-related hospitals admissions soar to close to 1000 per day. This prompted Alberta's transportation minister to ask the federal government for help in transferring sick patients out of Alberta because of capacity overload and request support for more nurses, critical-care staff, and respiratory therapists.[420] Alberta was not alone in the continued misuse of tax dollars during one of the worse health care crises in our history. The provinces cannot continue to squander tax dollars and expect Ottawa to keep handing over money in the form of health care transfers. FARE councils would be a first step in holding both levels of government accountable and restoring trust between Ottawa, the provinces, and the territories.

2. Provinces need to tackle long wait times for specialists by switching to pooled referral systems and virtual consults.

Thirty-year-old Greg Price of Alberta died of cancer. His referrals kept falling through the cracks. In 2011, Greg visited his family doctor for a routine physical, and a lump was found in one of his testicles. The attending physician decided it wasn't an issue. Eleven months later, Mr. Price returned because the lump was still there. A referral was sent to a surgeon, but it would take three more months before he was contacted about an appointment. When he started to suffer from lower back pain, fifty-one weeks after his first doctor's visit, Mr. Price decided to go to a walk-in clinic. An ultrasound and X-rays determined that he had a large abdominal mass. Afterwards, he was put on the list for an urgent CAT scan. The CAT scan (done at week fifty-six) determined that he might have stage-three testicular cancer with metastases to his lymph nodes. A week later, Greg called the walk-in clinic only to be told the attending doctor he saw was no longer there. He was given an appointment for later in the day. Another ultrasound confirmed that the results were consistent with testicular cancer. The clinic staff faxed the report to the consulting urologist. What the clinic staff did not know was that the urologist was away. After a week of waiting, Greg decided to call the urologist's office himself. A recorded voice message explained the consultant's absence. After it was determined that the urologist was unable to see him, Greg was referred to two other urologists, hoping he could see the specialist that would take him first. His symptoms continued to worsen and his legs started to swell. Fifty-nine weeks after seeing his family doctor, he finally underwent an orchidectomy (removal of a testicle). His swelling progressed. Greg Price died less than seventy-two hours after his surgery. His father explained that Greg was someone who was fit, capable of communicating, and very much in tune with his own health. None of that seemed to matter. Greg Price was caught in the non-system of medical referrals.[421]

For decades, referrals have been a mainstay in our health care system. Despite changes in technology and communication, much about how referrals are written and sent has not changed. The referral system remains fraught with chaotic miscommunication, politics, and disorder. This disorganization causes Canadians to die prematurely, become sicker, and endure a poorer quality of life. Often there is no consistency in the process. Protracted wait times to see a specialist continue to adversely affect patients and cost the system more money. In a 2011 Canadian Medical Association Survey, both family physicians and specialists said they were frustrated by insufficient information on referrals. Family physicians said there were difficulties finding specialists, not getting acknowledgement of referrals, and appointment-time issues. Some specialists also had idiosyncratic systems of referrals, such as only accepting referrals one day per month.[422] Family doctors often refer to specialists that they know the best or have a closer relationship with. While this may be beneficial at times, there is no way to ensure that this specialist doesn't have the longest waitlist in the area. Someone across town, not consulted, may have a much shorter wait time. In other jurisdictions, referrals continued to be faxed, paving the way for them to be lost or misplaced. Specialists assert that they are trying to triage patients with information that may not be accurate or clearly articulated or that could be missing altogether. The provinces and territories must move to electronic medical records with e-referrals, virtual referrals, and central referral intake systems.

A program called Alberta Netcare eReferral has added e-referrals to their electronic health records, making their referral system paperless. The system lets family doctors see what specialists have the longest waiting list and it also lets the doctor know when the referral has been received and allows for tracking of the referral.[423]

Sometimes conferring with a specialist for some general guidance may be all that a family doctor needs. The Rapid Access to Consultative Expertise (RACE) in British Columbia allows family doctors to call a central number throughout the week during business hours and a specialist will call them back. Fee codes allow both parties to be remunerated for their work. An analysis of the system found eighty percent of calls were returned within ten minutes. Both specialists and family doctors reported satisfaction with the system. It led to a fifty-percent reduction in referrals for face-to-face consults and a twenty-four-percent reduction in ER visits. Since the implementation of RACE, Calgary has started a similar program called Specialist Link and Ontario has launched the Champlain BASE e-Consult service. With BASE, family doctors send a referral form with test results to the specialist, who answers via a secure message system. An analysis of BASE use from 2010–2015 demonstrated there was an average wait time of two days to hear from specialists.[424]

Central intake referral systems (or pooled referrals) give family doctors the choice whether to consult a certain specialist or take the next one available. Often wait times are published, leaving patients and referring doctors a choice of who to see. In Newfoundland and Labrador, a central intake system for endoscopy successfully reduced wait times. Ontario has moved to centralized intake for joint replacements. Quebec, Saskatchewan, and Calgary have also launched pooled referral systems. Cardiologist Chris Simpson agrees central intake makes sense saying, "… it's like choosing your own line at the grocery store versus the single line at the bank." Anthony Graham, head of a central intake system for cardiology at St. Michael's Hospital, also agrees the new systems make sense, saying, "For those who practice in some sort of group environment, there's absolutely no question that central referral is the answer."[425]

While ongoing barriers may present a challenge and some practitioners may be reluctant to change, the provinces need to draw upon recent experiences with virtual consults and centralized referral systems. The systems should be designed to maintain consistently across the country and allow for some differences in specialty services and various geographic locations. One thing is certain, the current referral system must be overhauled and transformed to reduce wait times and get patients to the services they need as quickly as possible. We have the technology to accomplish this.

A 2017 CIHI report stated wait times for specialists in Canada were the highest among all eleven countries surveyed.[426]

3. Integrated community care models with an emphasis on prevention must become a priority.

Patient care in Canada is delivered primarily from a provider focus. The Canadian Medicare system has not kept pace with many socioeconomic changes. As a result, it has left patients to navigate a disjointed system that lacks both vertical and horizontal integration. Provincial systems are expensive, complex, incongruent, multi-layered, and non-communicative. They present patients with significant access barriers. Medical information is not readily shared among providers. The same questions are asked repeatedly by providers. Antiquated referral systems make wait times unsafe. Care remains episodic rather than continuous. Providers remain focused on crisis intervention rather than disease prevention. Covid-19 exacerbated all these issues. Provincial health care systems need to transition to highly integrated patient and family-care models, rather than remaining committed to provider-focused models.

Integrated health care involves systems that are coordinated, collaborative, and seamless when providing care for patients and families. The overarching goal of the integrated system is to provide patients with a series of optimal service providers who help transition patients and families along the health care continuum. It offers patients a continuous support service over time and is contraposed to an intermittent, crisis-intervention approach. Community clinics remain the best option for providing patients with an integrative care approach.

Key to this notion is early prevention of illness and the institution of health-promotion strategies. Practitioners agree that one of the best ways to improve health outcomes and save money is to prevent an illness before it happens. When prevention cannot be fully achieved, the earliest possible intervention serves to mitigate adverse outcomes and delay disease progression. This also has the potential to save valuable health care dollars in the long run. Community clinics should house a host of health care practitioners who are accessible and knowledgeable in assisting patients affected by social determinants of health.

Clinic access must be as central as possible. If patients cannot get to the care, care must go to them in the form of outreach. Anything that promotes health and abbreviates illness must be made available to patients. Treatments must be culturally relevant. Mental-health services must be included with community mental-health outreach available at all school levels and workplaces. Access must be designed around eliminating system barriers and advocacy must be assigned to older persons and those who lack support at home.

A truly integrated model is driven by patient-centred care, treatment, and oversight. Patients and families are involved in their own health care plans. These plans should begin at the pre-natal level and continue to end of life.

Management of integrated care should be consistent, harmonious, and transcend geographical, infrastructural, and informational barriers. Secure electronic health records should ensure practitioners have up-to-date patient information including all diagnostic data that can be readily shared. This includes allowing patients to view their own health records. Patient data must be regularly updated and should include cultural preferences, patient opinions, and automatic reminders pertaining to medication administration, appointments, and care changes. Management must include consistent health promotion information. Many of these programs can be offered virtually, and if that is not possible, health promotion must be made accessible to communities. Smoking cessation, cardiac rehab, recreation, and dietary plans are all examples of community programs that providers could recommend to patients.

Within an integrated model of community care, patients rely on the inter-professional team to help direct and guide their care. This means providers must build and cultivate long-standing relationships with community-resource programs and the people who run them. Funding remains crucial to the success of integrative care. Access to care cannot be precluded by funding. Informal caregivers must also be included in this model of care.

Across the country various groups have already demonstrated that integrative community clinics work. The Halifax North End clinic is an example of a community clinic servicing its community with quality primary care. With its dental clinic, mobile outreach street health, housing help, community programs, and mobile health clinic, the North End Community Health Centre is proof that community care works. Funding needs to be expanded for similar initiatives.

Provincial ministries of health need not reinvent the wheel. There are scores of integrated models of care already designed and some are in use. In 2012, the Canadian Nurses Association, in collaboration with the Canadian Medical Association, formed a steering committee to initiate a summit process that would establish guidelines to assist with the transformation of Canada's health care system towards a fully integrated model. The group outlined five foundational platforms that would fully support an integrated model of care. They also acknowledged that success in building a truly integrated model of care means addressing all the factors that affect and maintain health along a continuum. To achieve this goal, there must be a pan-Canadian effort to transition Medicare from its outdated, episodic-care trappings, into a fully integrated model of care. Imagine how Medicare would look today if policy makers had started implementing the changes as outlined in the 2013 document "Integration: A New Direction for Canadian Health Care."[427]

McMaster's Tapestry is another example. This program uses primary care to move patients away from a disease-focus model towards a more person-focused model. Tapestry accomplishes this by bringing together trained volunteers, technology, and inter-professional care teams that meet people in their own communities. A navigation system also helps people to access the system and helps patients to learn about their health and available community resources.[428]

Chronic disease rates are on the rise. Chronic diseases are

often linked to social determinants of health or those factors that place populations at risk for certain health conditions. Currently, Canadian provinces and territories do not have fully integrated health care systems. Their systems remain grounded in reactive, episodic care that seeks to extinguish whatever crisis may bring a patient to a doctor's office. Once the crisis is averted, the patient returns to their environment until the next episode occurs. Care among multiple providers remains siloed and uncoordinated. Current primary models of care are anything but patient-centred.

4. Provinces need to stop subsidizing physicians' liability costs and redirect the savings back into Medicare.

The Canadian Medical Protective Association (CMPA) supplies doctors with insurance coverage and a right to legal representation in malpractice lawsuits. The association has a war chest totalling approximately $5 billion.[429] Their resources are immense. Provincial governments currently reimburse doctors for a portion of those CMPA fees. In some jurisdictions, the rates of reimbursement are as high as *ninety percent*.[430] The process of physicians paying medical malpractice insurance and having those fees rebated via tax dollars is uniquely Canadian. This sets up an illogical scenario whereby taxpayers harmed via medical malpractice are actually funding the legal costs of those who may be responsible for their harm or, possibly, death. Medical malpractice lawyers representing plaintiffs have been quick to point out how this system continues to fail patients and families who suffered harm or death from medical negligence. Low to moderate-income patients often lack the resources to pursue litigation. In most cases they do not qualify for legal assistance. Litigators must impress upon prospective clients that the CMPA is flush with funds, and they are not shy to use those funds to drag proceedings out for as long as possible.

Paul Harte, who represents plaintiffs, told CTV that at one time his small firm, "... went up against twenty-seven lawyers in court, all paid for by the CMPA."[431] Should patients lose their case to the CMPA, the association may ask to have its legal fees covered. Its vast resources and its ability to aggressively recover legal fees remain disincentives to many patients and families seeking remuneration for damages. Kathleen Finlay, CEO of the Center for Patient Protection, described the association as a "Frankenstein-like creation." Finlay points out that a former CMPA insider remarked, "The CMPA would spend $100,000 protecting a doctor against a $5000 claim."[432] This is probably an easy thing to do when your defence is liberally subsidized by taxpayers. The amount of subsidization varies from province to province. In 2014, Ontario taxpayers paid almost $200 million dollars to subsidize the legal defences of doctors charged with medical malpractice in that province. According to the Ontario Ministry of Health, the amount has leaped by 3200 percent over a twenty-eight-year period and shows no signs of slowing down. Between 2013–2015, the cost to Ontario taxpayers of subsidizing the CMPA jumped by a whopping twenty-eight percent. Ontario currently subsidizes eighty-one percent of CMPA fees.[433] These statistics demonstrate the inordinate number of tax dollars that go into funding the CMPA. This subsidization gives doctors an enormous economic advantage over patients and families. In one of CMPA's own annual reports, documents showed that of all the cases that went to court in 2019, ninety percent were found in favour of the doctor.[434]

Imagine if those millions of dollars could be redirected back into Medicare instead of going to law firms. Imagine if the money saved could be invested towards making the system safer for patients or reducing hospital infection rates. As the system currently stands, it re-victimizes patients and families harmed by medical negligence and uses their own taxpayer money to obstruct closure and financial compensation. As Kathleen Finlay points out, the stories of patients harmed by medical malpractice are "... among the most poignant you will ever read," and "many involve marriage breakup, financial ruin, and even suicide."[435] In terms of Medicare dollars, it's an enormous loss. It's time provincial governments took a second look at an association that was founded in 1901 long before antibiotics were invented or women could vote. Making the CMPA rich should not be the mandate of provincial and territorial governments. Protecting patients and families of patients injured by the system should. The funnelling of millions of dollars annually into the CMPA must stop. If we are serious about reforming Medicare, the provinces must end this antiquated subsidization scheme and channel those dollars back into direct patient care.

5. Provinces and territories must vigorously expand home care, utilizing modern technology. Current ineffective home care models must be abandoned or drastically reformed.

It goes without saying, that if given a choice most people would rather recuperate or be treated at home rather than be in hospital. That's not to say all conditions can be treated at home. Obviously critical care, trauma, surgery, and emergency patients require access to hospital care. There does exist, however, a wide range of patients who can be treated or recover successfully at home.

During the mid to late-1990s, the federal government was practising serous deficit reduction. In its quest to slay the deficit dragon, it rewrote its fiscal transfer arrangement with the provinces and territories. The reaction was immediate. Provincial jurisdictions restructured health care systems dramatically. There was negative growth in health care spending, closure of hospital beds, closure of entire hospitals, staff reductions, and the movement of previous hospital services into the community. This type of restructuring was placing "the cart before the horse." Community infrastructure was not in place to transition much of the previously institutionalized care outwards to the community.

True home care services have never caught up and much like their facility-based cohort, home care services remain episodic and non-integrated. In study after study experts have demonstrated a litany of advantages to receiving care at home as opposed to care in a facility. It must be emphasized that this remains true only when care at home is accessible, flexible, affordable, and robust. In many jurisdictions across the country, home care remains fragmented, unaffordable, under-resourced, and immensely privatized. Moving patients to a home care model that remains outside Medicare will not work. It places pressure on patients to pay out-of-pocket or go without care. This often results in patients frequenting the emergency department, which is costly and, in many cases, unnecessary. The privatization of home care has created another tiering of care, particularly for the elderly. Older persons on fixed incomes or with limited financial capacity who cannot afford services may be forced to enter facility-based care. This move is often premature, may not be to the older person's benefit, and may occur when something as basic as ongoing home support is required. The move to facility-based care when home care supports have not been fully explored, is also more costly.

The days of housing older persons in high-rise complexes with ailing infrastructure have long since passed. Covid-19 has clearly demonstrated that traditional, long-term structures have numerous negative effects on the seniors they house. They perpetuate, rather than alleviate, alienation and loneliness for elderly occupants. Seniors need to be removed from run-down, ailing high-rises and moved into true community settings. Older persons need home-like facilities that are located within communities with amenities. Even if the dwellings are located within a larger community of older persons, they need to be modelled after regular subdivisions with ground-level facilities, including gardens, yards, and parks. If buildings are required for care requirements, they must be incorporated into regular community settings. Other countries have engaged in this transition.

The *Levensloopbestendige,* which translates into English as *Apartments for Life* (A4L), was founded in 1995 in the Netherlands to provide cost-efficient housing and care solutions to meet the demands of the country's elderly. The program focuses on mixing age groups while providing seniors with a maximum level of autonomy. Buildings accommodate all neighbourhood residents by offering public venues like restaurants, activity spaces, and local shops on the first floor. A4L structures include people who are fifty-five and independent, seniors requiring assisted living, and people who need medical care. The approach is based on four key values: autonomy; the value of "move it or lose it"; a "yes" culture (in direct contrast to a nursing home "rule culture"); and a family-centred approach to caregiving. The structures include rentals or condo-style apartments and are built so that they can easily accommodate lift-equipment, oxygen, modifiable infrastructure, and assistive devices like wheelchairs. While there is no hard and fast data surrounding cost-effectiveness, anecdotal evidence suggests the cost of these care providers is anywhere from ten to twenty-five percent lower than traditional care. Humanitas, the Dutch NGO that founded the project, went from running a loss to achieving a surplus of EUR54 million, which has been reinvested into the program.[436] Whatever way Canada decides to restructure home care, there are many more current, progressive models available.

Home care models for older persons must allow citizens to remain as healthy and independent as possible within their own homes and respective communities. Funds must be available for older persons to modify their homes. Transitional bridges must be developed to support older persons transitioning from hospital to home. The Transitional Care Bridge Project in the Netherlands seeks to interface hospital care with primary care. After older patients leave the hospital, a home care nurse visits them several times as part of this transitional follow-up program. The project found that there were thirty-seven percent fewer deaths among the seniors that received this care compared to those that did not thirty days after being discharged from hospital. The project has since been implemented in half of the hospitals in the Netherlands.[437]

Home care models vary across Canada. Variations exist in funding models, service delivery programs, and the use of co-payments and other fees. Home care continues to remain an extended service and is not included under the list of insured services covered under the Canada Health Act. As such, there are no federal standards or operational goals. This needs to change. Home care in Canada needs to work towards an integrated model of care that is flexible enough to meet the changing needs of patients and families. Services must go to the patient rather than the other way around. This includes lab services, physiotherapy, medication-delivery services, home support, and health care services.

This can be accomplished by embracing technology that assists people to remain at home. Telemedicine and Telehealth technologies have expanded greatly over the years. Portable diagnostic devices allow virtual physical exams for a growing number of medical conditions. The increased use of smartphones allows clinicians to provide patient follow-up via telephone. Remote monitoring now includes oxygen-saturation levels, blood pressure, heart rates, weight, blood sugars, and a host of additional diagnostic and screening data that can be downloaded directly to a patient portal. Sending secure emails makes it possible to share patient information in a safe and timely matter while providing collaborative care.

Machine learning allows a computer to learn how to do things previously done by humans. In one of its subdomains, computer vision, engineers are training computers how to see. Machine learning modules can look at skin lesions and determine if they are malignant with a high degree of accuracy.[438] Telecare services use alarms and sensors to check on patients at home and automatically report if something appears wrong. They include portable alarms to wear around your neck, movement sensors in case you fall, gas shut-off devices, fire detectors, flood detectors for under sinks and bathtubs, fixed alarms such as cord alarms in bathrooms, and medication dispensers to release pills at the correct time with a reminder alarm if medications have not been released.[439] Telehealth technologies also include devices that remind you to check your blood pressure or glucose, and prompt you to attend doctor's appointments.

Home care models must become integrative and holistic and incorporate technology that can keep patients safe at home.

This could help Canadians remain at home longer and as independent as possible. Expanded roles for health care providers must be embraced, including nurse practitioners, physician assistants, pharmacists, dieticians, registered practical nurses, home-support workers, paramedics, and nurses—all working to maximum scopes of practise. Patients who are elderly must experience wrap-around services within community settings. Home care models must be incorporated into the CHA to make them accessible, public, not-for-profit, holistic, and transformative.

6. Provinces and territories must set up centres to track data related to health care human resources such as recruitment and retention.

Crucial bedside nursing positions are continually vacated for non-bedside nursing positions and nurses retiring or changing careers. The same holds true for other health professionals and unregulated workers like housekeeping staff and continuing-care assistants. Data on why staff leave, where they go, and impediments to recruitment and retention are sketchy at best. Workloads and remuneration are key issues voiced by unions representing various health care workers. Data obtained from detailed exit interviews must be compiled to help health ministries provide long-lasting solutions to problems of recruitment and retention. Each province needs to establish a health care recruitment and retention division dedicated to enticing workers to enter and remain in the health care field. Such a program can also develop an active recruitment arm designed to connect ministries of health to provincial and territorial schools, colleges, and universities where health care programs are offered. Recruitment programs must also be able to assist with relocation and financial support for prospective health care workers.

Solutions to staff shortages must be driven by sound data. Otherwise, incorrect problem identification will only confound solutions. Data must be compiled from jurisdictions across each province and territory to identify where staff shortages are more pronounced. Provincial recruitment and retention centres must collaboratively liaise with groups that represent front-line staff. Input from front-line staff is crucial to solving staff shortages. Centres must also liaise with organizations responsible for developing professional health care standards to share data pertaining to retirement, workload, and retention of health care workers. The newly-minted Progressive Conservative government in Nova Scotia has already implemented a provincial health care recruitment and retention department. Health care workers appear optimistic that this is a step in the right direction. Other provinces must follow Nova Scotia's lead.

Individual Citizen Action

1. Reject the narrative. Force a counter-narrative. Demand accountability.

In 2013–14, Canadian garbage containers were incorrectly labelled as plastics and shipped to the Philippines. In 2019, Bolloré Logistics were awarded the contract to retrieve the trash, which cost $1.14 million.[440] Canadian grocery giant Loblaws fought against raising the minimum wage, admitted to a fourteen-year bread price fixing scheme, and fought a tax battle with CRA, which eventually made them pay $368 million in "back taxes." Loblaws had net earnings of approximately $800 million in 2018.[441] In April of 2019, the Canadian government gave Loblaws $12 million to install energy-efficient fridges. These (and innumerable other examples) are examples of why taxpayers must not accept the argument that there isn't enough money to support public health care.

Canadians have become inured to this level of waste. Tax dollars are continuously squandered, leaving taxpayers numb to the gross mismanagement and repeated lack of accountability for wasteful spending. When it comes to funding the public health care system, funders seem more likely to believe that there are not enough tax dollars to support Medicare. Much of this flows from the neoliberal discourse espoused by politicians, lobbyists, and influencers. I'm not sure that Canadians understand the power they collectively possess as both funders and voters within the system. We can counter the affordability narrative by demanding change. We can also push back by insisting that Canadian health care is a priority. Covid-19 demonstrated the vitalness of public health care systems.

The Covid crisis illuminated one essential element that neoliberal policy makers have avoided acknowledging—without a healthy society, supported by a robust public health system, all other systems fail. Covid taught us that people, not capital, are our greatest resource. Covid-19 has reaffirmed that health is the universal egress from which everything emanates—education systems, economic systems, transportation systems, political systems, private enterprise, supply chains—all of it. For proponents of neoliberalism driving the sacrosanct economic engine, one certainty has emerged—healthy workers are the single most important ingredient in keeping that engine operational.

By January of 2022, the International Monetary Fund (IMF) came out with a number showing just how much a healthy workforce is worth to the global economy—about $14 trillion. In a CNN report, the IMF confirmed that it expects "the pandemic to have cost the world $13.8 trillion in lost economic output by 2024."[442] This proves yet again that our "global community" requires healthy people supported by vigorous health care systems if it is to survive at all.

Exasperated and beaten down with ongoing neoliberal greed and governmental fiscal waste, taxpayers are tired. The fatigue is palpable. We no longer have the time to feel powerless. In instances where people collectively joined forces to send government a message, policies have been changed. We need to send the government a message that reckless abandon in spending tax funds that precludes health care investment is not responsible government. A grass-roots diligence helped create Medicare. Our current situation commands the same diligence. Observe where your tax dollars are going. Insist that health care spending is a priority. Ask yourself who is benefitting from the messaging that public health care is not sustainable. Demand financial accountability in the name of Medicare.

2. Funders must practice health care activism.

In the spring of 2015, the Liberal government in New Brunswick attempted to put forth a new policy that would change how seniors were assessed for nursing-home care in the province. Under the new legislation, the savings and investments of seniors would no longer be exempt as prospective sources to fund care. A capped maximum payment of $113 dollars per day for nursing home care would also be raised to $175 per day.[443] From the spring through to the fall of 2015, seniors, advocates, and families came out in droves to oppose the new policy. Rallies and meetings sprung up across the province.

Adult children of seniors packed local Legions and halls to protest this budget-balancing blow against their elderly parents. Many attendees were using walkers and canes. Others were in wheelchairs. Advocates like New Brunswick's Cecile Cassista, executive director of the Coalition for Seniors and Nursing Home Residents' Rights, took to social media, television, and radio to express her unhappiness with the attack on the province's seniors. At the height of the demonstrations, seniors also fought back with an unparalleled tenacity. They wrote letters and gave testimony stating that they would sell their family homes and leave New Brunswick. The pressure imposed by older persons, their families, and advocacy groups was unrelenting. By September of 2015, it seemed that the provincial government of Brian Gallant had gotten the message. The government recanted its position and announced it would not advance contentious reforms to long-term care. Some pundits admit that the groups who took on the government were lucky that they had a premier who listened. Others pointed out that the spirit and diligence of the pro-senior groups demonstrated one undeniable fact—when people come together for a collective cause, governments are forced to listen.

The New Brunswick example demonstrated that power rests in collective action. As funders of Medicare, we must become comfortable at speaking out and becoming advocates for ourselves and our neighbours. As individuals, there is a list of ways we can become proactive. We can write letters to our local MLAs, newspapers, and health ministries voicing our concerns about policies that will affect us and the future of health care. We can utilize social media platforms and follow like-minded individuals. We can volunteer to sit on boards for local health authorities. Anytime we have an unpleasant experience at hospitals, these experiences should be relayed to managers or patient-advocate services. Every day there are individuals and organizations across Canada working to save Medicare. They need our help.

The Canadian Health Coalition (CHC) is a non-partisan organization dedicated to saving Canadian Medicare. Since 1979, the coalition has been dedicated to the maintenance of a universal public health care system and opposes its privatization.[444] The CHC has provincial affiliates across the country. The coalition is composed of academics, health care workers, unions, seniors, and various community organizations. If funders are serious about opposing the forces that are undermining Medicare, they can help by joining the CHC or one of its provincial affiliates. Individuals can help by taking the time to read the work done by the CHC, which includes research and information specific to the advancement of Medicare.

Bloodwatch.org is a non-profit organization committed to upholding the findings in the *Krever Inquiry*. The organization advocates for a safe, volunteer, public blood system in Canada. It is instrumental in exposing the pitfalls of the privatization of blood donation in Canada. It is also fastidious in following the worrisome development of private plasma clinics throughout the country. The organization is made up of safe-blood advocates, tainted-blood survivors, and regular citizens. Bloodwatch.org is committed to maintaining blood as a public resource and is against the commodification of plasma and the establishment of private plasma clinics. If funders are interested in preserving our current public blood transfusion system, they can email bloodwatch.org and sign up for newsletters.[445]

The Center for Patient Protection is an organization that was initially created to address avoidable medical errors within our health care system. These include the litany of patient safety breakdowns that claim lives and harm patients every day. The center has become one of the foremost voices for improving patient outcomes. It also has become a leading advocacy group for improved mental-health services, suicide-prevention practices, and reduces gender-related barriers to safe health care for women. Founder Kathleen Finlay has become one of Canada's most passionate voices for patient safety.[446] If funders are serious about advocating for patient safety policies or have a story to tell about being harmed by the health care system, they can follow or contact the Center for Patient Protection.

Canadian Doctors for Medicare is a physician-led organization. The organization is committed to advocating for a health care system based on need, not on the ability to pay. The organization formed around a central theme in 2006—a two-tiered health care system that allows the wealthy to purchase private insurance at the expense of most Canadians who cannot. The organization believes reform must continue within the public domain. Individuals interested in supporting Medicare can follow the work of Canadian Doctors for Medicare or donate to their cause.[447]

In *Requiem for the American Dream*, Noam Chomsky echoes the sentiments of his late friend, Howard Zinn: "What matters is the countless small deeds of unknown people, who lay the basis for the significant events that enter history."[448] Chomsky adds, "They're the ones who've done things in the past. They're the ones who'll have to do it in the future."[449] Canadians must understand the strength of their collective voices. Whether on an individual or group basis, adding your voice to support Medicare has never been more urgent.

3. Funders must practise health promotion and illness prevention in a broader sociological sense.

As shareholders in the Medicare system, each of us has a very important stake. We owe it to ourselves and the system to stay healthy and mitigate illness. Smoking cessation, watching our weight, monitoring our blood pressure, eating wisely, and exercising regularly are all ways that we can promote our own health. While these individual choices all have the potential to positively affect health outcomes, research demonstrates that focusing solely on individual choices is reductionistic. Restricting health promotion in this way oversimplifies the relationship between personal choices and the social circumstances that restrain lifestyle choices.

Authors Bolaria and Dickinson emphasize the relationship between individual lifestyle choices and the social-structural conditions that shape them. "The literature on lifestyles and life chances indicates that lifestyles are shaped by life chances. Social and material conditions both enable and constrain chosen lifestyles. A focus on lifestyles and self-imposed risks ignores the social basis of lifestyles and health and illness. The empirical reality is that socioeconomic inequalities produce social variability in health status."[450] Focusing solely on individual choices also places the full burden of health and illness upon the shoulders of individuals, separating them from the social conditions that influence health and illness. Isolating individual choices from the social conditions that shape them places an undue amount of shame and guilt on individuals. It arguably perpetuates, rather than alleviates, marginalization, stigmatization, and ill health. Individual lifestyle choices are moored to social contexts.

This is borne out by the evidence surrounding the social

determinants of health. We know that economically advantaged Canadians tend to live longer than their less privileged cohorts. Many Indigenous communities demonstrate how poverty vis-à-vis colonialism restricts healthy lifestyle choices. If we are serious about improving Medicare and saving tax dollars, we must recognize the interconnectedness between social determinants of health and individual lifestyle choices. Health promotion and illness prevention policies must also recognize the intricacies of this interconnectedness. We must learn to consider, "… the combined impact of life circumstances and life choices."[451]

These are foundational steps that individuals, federal, and provincial governments can take to help restore Medicare. Critics may insist that this type of restoration in unaffordable. I believe they are incorrect.

CONCLUSION

As Canadians, we tend to think of Medicare as a stand-alone social policy. We forget that Medicare was part of a larger platform of social-welfare systems that swept across post-war Canada. As countries sought to develop an array of social policies to offer protection against the vulgarities of the market, universal health care became a vital part of the evolution of the welfare state. Medicare founders like T. C. Douglas, were dedicated to the greater ideal of equality for all Canadians. This included improving labour standards for workers, aiding seniors and the unemployed, reducing social inequity, and helping families keep food on the table. Lack of accessibility to health care was one of many social problems they sought to overcome. Author Michael Bradley points out their dedication to equality: "These men... were fighters. They recognized Canadian problems and were personally affronted by the human suffering caused by them... they were dedicated to improving the world, correcting inequalities and injustices, and their instrument was democratic political action."[452]

This is a crucial feature of Medicare's evolution. Health care has drifted further away from the network of social policies crucial to its existence. It has become estranged from, and a competitor of, its social program partners. It is now relegated to being yet another greedy cost driver. Among all the inimical effects neoliberalism had on our universal health care system, this is the cruellest. Divorcing health care from other social amenities created a great chasm. This has fostered a competition among social programs that were once united in their pursuit of a comprehensive welfare state. This division is now entrenched and has created the only environment that young physicians, nurses, and health care workers know. As baby boomers age, stories of what life was like pre-Medicare and how it evolved alongside social provisions are fading. A new crop of health professionals now accepts the isolation of health care from the social welfare state.

In the past few years, friends of mine required surgery for some serious issues. In some cases, along with medications and treatments, they were given a list of directions of what to do to prepare at home the night before. This resulted in patients staying awake all night to follow pre-op directions for surgeries scheduled at six a.m. the next day. When one of my friends pointed out that this regime meant he would be awake the entire night before surgery, his young surgeon replied, "Yes, I know, but it is not 1980 anymore." The young doctor was correct. It would be unheard of to expect this of a patient on the night prior to surgery during the late 1970s or '80s. In light of all the squandered tax dollars, we remain convinced that supporting patients pre-operatively is something we can no longer afford. This is the only system that a new generation of health professionals have ever worked under: one where they've been educated to cut costs and place as much responsibility as possible onto the patient, and where a patient's fears and anxieties surrounding an impending surgery are no longer relevant.

Despite all its might and wealth, neoliberalism seems to have met its match when it comes to dismantling Canada's health care system. While it continues its persistent assault on public health care, there is hope that the people of Canada will do what they always have done in the face of adversity—unite. Defunding, defrauding, deregulation, and deliberate disintegration have already taken a stranglehold. Unless Canadians harness their collective strength, Medicare will slip from our grasp. We must look to the past to conjure that strength. We must ask why the values that Medicare embodies withstood the test of time and continue to remain relevant to Canadians. The answers are entrenched in our evolutionary history.

The US aside, all Western countries have a system of universal health care. It seems that in nations around the world, caring for the sick and disabled is more the rule than the exception. This positions the US system as a distinct outlier when it comes to providing health care services. But the commodification of health care is more dire than simply being an outlier. Human evolution demonstrates that it is an unnatural phenomenon.

Caring for the sick is as old as humanity itself. Archaeologists studying ancient remains concluded that the "archaeology of health care" does indicate that pre-historic people took care of their sick and disabled. One of the cases that led to this conclusion was the discovery of the 4000-year-old remains of a profoundly ill young man. While other skeletal remains were found lying straight, the remains of Burial 9 (as they were known) were curled up in a fetal position. The archaeologists found that the body of Burial 9 was lying in the grave much the same it lay while he was alive. Examination revealed that he had weak bones and fused vertebrae. The evidence also suggested he had been paralyzed from the waist down at an early age as the result of a disease called Klippel-Feil syndrome. The archeological team concluded that he probably lived ten years after his disease started but had little use of his arms and couldn't have fed or washed himself.

The archaeologists described Burial 9's disability in a 2009 *Anthropological Science* article. They reaffirmed that "… not only does his care indicate tolerance and cooperation in his culture but suggests that he himself had a sense of his own worth and a strong will to live. Without that… he could not have stayed alive." The case of Burial 9 is not unique. Archaeologists were aware of "about 30 cases in which the disease or pathology was so severe, they must have had care in order to survive." These cases include that of 45,000-year-old Shanidar 1 found in Iraq. He died at approximately fifty years old, had one arm, loss of vision in one eye, and other injuries. The approximately 7,500-year-old remains of a boy found in Florida had what archaeologists believed to be spinal bifida. He lived to be approximately fifteen years old. D. N. Dickel and G. H. Doran, from Florida State University, concluded, "Under some conditions life 7,500 years ago included an ability and willingness to help and sustain the chronically ill and handicapped."[453]

Dr. Martin, associate professor of biological anthropology at the University of Nevada, gives a similar example from her work. A young woman's 4,000-year-old skeletal remains indicate that she suffered from a degenerative neuromuscular disease that was likely polio. Dr. Martin asserts, "Her condition likely made it difficult for her to walk… she had exceedingly thin arm and leg bones with very little buildup of normal muscle attachments… she probably received round-the clock care." Dr. Martin also observed that she had extensive periodontal disease unrelated to her condition, with teeth that had many cavities. She was also, "missing teeth from abscesses and periodontal disease." Her culture cultivated dates. Dr. Martin suggested the people caring for her may have been overly kind, giving her lots of "sticky yummy dates."[454]

CONCLUSION

Archaeological evidence abounds with examples of how prehistoric groups catered to their sick and disabled. Even a human from the species *Homo heidelbergensis* dating back 500,000 years appears to have been cared for by his hunter-gatherer group. Elvis, one of the oldest disabled remains to be uncovered, was discovered in Northern Spain. Studies indicate Elvis had a spine that was probably bent forward. He possibly used a cane. Analysis of his lower spine showed he had a slipped vertebrae and a boney growth on another vertebrae. Although it is unlikely he could have been an active hunter or carrier of heavy loads, he lived to be forty-five years old. Anthropologist Dr. Stringer tells us, "This individual probably could move around, but couldn't get his own food, so it implies a level of social support, and that he was valued by his contemporaries."[455]

Caring for the sick and disabled is part of our evolutionary history. Is it possible that Canadians feel strongly about our Medicare system because it is such a natural part of who we are as humans? Attending to the weak and sick dates back through the millennia.

Attacks on Medicare are seen as an assault on equity, fairness, and compassion but, most importantly, an assault on our solidarity as a society. Forcing Canadians to be entirely self-reliant within a market-system of health care pulls them apart from their social fabric. It dissolves the social solidarity that brought about Medicare in the first place. The concept of health as a human right that Tommy Douglas fought for was later incorporated into the 1966 United Nations General Assembly.[456] While this may appear as a contemporary ideology, it is actually part of our evolutionary history. Evidence supports creating a private-pay system for health care results in a synthetic system that defies the natural evolution of mankind. Privatized systems like those in the US should proceed with caution, as biologist Rachel Carson warns, "... man is a part of nature, and his war against nature is inevitably a war against himself."[457]

Professor Antonia Maioni relays the story of how every year she asks students this question: What is it that makes Canada "unique"? Professor Maioni tells us, "... the most frequent items the students come back to... are a variation of the three 'Hs': (Tim) Hortons, hockey, and health care."[458] So what is it about the concept of public health care that keeps Maioni's students identifying it as a uniquely Canadian trait? The answer could be that Medicare, and the values it espouses, have become entrenched into our national identity as a means of preserving relevance. This preservation of identity is crucial to the future of Canada.

Author Michael Bradley believes that the drive to be relevant is organic in all animals. He recounts a 1949 experiment done by behavioural researcher J. C. Braddock with the aquarium fish platys. Braddock demonstrated that the fish continued to defend their territories to remain relevant, despite the consistent lowering of water temperature. Even when the temperature became too low for the platys to eat, breed, or live, they died defending their territories. Although the assertion of territory has reproductive relevance, Bradley concluded there was more at play than a reproductive mechanism. Even when predicaments resulted in their dying, the platys fought to maintain an identity—a drive to be relevant to the future. Thousands of other experiments with other species have revealed the same tendency. The platys experiment demonstrated the significance of this "intangible"—to be relevant to the future. In Bradley's opinion, "for individuals the need to be 'relevant,' to have an identity, is the most important thing in life. This intangible persists to motivate when there is

CONCLUSION

no biological-reproductive way of influencing the future."[459]

It shouldn't strike us as odd when Maioni's students view the concept of universal public health care as part of our national identity. It is about preserving our identity as a nation and maintaining our relevance into the future. As Bradley reminds us, "This intangible identity-drive is likely to be the last, and most powerful, motivator of Canadians as a social unit... long after they have given in to temptations of short-sighted economic security..."[460] Revitalization of Medicare assures our relevance into the future. I believe Canadians will cling to this identity. Many of us are doing so now. I believe that after careful examination of the privatization option and understanding the threat it poses to our identity, Canadians will fight—like the platys in Braddock's ice-cold aquarium.

Author Shirley Abbott once said, "... our ancestors dwell in the attics of our brains as they do in the spiralling chains of knowledge hidden in every cell of our bodies."[461] This idea brings me to the last reason why I believe it is so critical to defend Medicare at this time—our past.

The irony is not lost upon me that during the writing of this work, the world celebrated the seventy-fifth anniversary of the Normandy Invasion. On the evening of June 6, 2019, I took some time out from writing to watch the news coverage of this historic day. I had been thinking a lot about Canada's veterans in the lead-up days to the anniversary of Operation Overlord. A black-and-white photo has been sitting on my desk for the entirety of my work life. It is a photo of my father and another Canadian serviceman digging a slit trench during the Normandy invasion. Beside them is a sign that reads, "Old soldiers never die, they just dig and fade away into a slit trench." Shortly after that trench was completed, my father and his friend sought refuge within it after coming under attack from enemy shelling. So, it was with a certain air of revery and sadness that I tuned in to watch the anniversary celebrations honouring our soldiers. Watching the grainy footage of young men storming the beach, wading through waist-high water, and parachuting from the sky, I was reminded of the bravery and fortitude that once shaped the greatness of this country. Perhaps like my own father, these young men embarked on an incredible journey—a journey that posed such extraordinary risk and assured no soldier any guarantee of a safe return home. Despite the risk, they set out and did so because the future of the country was at stake. Their strength and solidarity are reflected in every vestige of freedom that we enjoy today. It is difficult to envision a Canada bereft of their heroic sacrifices.

Today, they are gone. As their descendants, we are left to carry on their legacy. Medicare, more than any other social policy, embodies the egalitarian vision of our ancestors. What social pillar could be more definitive of the better world Canada's veterans envisioned than Medicare? We must draw upon the wisdom, the strength, and the example of the people who came before us. Yet we have resisted doing so. Maybe this inertia stems from a fear that we will appear fragile—unable to carry our own weight. Maybe it's a fear that in reaching back into the past, we will somehow surrender our own identity. The question we must ask ourselves is: Are we content to leave the legacy of our ancestors to atrophy?

Derrick Smith was a nurse anesthetist in a New York City hospital during the Covid-19 pandemic. He was no stranger to the respiratory failure Covid-19 patients are forced to endure. In the spring of 2020, one such patient was rapidly deteriorating and required mechanical ventilation. With the mortality rate of

CONCLUSION

ventilated Covid-19 patients hovering around eighty percent, Smith called the patient's wife, fearful that this might be the sick man's last opportunity to speak with her. But while awaiting the life-saving procedure of intubation, something else was preoccupying the dying patient's mind. Between his laboured breaths, he looked up and asked staff, "Who's going to pay for it?" Derrick Smith said the incident was "by far the worst thing" he had seen in twelve years of being a critical care and anesthesia nurse. He said that moment "shed light on a health care system that… has been and still is failing its people."[462] It's a system that doesn't remotely resonate with the values and spirit of Canadian Medicare and with those who fought to build a better Canada.

Neil "Charlie" Gillis was sick. Born in 1879, he was a small man who lived somewhat of a dichotomous life. During work hours, he laboured as a coal miner at the number-eleven colliery in Glace Bay, Nova Scotia. When not at work, he was an actor. He recited lines, donned costumes, and wore face makeup. He loved the stage.

As a child, he had suffered from rheumatic fever, which damaged his heart valves. As he aged, the damaged valves gave way to a chronic state of heart failure. From his home in the number-eleven coal-mining district of Glace Bay, he walked along railroad tracks to get to work. This was normally a fifteen-minute walk. As he suffered from chronic heart failure and shortness of breath, though, the walk became longer and more laboured. Twice he passed out on the number-eleven train tracks. Near the end of his working days, his fifteen-minute walk was taking him upwards of an hour. These were the late 1930s and early 1940s. Canada's pension plans were not yet developed, and Medicare had not been implemented across the country. Neil Charlie walked to work until he couldn't walk anymore.

Times were tough. He needed the doctor, but seeing the doctor required money.

My father told me this story many times. Neil Charlie Gillis was my grandfather. He died in 1943 close to the age I am now. His days of crawling to work breathless were finally over.

The circumstances surrounding the suffering of my grandfather are not unique to me. Every one of us has our own story: stories of parents and grandparents who worked and sacrificed so that successive generations could live better, more fulfilling lives.

Pause to reflect on your own story. It's imperative to establish the vision of what is at risk before you read one more line.

I make a point to walk several kilometres every day. My route includes a couple of steep hills. As I reach the crest of the first hill, my mind often wanders to the image of Neil Charlie walking breathlessly to work. Unlike him, I have no trouble breathing. At the highest point of my walk, I take pause and inhale the biggest, deepest, breath I can muster. On some days, I feel as if I must replicate the breaths he was unable to take. I have a keen awareness that my cardio-respiratory system is in far better shape than his must have been at this age. These are different times. I had the good fortune of growing up with Canadian Medicare. There were people who came before me who worked to ensure that we would have access to such a system. It is unlikely that I will ever be forced to crawl to work breathless. Should I lapse into heart failure, I have the luxury of walking into an emergency department, seeing a cardiologist, and having a comprehensive diagnostic workup with a treatment plan. This is the legacy of our forefathers. It is a legacy that I do not take for granted. It is not a history that belongs to me alone. It is all our histories—our collective history. We carry that history with us, and it should not be forgotten. To forget it is to launch future generations into a deeper aberration of poverty—a poverty bereft of our own past. Our history, Canada's history, is worth defending.

Far from the strength and tenacity of Tommy Douglas, Canada's veterans, and our grandparents, capitalism threatens to buy out the Canadian Medicare system. Canadians can now sell their blood in private plasma clinics. Much of the long term-care sector is privatized and fragmented. More and more care is being transferred onto the shoulders of patients. Executive private clinics now dot the Canadian landscape. Medicare services continue to be delisted. Ancillary hospital services are contracted out. Canadians, many of them seniors, cannot afford their medications. Hospital food is prefabricated. People having quadruple bypass surgery are coming to the hospital carrying their suitcases the day of surgery. Patients are self-administering their own pre-op treatments. Emergency services are crumbling. Within the system, there is no time, empathy, validation, compassion, or dignity, and there are no explanations. Just keep the costs down. The system is disjointed, uncoordinated, and competitive. It's cold. Transactional. Deliberate disintegration is ravenously eating through to the heart of Medicare.

The health care market is an inexhaustible one. There are billions of dollars in profit to be made if the public system collapses. Just ask the corporate health care profiteers in the US. As long as there are people, they will need health care. If sickness, disease, accidents, and pandemics prevail, people will need to be treated. Big pharma, health care-insurance conglomerates, and their profiteers, view health care as an infinite source of wealth. Neoliberalism supplies the oxygen for this conquest. Will Canadians allow capitalism to dig Medicare's grave?

I was recently walking against a cold Canadian winter wind. An ambulance roared by with sirens blaring. For most of my career, I have been a critical-care nurse. So, when emergency vehicles pass by, I'm always curious about the patient inside. Are they headed to my former ER? What's the story? What's the patient's condition? Will they be ok? My mind drifts back to that one important emergency-department screen called the "to be seen" (TBS) screen. As a well-illuminated dashboard, this screen indicated how many patients were still waiting in the emergency department queue. It's the all-important screen with a very important number. A large number of "TBS patients" means the ER is overcrowded, things are going slowly, and sick people are waiting. Their treatment may be delayed, and their outcomes adversely affected. The patient inside the ambulance is about to be added to someone's TBS screen.

I worry that unless we act now, we will be unable to pull Medicare from the clutches of those who seek to dismantle it. I remain hopeful we can successfully change the tide and counter the narrative that Medicare is for sale. I hope that we can transform Medicare into the universal, egalitarian system our forefathers envisioned. I hope this work will, at some level, make Canadians take pause in understanding what is truly at stake. In rescuing Medicare, we make Canada relevant to the future. We honour the sacrifices of our past. We unite with the natural forces of our evolution as a species, and we prevent the next generation from succumbing to the same fate as our Indigenous brother Brian Sinclair—slumped in an emergency room waiting area, dying to be seen.

ENDNOTES

1. In the Beginning

1 https://www.ncbi.nlm.nih.gov/pmc/articles/PMC6459437/

2 Public Opinion. "Canadians Want Health Care to be the Focus for Political Parties in the Lead Up to the Election This Fall," *Ipsos* (Canada), June 13, 2019.

3 *CBC Arts*. "Tommy Douglas Crowned Greatest Canadian," CBC, November 29, 2004.

4 H. C. Pentland, "The 1919 Winnipeg General Strike," *The Canadian Dimension*, October 16, 2018.

5 Ibid.

6 Ibid.

7 Ibid.

8 Ibid.

9 Ibid.

10 J. Nolan Reilly, "Winnipeg General Strike of 1919," *The Canadian Encyclopedia*, February 7, 2006.

11 Ibid.

12 Michael Bradley, *Crisis of Clarity* (Toronto: Summerhill Press, 1987), 65.

13 Antonia Maioni, *Health Care in Canada* (Don Mills: Oxford University Press, 2015), 19.

14 Linda McQuaig, *The Wealthy Banker's Wife* (Toronto: Penguin Books, 1993), 26.

15 Bradley, 77.

16 Maioni, 20–21.

17 Bradley, 52.

18 Bradley, 67.

19 Ibid.

20 Ibid.

21 Bradley, 69.

22 Bradley, 81.

23 Bradley, 74.

24 Bradley, 78.
25 Bradley, 86.
26 Bradley, 87.
27 Ibid.
28 Bradley, 88.
29 Bradley, 89.
30 McQuaig, 161.
31 Bradley, 34.

2. The Healthcare Privatization Myth

32 C. J. Polychroniou, "Noam Chomsky: The US Health System is an "International Scandal"—and ACA Repeal Will Make It Worse," *Truthout*, January 12, 2017.

33 Annalisa Merelli, "A History of Why the US is the Only Rich Country Without Universal Health Care," *Quartz*, July 18, 2017.

34 C. J. Polychroniou, "Noam Chomsky: The US Health System is an 'International Scandal'—and ACA Repeal Will Make It Worse," *Truthout*, January 12, 2017.

35 Ibid.

36 Annalisa Merelli, "A History of why the US is the Only Rich Country Without Universal Health Care," *Quartz*, July 18, 2017.

37 "Progressive Party (United States, 1912)," Wikipedia, last modified August 15, 2021, https://en.wikipedia.org/wiki/Progressive_Party_(United_States,_1912).

38 Antonia Maioni, *Health Care in Canada*. Don Mills: Oxford University Press, 2015, 62.

39 Annalisa Merelli, "A History of why the US is the Only Rich Country Without Universal Health Care," *Quartz*, July 18, 2017.

40 Maioni, 63

41 Annalisa Merelli, "A History of Why the US is the Only Rich Country Without Universal Health Care," *Quartz*, July 18, 2017.

42 Roosa Tikkanen and Melinda K. Abrams, "U.S. Health Care from a Global Perspective, 2019: Higher Spending, Worse Outcomes," *The Commonwealth Fund*, January 30, 2020.

43 Edward R. Berchick, Jessica C. Barnett, and Rachel D. Upton, "Health Insurance Coverage in the United States: 2018," *United States Census Bureau*, November 8, 2019.

44 Edward R. Berchick, and Larissa Mykyta, "Uninsured Rate for Children up to 5.5 Percent in 2018," *United States Census Bureau*, September 10, 2019.

45 Joan Alker and Olivia Pham, "Nation's Progress on Children's Health Coverage Reverses Course," *Georgetown University Center for Children and Families*, November 21, 2018.

46 Edward R. Berchick, Emily Hood, and Jessica C. Barnett, "Health Insurance Coverage in the United States: 2017," *United States Census Bureau*, September 2018.

47 Melissa Patrick, "Study Finds More Than 1/4 of Adults in the U.S. are Underinsured Because of High Deductibles," *Northern Kentucky Tribune*, October 23, 2017.

48 Ed Woods, "Health Care Costs Number One Cause of Bankruptcy for American Families," *Bond and Botes Law Offices*, January 20, 2017.

49 Wendell Potter, "The $140 Billion the *New York Times* Says Americans Owe in Medical Debt is Just the Tip of the Iceberg," *Now*, July 21, 2021.

50 Irene Papanicolas, Liana R. Woskie, and Ashish K. Jha, "Health Care Spending in the United States and Other High-Income Countries," *Jama*, March 13, 2018.

51 David U. Himmelstein et al., "A Comparison of Hospital Administrative Costs in Eight Nations: US Costs Exceed All Others by Far," *Health Affairs* 33, no. 9 (September 2014).

52 Ibid.

53 "Woman Says Her Son Couldn't Afford His Insulin—Now He's Dead," *CBS News*, January 4, 2019.

54 Ibid.

55 "Americans Stage 'Caravan to Canada' to Buy Cheaper Insulin," *As It Happens*, CBC, May 8, 2019.

56 Julia Belluz, "The Absurdly High Cost of Insulin Explained: Why Americans Ration a Drug Discovered in the 1920s," *Vox*, November 7, 2019.

57 Duane Pohlman, "The Cost of Living: The Skyrocketing Price of a Lifesaving Medication," *WKRC Indianapolis*, November 6, 2018.

58 Sarah Jones, "Another Person Has Died After Rationing Insulin," *Intelligencer*, July 15, 2019.

59 William Rivers Pitt, "Insulin Prices Killed Josh Wilkerson. Now His Mother is Taking on Big Pharma," *Truthout*, August 24, 2019.

60 Reuters staff. "Eli Lilly Sees 2019 Profit, Revenue Above Estimates; Shares Rise," *CNBC News* via Reuters, December 20, 2018.

61 Angelica Lavito, "Eli Lilly Falls 5 Per Cent on Sluggish Growth in Animal Health, as it Weighs Options for the Unit," *CNBC News*, January 31, 2018.

62 Judy George, "Out-Of-Pocket Costs Go Through the Roof for Neurology Drugs—MS patients with private insurance paid 20 times more in 2016 vs 2004," *MedPage Today*, May 2, 2019.

63 Ibid.

64 Linda McQuaig, *The Wealthy Banker's Wife* (Toronto: Penguin Books, 1993), 9.

65 Alternet and Liz Posner, "For Profit Medical Companies are Making Tons of Money Taking Poor People's Blood," *Alternet*, December 8, 2017.

66 Nicholas Scheffler, "Plasma Centers Profit Off the Working Poor," *USW 9460—Northlands Health care Workers Union*, August 10, 2018.

67 Alexa Valiente, Mark Abdelmalek, and Lauren Pearle, "Why Thousands of Low-Income Americans 'Donate' Their Blood Plasma to For-Profit Centers," *ABC News*, January 13, 2017.

68 David Cecere, "New Study Finds 45,000 Deaths Annually Linked to Lack of Health Coverage," *Harvard Gazette*, September 17, 2009.

69 Arthur Delaney, "Yes, People Die When They Don't Have Access to Health Care," *HuffPost*, May 9, 2017.

70 Wendell Potter, *Deadly Spin* (New York: Bloomsbury Press, 2010), 65.

71 Ibid., 68

72 Ibid., 69

73 Ibid., 70

74 Rajah Kamal, Cynthia Cox, and Erik Blumenkranz, "What Do We Know About Social Determinants of Health in the U.S. and Comparable Countries?" *Peterson-KFF Health System Tracker*, November 21, 2017.

75 Joshua Cohen, "U.S. Maternal and Infant Mortality: More Signs of Public Health Neglect," *Forbes*, August 1, 2021.

76 Cynthia Cox and Selena Gonzales, "The U.S. has Highest Rate of Disease Burden Among Comparable Countries, and the Gap is Growing," *Health System Tracker*, June 7, 2015.

77 "The Effects of Rising Health Insurance Premiums on Employment," *The National Bureau of Economic Research, Bulletin on Aging & Health*, no. 2 (June 2005).

78 Lorie Konish, "This is the Real Reason Most Americans File for Bankruptcy, "*CNBC*, February 11, 2019.

79 Terri Cullen, "Malpractice Liability Costs U.S. $55.6 Billion a Year," *HCP Live*, September 8, 2010.

80 Austin Frakt, "The Astonishing High Administrative Costs of U.S. Health care," *New York Times*, June 9, 2019.

3. Why the Emergency Department Mattered

81 Vanessa Milne, Joshua Tepper, and Jeremy Patch, "Emergency Room Overcrowding: Causes and Cures," *Healthy Debate* (Canada), June 15, 2017.

82 "Our Promise Strategy," Capital Health, accessed May 8, 2021, https://www.cdha.nshealth.ca/system/files/sites/343/documents/our-promise-strategy.

83 "Number of Doctors Per Capita in Canada Reaches Record High," *The Canadian Press* (Canada), September 26, 2019.

84 "Finding a Primary Care Provider in Nova Scotia—March 2021," Nova Scotia Health, accessed May 8, 2021, http://www.nshealth.ca/files/finding-primary-care-provider-nova-scotia-march-2021.

85 Scot H. Simpson, "Of Silos and Systems: The Issue of Regionalizing Health Care," *The Canadian Journal of Hospital Pharmacy* 64, no. 4 (July–August 2011): 237–238.

86 *CBC News*, "80M Allocated for Health Super Board Startup Costs," CBC, August 27, 2008.

87 *CBC News*, "$3.2M in Severance for Ex-CEOs of Calgary, Edmonton Health Boards," CBC, October 8, 2008.

88 Marieke Walsh, "Health District Merger Costs Jump to $9 Million," *Global News*, November 17, 2015.

89 Corpus Sanchez, "Changing Nova Scotia's Health care System: Creating Sustainability Through Transformation," December 2007.

90 *CBC News*, "103 Ways to Fix Health Care in N.S.," CBC, January 17, 2008.

91 Corpus Sanchez, 37.

92 *CBC News*, "103 Ways to Fix Health Care in N.S.," *CBC*, January 17, 2008.

93 Corpus Sanchez, 40.

94 André Picard, *Matters of Life and Death* (British Columbia: Douglas & McIntyre, 2013), 38.

95 Corpus Sanchez, 33.

96 Picard, 39.

97 Michael Tutton, "Halifax Doctor Defends Use of 'disaster alert' for Overflow in Emergency," *The Globe and Mail*, January 24, 2009.

98 Ibid.

99 Ibid.

100 Keith Doucette, "Halifax Woman Blames Slow Ambulance Response in Death of Husband," *CTV News*, March 31, 2021.

101 Michael Gorman," Long-Awaited Report into N.S. Ambulance System Released," *CBC News*, March 8, 2021.

102 Picard, 38.

103 Vanessa Milne, Joshua Tepper, and Jeremy Patch, "Emergency Room Overcrowding: Causes and Cures," *Healthy Debate (*Canada), June 15, 2017.

104 Kelly Grant, "Hospital Overcrowding has Become the Norm in Ontario, Figures Show," *The Globe and* Mail, May 21, 2017.

105 Ibid.

106 André Picard, "Bedlam Over Beds :We Can No Longer Ignore Our Long-Term-Care Crisis," *The Globe and Mail*, May 28, 2019.

107 Ibid.

108 Ibid.

109 Ontario Ministry of Long-Term Care, "Hallway Health Care: A system under strain," First *Interim report from the Premier's council on Improving health care and ending hallway medicine,* January 2019.

110 *CTV Atlantic News*, "Valley Doctors Start Go-Fund-Me Page to Raise Awareness of Growing Health-Care Crisis," CTV, May 3, 2019.

111 *CBC News.* "Treating Patients in Supply Closets Final Straw for ER Doctors in Kentville," CBC, January 15, 2020.

112 *CBC News*. "Campbellton Hospital Takes Extreme Steps After Running Out of Beds," CBC, November 21, 2019.

113 Philip Lee-Shamrock, "Daily Bed Census May Not Capture Full Extent of Hallway Health Care," *CBC News*, February 3, 2019.

114 "Coon Calls for Public Inquiry in Wake of Fredericton Teen's Suicide," *CBC News*, March 2, 2021.

4. The Four Horsemen

115 Stephen Metcalf, "Neoliberalism: The Idea that Swallowed the World," *The Guardian*, April 18, 2017.

116 Jim Stanford, "Canada's Transformation Under Neoliberalism," *Canadian Dimension*, March 29, 2014.

117 Ibid.

118 Ibid.

119 Ibid.

120 Kevin CarMichael, Richard Blackwell, and Greg Keenan, "Free up 'dead money,' Carney Exhorts Corporate Canada," *The Globe and Mail*, August 22, 2012.

121 Colleen Fuller, "20 Years Later : How Corporations Took Over Canada's Health Care System," *Policynote*, September 26, 2017.

122 Andrew Jackson, "Corporate Tax Cuts, Lost Revenues and Lagging Business Investment," *The Broadbent Institute,* last modified September 10,

2022, https://www.broadbentinstitute.ca/corporate_tax_cuts_lost_revenues_and_lagging_business_investment.

123 Stephen Metcalf, "Neoliberalism: The Idea That Swallowed the World," *The Guardian*, April 18, 2017.

124 Bruce Livesey, "Is Neoliberalism Destroying the World?" *CBC*, September 26, 2018.

125 Effective Public Health care Panacea Project, "How Much Does Canada Spend on Health care?" accessed September 26, 2021, https://www.ephpp.ca/health care-funding-policy-in-canada/.

126 Canadian Institute for Health Information, "National Health Expenditure Trends 2020," *CIHI*, 2021.

127 Haizhen Mou, "What Now?/Canada Health Transfer: Background and Future," *Canada West Foundation 50*, May 13, 2021.

128 Antonia Maioni, *Health Care in Canada* (Don Mills: Oxford University Press, 2015), 55.

129 Ibid., 56.

130 Canadian Institute for Health Information, "Hospital Trends in Canada—Results of a Project to Create a Historical Series of Statistical and Financial Data for Canadian Hospitals Over Twenty-Seven Years," *National Health Expenditure Database, CIHI*, 2005, 2.

131 Canadian Institute for Health Information, "Hospital Trends in Canada—Results of a Project to Create a Historical Series of Statistical and Financial Data for Canadian Hospitals Over Twenty-Seven Years," *National Health Expenditure Database, CIHI*, 2005, 3.

132 Gabriel Yiu, "Corporate Tax Cuts Have Made Canada a Poorer Country," *HuffPost*, September 16, 2016.

133 Brian DuBreuil, "Reality Check: Are Hospital Bed Claims Accurate?" *CBC News*, October 4, 2013.

134 Canadian Museum of History, "Explosive Changes in Klein's Alberta, 1992–2000," Chapter 11, April 21, 2010.

135 Brian Bergman, "McKenna Retires," *The Canadian Encyclopedia*, December 15, 2013.

136 Natalie Mehra, "$22 Billion in Cuts to Funding for Public Services Planned by Mr. Ford, Worse Than Harris, We are 'Extremely Worried,'" *Ontario Health Coalition*, June 3, 2018.

137 Briefing Note, "Gordon Campbell—Canada's Arch Health Care Privateer and Author of the Worse Cuts in BC's History," *Ontario Health Coalition*, September 20, 2018.

138 Camille Bains, "Health Care Battle in Judge's Hands but Expected to Land in Canada's Top Court," *The Canadian Press for CBC News*, February 28, 2020.

139 Paul Chiasson, "Health Spending Fails to Keep Pace with Inflation, Population Growth," *The Canadian Press for the Globe and Mail*, December 15, 2016.

140 Gabriel Yiu, "Corporate Tax Cuts Have Made Canada a Poorer Country," *HuffPost*, September 16, 2016.

141 Justin Tang, "Provinces Irate Over Health Funding Talks with Morneau," *The Canadian Press for the Globe and Mail*, December 18, 2016.

142 Bob Hepburn, "Why Doug Ford's to Blame for Health-Care Mess," *The Toronto Star*, July 15, 2020.

143 Dean Bennett, "UCP Leader Jason Kenney Wants to Explore Private Health-Care," *The Canadian Press for Global News*, February 20, 2019.

144 Mike Parker, "HSSA Criticizes Kenney's Plan for Potential $1.2B Cut to Health Care," *The National Union of Public and General Employees*, accessed September 21, 2022, https://nupge.ca/content/hsaa-criticizes-kenney%E2%80%99s-plan-potential-12b-cut-health-care.

145 Graham Thomson, "MacKinnon Report Gives Kenney Roadmap for Klein-Style Cuts," *CBC News*, September 4, 2019.

146 Michael Gorman, "Long-Term Care Homes Feeling Impacts of Budget Cuts," *CBC News*, August 17, 2016.

147 Christine Saulnier, "Nova Scotians Made to Wait for the Trickle-Down That Will Never Come," *The Monitor*, February 25, 2020.

148 Colleen Fuller, "20 Years Later: How Corporations Took Over Canada's Health Care System," *Policynote*, September 26, 2017.

149 Jason Kirby et al., "99 Stupid Things the Government Did with Your Money: Parts I, II, and III," *Maclean's*, January 7, 2013.

150 Paige MacPherson, "Government Must Come Clean About Yarmouth Ferry Costs," *Canadian Taxpayers Federation News Release*, July 16, 2019.

151 Armine Yalnizyan, "Five Reasons to Say No to More Corporate Tax Cuts," *The Globe and Mail*, January 28, 2011.

152 Trish Hennessy, "Hennessy's Index, Tax Cuts 101," *The Canadian Centre for Policy Alternatives*, March 2014.

153 Marco Chown Oved, Toby A. A. Heaps, and Michael Yow, "The High Cost of Low Corporate Taxes," *The Star & Corporate Knights Project*, December 14, 2017.

154 Ibid.

155 Ibid.

156 David MacDonald, "The History of Tax Exemptions, Credits, and Loopholes in Canada," *The Canadian Centre for Policy Alternatives*, May 25, 2017.

157 Zach Dubinsky, "Wealthy Canadians Hiding up to 240B Abroad, CRA says," *CBC News*, June 28, 2018.

ENDNOTES

158 Zach Dubinsky and the International Consortium of Investigative Journalists, "Huge 'Pandora Papers' Leak Exposes Secret Offshore Accounts of Politicians, Celebrities, and Billionaires," *CBC News,* October 3, 2021.

159 Jim Grieshaber-Otto and Scott Sinclair, "Bad Medicine: Trade Treaties, Privatization and Health Care Reform in Canada," *Canadian Centre for Policy Alternatives*, 2004, 2.

160 Ibid., 147.

161 Sumatra Dey, "The Good, the Bad, and the Ugly on NAFTA 2.0," *The Council of Canadians*, 2018.

162 Ronald Labonte et al., "The New NAFTA's Assault on Public Health," *The Conversation*, May 21, 2019.

163 Ibid.

164 Sumatra Dey, "The Good, the Bad, and the Ugly on NAFTA 2.0," *The Council of Canadians*, 2018.

165 Zoe Greenberg, "What is the Blood of a Poor Person Worth?" *The New York Times*, February 1, 2019.

166 *George Stroumboulopoulos Tonight*, "A Look Back at Canada's Tainted Blood Scandal," *CBC News*, October 4, 2013.

167 Anne Kingston, "A Bloody Mess: The Story Behind Paid Plasma in Canada," *Maclean's*, November 22, 2017.

168 Ibid.

169 The WHO Database on Blood safety, "Blood Safety and Availability," *World Health Organization*, June 10, 2020.

170 Tori Weldon, "After One Year, Pay-for-Plasma Clinic in Moncton Sees Almost 300 Visits Weekly," *CBC News*, July 19, 2018.

171 Anne Kingston, "A Bloody Mess: The Story Behind Paid Plasma in Canada," *Maclean's*, November 22, 2017.

172 Ibid.

173 Ibid.

174 Danyaal Raz, "Why is Health Canada Aiding a Private Company Instead of Safeguarding Canadian Blood Supplies?" *Ottawa Life Magazine*, January 5, 2018.

175 Kathy Tomlinson, "Some Doctors are Charging Both Government and Patients Privately in Illegal Double-Dipping Practice," *The Globe and Mail*, June 10, 2017.

176 Ibid.

177 Ibid.

178 177 Ibid.

179 Ibid

180 Ibid.

181 Natalie Mehra, "Private Clinics and the Threat to Public Medicare in Canada. Results of Surveys with Private Clinics and Patients," *The Ontario Health Coalition,* June 10, 2017.

182 Ibid.

183 Ibid.

184 Ibid.

185 Ibid.

186 Lauren McKeon, "Five of Toronto's Most Exclusive Private Medical Clinics," *Toronto Life,* February 26, 2014.

187 Robert Cribb, Vjosa Isai, and Maham Shakeel, "Should the Wealthy be Allowed to Buy Their Way to Faster Health Care at Private Clinics?" The *Toronto Star* and the *Ryerson School of Journalism,* March 18, 2017.

188 Ibid.

189 Ibid.

190 CBC, "Quebec Coroner Urges Stricter Rules for Private Clinics After Man Dies in Wait Room," *CBC News,* April 22, 2009.

191 Emily Yahr, "What Went Wrong with Joan Rivers's Last Medical Procedure: Lawsuit," *The Washington Post,* January 28, 2015.

192 Tom Winter, "Civil Case in Joan Rivers' Death Settled," *NBC News,* May 12, 2016.

193 Amy Stoodley Files, "Elderly N.S. Couple Hard-Pressed to Pay $309 to Access Medical Records," *CTV eNews,* September 26, 2019.

194 André Picard, "Want Your Medical Records? Be Prepared to Pay—a Lot," *Globe and Mail,* March 13, 2013.

195 Karin Larsen, "Third BC Seniors Home Owned by Chinese Company Fails Standard of Care, Placed Under Health Authority Control," *CBC News,* December 12, 2019.

196 Ibid.

197 Lindsay Kines, "Island Health Takes Control of Nanaimo Seniors Home; Cites Inadequate Care of Residents," *Times Colonist,* November 28, 2019.

198 Ibid.

199 Courtney Dickson, "Health Authority Takes Over Operations at Private Seniors Care Home in Okanagan Town," *CBC News,* February 25, 2020.

200 Bethany Lindsay, "For-Profit Homes Fail to Deliver on Direct Care Funded by the Public, BC Seniors Advocate Says," *CBC News,* February 4, 2020.

201 Erica Johnson, "Nursing Home Rationed Diapers While Residents Suffered Rashes, Infections," *CBC News,* February 23, 2020.

ENDNOTES

202 Michael Gorman, "Death of Woman Hospitalized for 'Horrific' Bedsore Sparks Criminal Investigation," *CBC News*, June 15, 2018.

203 Trish Hennessy, "Disaster in the Making. The Quiet Erosion of Canada's Regulation System," *Canadian Centre for Policy Alternatives*, February 22, 2011.

204 "Private Public Partnerships (P3s) or Private Over Patients? The Facts About For-Profit Hospitals." *The Ontario Health Coalition*, PDF.

205 Ibid.

206 André Picard, "In This PPP, Taxpayers are the Ones Who Paid," *The Globe and Mail*, February 5, 2009.

207 Natalie Mehra, "Ontario Will Pay $3.5 Billion Over 25 Years for One P3 Hospital," *The National Union of Public and General Employees*, accessed August 27, 2022, https://nupge.ca/content/ontario-will-pay-35-billion-over-25-years-one-p3-hospital.

208 Nick Westoll, "Brampton Council Declares Health-Care Emergency Amid Hospital Overcrowding, Wait Times," *Global News*, January 22, 2020.

209 Walter Strong, "Public Protected from Potential Collapse of Company Part of Stanton Hospital Project, Says N.W.T. Government," *CBC News*, February 2, 2018.

210 Hilary Bird, "Yellowknife's New Hospital Comes in Millions Over Budget Due to Property Tax Flub," *CBC News*, February 17, 2020.

211 Randi Beers, "Mould Clean Up at Yellowknife's New Hospital Could Have Put Patients at Risk, Warn Staff," *CBC News*, October 30, 2019.

212 Adam Hunter, "Roof Replacement for New $400M North Battleford Hospital 'ridiculous,' Says Sask. NDP," *CBC News*, May 23, 2019.

213 Laura Woodward, "'A Serious Bone of Contention': Emails Reveal Details About Faulty Sask. Hospital Roof," *The Saskatoon News*, January 21, 2020.

214 CUPE, "Five Times Provincial Governments Failed with P3 Hospitals," *CUPE Nova Scotia*, February 10, 2017.

215 Jane Gerster, "A Man was Ignored to Death in an ER Ten Years Ago. It Could Happen Again," *Global News*, September 21, 2018.

216 Ibid.

217 The Canadian Press, "Man's Death After 34-hour ER Wait Must be Ruled Homicide, Family's Lawyer Tells Inquest," *The Canadian Press for The National Post*, January 24, 2015.

218 Jeff Keele, "Inquest Hears ER was Short Three Nurses the Night Brian Sinclair Died," *The Canadian Press for CTV News Winnipeg*, October, 2013.

219 Kelly Geraldine Malone, "Family of Brian Sinclair, Who Died During 34-Hour ER Wait, Says Racism Still an Issue," *The Canadian Press for CBC News*, September 21, 2018.

220 "Brian Sinclair Inquest Recommendations Slammed by ER Doctors," *CBC Manitoba*, March 20, 2015.

221 Jane Gerster, "A Man was Ignored to Death in an ER Ten Years Ago. It Could Happen Again," *Global News*, September 21, 2018.

222 Robin McGee, *The Cancer Olympics*, (Victoria, British Columbia: Friesen Press, 2014), 4.

223 Ibid., 5.

224 Ibid., 6.

225 Ibid., 11.

226 Ibid.

227 Ibid.

228 McGee, 13.

229 Ibid., 31.

230 Erica Johnson, "Seniors' Home Confines 94-Year-Old Blind Woman to Bedbug-Infested Room for Two Weeks," *CBC News*, November 3, 2019.

231 Jen White, "This Man Lost His Leg After Seven Years Waiting for a Kidney in N.L.—and Now He's Losing Hope," *CBC News*, May 30, 2019.

5. The Reward Puppets

232 Yuval Noah Harari, *Sapiens*, (Canada: McClelland & Stewart, 2016), 367.

233 Ibid., 368.

234 Ibid.

235 William Lazonick, "To Boost Investment, End S.E.C. Rule That Spurs Stock Buybacks," *The New York Times*, March 6, 2015.

236 Kevin Carmichael, Richard Blackwell, and Greg Keenan, "Free up 'Dead Money,' Carney Exhorts Corporate Canada," *The Globe and Mail*, August 22, 2012.

237 Harari, 368.

238 Ibid.

239 Harari, 369.

240 Ibid., 370.

241 Nova Scotia Health/Need a Family Practice Registry/Monthly Reporting on Finding a Primary Care Provider in Nova Scotia, accessed November 15, 2021.

242 Jean Laroche, "It Cost $130K to Renovate Seven Steps at Province House," *CBC News*, February 2, 2018.

ENDNOTES

243 Alex Cooke, "This is the Face of the Health-Care Crisis: Woman Issues Plea to N.S. Premier," *CBC News,* April 25, 2019.

244 Trevor Nicholas, "Nova Scotia Premier Announce Business Tax Cuts," *Huddle,* February 12, 2020.

245 Ibid.

246 Ibid.

247 Jesse Thomas, "Young People, Jobs are Coming Back to Halifax in Record Numbers," *Global News,* June 17, 2019.

248 Ibid.

249 Ibid.

250 Ibid.

251 Ibid.

252 Toby Sanger, "Who Would Really Benefit from Kenney's Corporate Tax Cuts?" *The National Observer,* April 12, 2019.

253 Ibid.

254 Ibid.

255 Canadian Institutes of Health Research, "Showcasing a Canadian Success Story: The Ebola Vaccine," November 26, 2015.

256 Avis Favaro, Elizabeth St. Philip, and Alexandre Mae Jones, "Canadian Doctors Help Critically Ill Pregnant Woman Survive and Save Baby's Life," *CTV News,* October 2021.

257 Peter Armstrong, "Where Your Tax Dollar Goes," *CBC News,* February 23, 2018.

258 Canadian Health Services Research Foundation, "Myth: A Parallel Private System Would Reduce Waiting Times in the Public System," *CHSRF,* March 2005.

259 Mickey Djuric, "Saskatchewan's Private MRI System Not Meeting Provincial Requirement Auditor Says," *Global News,* June 25, 2020.

260 Adam Hunter, "Saskatchewan's MRI Wait-List Doubled From 2015 to 2019," *CBC News,* January 30, 2020.

261 Dr. Bob Bell and Stefan Superina, "Does Hybrid Health Care Improve Public Services? Lessons Learned from Australia," *Health care System Profiles,* July 4, 2019.

262 Ibid.

263 Ibid.

264 N. Gregory Mankiw, "The Economics of Health care," *Harvard University,* 2017.

265 Joseph Heath, "Health Care as a Commodity," *Policy Options,* February 1, 2003.

266 Christos Iliadis et al., "Theories of Supply and Demand, Problems of Peculiarities in the Health care Sector: Its Effects on Health Policy," *Journal of Health care Communications* 4, no. 3 (November 22, 2019): 5.

267 Wendell Potter, "Free Market Ideology Doesn't Work for Health Care," *Yahoo News*, June 8, 2015.

268 Abdulrahman El-Sayed, "Five Reasons Free Markets Don't Work in Health Care," *HuffPost*, June 5, 2012.

269 Bethany Lindsay, "For-Profit Homes Fail to Deliver on Direct Care Funded by the Public, B.C. Seniors Advocate Says," *CBC News*, February 4, 2020.

270 Naomi Lightman and Lorain Hardcastle, "How Private Long-Term Care Facilities Handled Covid Needs Scrutiny," *The Edmonton Journal*, February 12, 2021.

271 Michael Sainato, "'I Live on the Streets Now': How Americans Fall into Medical Bankruptcy," *The Guardian*, November 14, 2019.

272 Linda McQuaig and Neil Brooks, *The Trouble with Billionaires* (Toronto: Penguin Books, 2010), 88.

273 Daniel R. Hoffman, "How Today's Corrupt Health Care System is About to Get Worse," *The Philadelphia Inquirer*, December 5, 2016.

274 Emily Payne, "Top Health Insurers' Revenues Soar to Almost $1 Trillion in 2019," *Benefits Pro*, February 24, 2020.

275 Elsie Reuter, "Kaiser Permanente Tripled Income in 2019," *MedCity News*, February 10, 2020.

276 Edward R. Berchick, Jessica C. Barnett, and Rachel D. Upton, "Health Insurance Coverage in the United States 2018," *The United States Census Bureau*, November 8, 2019.

277 Berkeley Lovelace Jr., "Three Major Pharmaceutical Companies Just Reported Earnings—Here's How They Did," *CNBC News*, April 30, 2019.

6. Covid-19 Makes the Case

278 Andrew Joseph, "WHO Declares Coronavirus Outbreak a Global Health Emergency," *Stat News*, January 30, 2020.

279 William Wan, "WHO Declares a Pandemic of Coronavirus Disease Covid-19," *The Washington Post*, March 11, 2020.

280 Erica Alini, "Coronavirus: Canada Lost 1 Million Jobs in March," *Global News*, April 9, 2020.

281 CBC, "Canada Tops 100,000 Reported Coronavirus Cases," *CBC News*, June 18, 2020.

ENDNOTES

282 Staff for the Canadian Press, "Canada's Unemployment Rate Reaches 13.7%," *The Canadian Press for Global News*, June 5, 2020.

283 Canadian Institute for Health Information, "Pandemic Experience in the Long-Term Care Sector: How Does Canada Compare with Other Countries?" *CIHI*, Ottawa: CIHI, 2020.

284 Sigal Samuel, "Canada's 'National Shame': Covid-19 in Nursing Homes," *Vox*, July 7, 2020.

285 Roger E. Riendeau, *A Brief History of Canada* (New York: Infobase Publishing, 2007), 330.

286 Aaron Wherry, "Leaving out Long-Term Care was Medicare's Original Sin—and We're Paying For It Now," *CBC News*, May 28, 2020.

287 Madeleine Ritt, "The Crisis of Privatized Care in Ontario," *Healthy Debate*, December 4, 2020.

288 Pat Armstrong et al., *They Deserve Better: The Long-Term Care Experience in Canada and Scandinavia* (Canada: The Canadian Centre for Policy Alternatives, 2009, 12.

289 Aaron Wherry, "Leaving out Long-Term Care was Medicare's Original Sin—and We're Paying For It Now," *CBC News*, May 28, 2020.

290 Th Thanh Ha, "Herron Long-Term Care Residents Died of Thirst and Malnourishment Quebec Coroner's Inquest Told," *The Globe and Mail*, September 14, 2021.

291 Shayla Vize, "'A Mistake was Made.' Man Left Behind During Evacuation of Hamilton Retirement Home," *CHCH News*, May 20, 2020.

292 Emma Paling, "Military Says it Found Disturbing Conditions in Ontario Care Homes," *HuffPost*, May 26, 2020.

293 Tara Carman, "Canada's Hardest Hit Nursing Homes Lost 40% of Residents in just 3 Months of the Pandemic," *CBC News*, July 10, 2020.

294 Samuel Riches, "What Went Wrong in Bobcaygeon: How Covid Killed 29 People in an Ill-Prepared Nursing Home," *The National Post*, April 10, 2020.

295 Tara Carman, "Canada's Hardest Hit Nursing Homes Lost 40% of Residents in just 3 Months of the Pandemic," *CBC News*, July 10, 2020.

296 Judy Havien, "Northwood, a Blueprint for How Covid-19 Raged Through Long-Term Care Homes," *National Observer*, May 14, 2020.

297 Ibid.

298 Stephanie Nolen, "What Happened at Northwood?" *The Coast*, April 15, 2021.

299 Ibid.

300 Ibid.

301 Adam Miller, "The Key Lesson from SARS That Canada Failed to Heed When Covid-19 Hit," *CBC News*, October, 17, 2020.

302 Ibid.

303 Stephanie Nolen, "What Happened at Northwood?" *The Coast*, April 15, 2021.

304 John McCracken, "Authorities Ignored Early Warnings from Northwood's Long-Term Care Workers and Unions," *The Nova Scotia Advocate*, May 8, 2020. z

305 Laura Eggertson, "Review Uncovers Fatal Flaws in Long-Term Care Infection Control," *CMAJ* 192, no. 41 (October 13, 2020): E1221–E1222.

306 Karin Larsen, "Third B.C. Seniors Home Owned by Chinese Company Fails Standard of Care, Placed Under Health Authority Control," *CBC News*, December 12, 2019.

307 Paul Curry, "Broken Homes," *Nova Scotia Nurses Union*, December 2015.

308 Bobbi-Jean MacKinnon, "Nurses Union Calls for Independent Inquiry into Long-Term Care Sector," *CBC News*, October 15, 2020.

309 Thomas Gabor and John Kiedrowski, "Crime and Abuse Against Seniors: A Review of the Research Literature with Special Reference to the Canadian Situation," *The Research and Statistics Division of the Justice Department of Canada*, 2009.

310 Sandie Ronaldo and Litsa Sourtzis, "W5 Investigation Reveals National Crisis: Homicide in Care Homes," *CTV News*, September 28, 2013.

311 Melissa Mancini, "At Least 29 Long-Term Care Residents Killed by Fellow Residents in 6 Years," *CBC News*, January 20, 2019.

312 Ibid.

313 Geoff Leo, "Depleted National Stockpile Leaves Canada Reliant on China for Masks, Gowns and Other Supplies During Pandemic," *CBC News*, May 6, 2020.

314 Avery Haines, "Whistleblower Says Workers at Nursing Homes Aren't Being Given Protective Gear," *CTV News*, March 31, 2020.

315 Ainslie MacLellan, "PPE Shortages Persist at Quebec Long-Term Care Home with More Than Half of the Residents Infected," *CBC News*, April 23, 2020.

316 Julie Ireton, "Field Visits by Phone, Locked-Up PPE Flagged by Nursing Home Staff in 1st Wave, Documents Show," *CBC News*, October 7, 2020.

317 CBC, "Survivor Stories from a Deadly Covid-19 Outbreak at a New Brunswick Nursing Home," *CBC News*, December 8, 2021.

318 James Keller, "How Prepared are Our Hospitals for the Coronavirus Outbreak?" *The Globe and Mail*, March 15, 2020.

319 Kerri Breen, "Coronavirus Pandemic Puts Canada's Supply of Ventilators in the Spotlight," *Global News*, March 17, 2020.

ENDNOTES

320 Mike Crowley, "Some of Ontario's Biggest Hospitals are Filled Beyond Capacity Nearly Every Day New Data Reveals," *CBC News*, January 22, 2020.

321 Elizabeth Fraser, "Campbellton Hospital Takes 'Extreme' Steps After Running Out of Beds," *CBC News*, November 21, 2019.

322 Jim Vibert, "Covid Lockdown Leaves Long Surgical Delays in Nova Scotia," *Saltwire News*, July 29, 2020.

323 Chris Stoodley, "Health Authority Handling Backlog of Colonoscopies," *City News (Halifax)*, August 30, 2020.

324 Allison Jones, "Delayed Cardiac Surgeries Due to Coronavirus May Have Caused 35 deaths in Ontario: Minister," *The Canadian Press for Global News*, April 28, 2020.

325 Licia Corbella, "Corbella: Alberta Man Died from the Lockdown, Not Covid-19." *The Calgary Herald*, June 30, 2020.

326 Nicole Bogart, "'He Never Got a Chance': B.C. Man Dies After Surgery Cancelled Due to Covid-19," *CTV News*, May 3, 2020.

327 Aaron D'Andrea, "Covid-Strained Health Care Led to 4K Deaths. How Do We Stop It From Happening Again?" *Global News*, November 30, 2021.

328 Jennifer Henderson, "Hospitals Empty Beds Before Wave of Covid-19 Admissions," *The Halifax Examiner*, April 2, 2020.

329 Rachel Cave, "Fifty Hospital Patients Waiting for Nursing Home Beds Have Been Transferred, Says Province," *CBC News*, March 24, 2020.

330 Kelly Grant and Tu Thanh Ha, "How Shoring up Hospitals for Covid-19 Contributed to Canada's Long-Term Care Crisis," *The Globe and Mail*, May 20, 2021.

331 Ibid.

332 Frances Woolley, "Coronavirus Is About to Reveal How Fragile Our Health System Is," *Policy Options*, March 19, 2020.

333 Barbara Sibbald, "What Happened to Hospital Patients That Had "Nowhere to Go?" *CMAJ News*, May 15, 2020.

334 Kelly Grant and Tu Thanh Ha, "How Shoring up Hospitals for Covid-19 Contributed to Canada's Long-Term Care Crisis," *The Globe and Mail*, May 20, 2021.

335 Rachel Cave, "Senior Sent Home from Hospital Was Waiting for a Nursing Home Bed, Says Family," *CBC News*, March 24, 2020.

336 Kelly Grant and Tu Thanh Ha, "How Shoring Up Hospitals for Covid-19 Contributed to Canada's Long-Term Care Crisis," *The Globe and Mail*, May 20, 2021.

337 Ibid.

338 Ibid.

339 Stephanie Nolen, "What Happened at Northwood?" *The Coast,* April 15, 2021.

340 Ibid.

341 Kelly Grant and Tu Thanh Ha, "How Shoring Up Hospitals for Covid-19 Contributed to Canada's Long-Term Care Crisis," *The Globe and Mail,* May 20, 2021.

342 Ibid.

343 The Canadian Press, "Lawsuits Over Covid-19 Handling in Nursing Homes Raise Questions About Standards of Care," *CTV News,* May 3, 2020.

344 Heidi Petracek, "Proposed Northwood Lawsuit Expanded to Seek Damages from Nova Scotia Government," *CTV Atlantic,* June 24, 2020.

345 Miriam Katawazi, "$40M Class Action Lawsuit Alleges Ontario Long-Term Care Home Did Not Follow Provincial Covid-19 Orders," *CTV News Toronto,* May 26, 2020.

346 Allison Hanes, "Doctor's Suicide a Tragic Wake-Up Call," *The Montreal Gazette,* January 12, 2021.

347 Catherine McDonald, "Coronavirus: Toronto Hospital Nurse Who Died by Suicide Remembered as Caring, Dedicated," *Global News,* January 25, 2021.

348 Canadian Institute for Health Information, "Covid-19 Cases and Deaths in Health Care Workers in Canada," *CIHI,* August 19, 2021.

7. The Road Forward

349 Doug Ford (@fordnation). 2020. "Nothing is more important than health care." Twitter, September 18, 2020, 3:58 p.m. https://twitter.com/fordnation/status/1307029959177908225/video.

350 CBC, "'Extremely Concerned': Protesters Decry Ontario Health-Care Cuts, Changes." *CBC News,* November 9, 2019.

351 Charles Russell and Jennie Russell, "Proposed $200M Private Orthopedic Surgery Facility Would be Largest in Alberta's History," *CBC News,* August 10, 2020.

352 James Wilt, "The Devastation of Manitoba: An Autopsy of Pallister's Austerity Regime," August 28, 2019.

353 Jocelyne Richer, "'We Will Not be Dictated to': Quebec Premier Legault Warns Ottawa Over Health Care," *The Canadian Press for The National Post,* November 14, 2018.

354 Matt Haig, "10 Eternal Reasons to Feel Hopeful, According to Matt Haig," *British Vogue,* August 30, 2020.

ENDNOTES

355 Ibid.

356 Jon Tattrie, "Cape Breton Boasts 3 of Canada's Top 5 Public Golf Courses," *CBC News*, August 1, 2017.

357 Tom Ayers, "Political Heavyweights Back Campaign for Airport Near Inverness Golf Course," *CBC News*, June 25, 2019.

358 Michael Gorman, "Nova Scotia Sees Spike in Child Poverty Rates," *CBC News*, February 28, 2019.

359 Statista Research Department, "Average Tuition Fee for Full-Time Canadian Undergraduate Students in Canada in the 2021/22 Academic Year, by Province," *Statista*, November 22, 2021.

360 Statistics Canada, "Canadian Income Survey 2019," March 23, 2021, https://www150.statcan.gc.ca/n1/daily-quotidien/210323/dq210323a-eng.htm.

361 Nicole Sturgeon, "Why Governments Should Prioritize Well-Being," filmed July 2019, Scotland, TEDSummit 9:51, https://www.ted.com/talks/nicola_sturgeon_why_governments_should_prioritize_well_being?language=en.

362 Lucy Bennett, "Budget 2019: Massive Boost for Mental health," *nzherald.co.nz*, May 29, 2019.

363 Dougal Sutherland, "Mental health Wins Record Funding in New Zealand's First 'Well-Being Budget,'" *The Conversation*, May 30, 2019.

364 Andre Mayer, "Buying our way Out of Pandemic Malaise is Hurting the Planet, Experts say," *CBC News*, August 14, 2021.

365 Michael Bradley, *Crisis of Clarity* (Toronto: Summerhill Press, 1987), 86.

366 Ibid., 80.

367 C. David Naylor, Andrew Boozary, and Owen Adams, "Canadian-Federal/Provincial /Territorial funding of Universal Health care: Fraught History, Uncertain future," *CMAJ* 192, no. 45 (November 2020): E1408–E1412, https://doi.org/10.1503/cmaj.200143.

368 Ibid.

369 Tom McIntosh, "The disingenuous demands of Canada's Premiers for $28 Billion in Health-Care Funding," *The Conversation*, March 28, 2021.

370 C. David Naylor, Andrew Boozary, and Owen Adams, "Canadian-Federal/Provincial /Territorial funding of Universal Health care: Fraught History, Uncertain future," *CMAJ* 192, no. 45 (November 2020): E1408–E1412, https://doi.org/10.1503/cmaj.200143.

371 Tom McIntosh, "The disingenuous demands of Canada's Premiers for $28 Billion in Health-Care Funding," *The Conversation*, March 28, 2021.

372 C. David Naylor, Andrew Boozary, and Owen Adams, "Canadian-Federal/Provincial /Territorial funding of Universal Health care: Fraught

History, Uncertain future," *CMAJ* 192, no. 45 (November 2020): E1408–E1412, https://doi.org/10.1503/cmaj.200143.

373 Jennifer Brady, "167 Canadian Health Professionals Call for a Basic Income," *UBI Works*, May 2020.

374 Ibid.

375 B. Singh Bolaria and Harley Dickinson, *Health, Illness, and Health care in Canada* (Scarborough: Nelson Thompson Learning, 2002), 38.

376 Claire Conway, "Poor Health: When Poverty Becomes Disease," *University of California News*, January 7, 2020.

377 André Picard, *Matters of Life and Death*, (British Columbia: Douglas & McIntyre, LTD. 2013), 187

378 Ibid., 186.

379 Ibid., 187.

380 Christian H. Cooper, "Why Poverty Is Like a Disease," *Nautilus*, April 17, 2017.

381 Ibid.

382 Brian Goldman, "The Health Cost of Being Poor," *CBC News*, February 3, 2020.

383 Marcelo Tonelli, Kwok-Cho Tang, and Pierre-Gerlier Forest, "Canada Needs a "Health in All Policies" Action Plan Now," *CMAJ* 192, no. 3 (January 20, 2020): E61–E67, https://doi.org/10.1503/cmaj.190517

384 Ibid.

385 Ibid.

386 Richard Cannings, "Time to Take a Serious Look at Basic Income," last modified May 24, 2020, https://richardcannings.ndp.ca/news/time-take-serious-look-basic-income.

387 Jennifer Brady, "167 Canadian Health Professionals Call for a Basic Income," *UBI Works*, May 2020.

388 Claire Conway, "Poor Health: When Poverty Becomes Disease," *University of California News*, January 7, 2020.

389 Heidi Petracek, "'No Heart Medication, No Food': N.S. Woman Says That Will be Her Choice After Rent Increase," *CTV News*, October 29, 2020.

390 Stephen Cooke, "Hundreds Attend Rent Control Rally in Halifax's Parade Square," *Saltwire*, November 7, 2020.

391 Leslie Young, "Hundreds of Canadians Die Every Year Because They Can't Afford Medications: Nurses' Union," *Global News*, May 1, 2018.

392 Shikha Gupta and Mary Ann McColl, "Without Pharmacare, Canadians with Disabilities Rationing Drugs Due to High Prescription Costs," *The Conversation*, December 6, 2020.

ENDNOTES

393 Editorial, "Canada Needs Universal Medicare," *The Lancet*, October 19, 2019, https://doi.org/10.1016/S0140-6736(19)32324-4.

394 Lee-Anne Goodman, "Canada Pays Too Much for Generic Drugs: Study," *The Canadian Press for Global News*, October 14, 2014.

395 André Picard, "Action Not Excuses on Drug Coverage," *The Globe and Mail*, April 6, 2011.

396 M. Sorin, E.L. Franco, and A. Quesnel-Vallée, "Inter-and Intraprovincial Inequities in Public Coverage of Cancer Drug Programs Across Canada: A Plea for the Reestablishment of a Pan-Canadian Pharmacare Program," *Current Oncology (Toronto, Ontario)* 26, no. 4 (2019): 266–269, https://doi.org/10.3747/co.26.4867.

397 Eric Hoskins et al., "A prescription for Canada: Achieving Pharmacare for All," *Health Canada*, June 2019.

398 Jan Malek, "Covid-19 Shows That Pharmacare is Needed Now," *Council of Canadians*, 2021.

399 Heart & Stroke Canada, "Atrial Fibrillation," last modified September 18, 2022, https://www.heartandstroke.ca/heart-disease/conditions/atrial-fibrillation.

400 CBC, "5 Pharmacare Question and Answers," *CBC News*, February 27, 2018.

401 CHC, "Pharmacare," *The Canadian Health Coalition*, July 24, 2021.

402 Eric Hoskins et al., "A prescription for Canada: Achieving Pharmacare for All," *Health Canada*, June, 2019.

403 Ibid.

404 Theresa McManus, "New Westminster-Burnaby MP Not Giving Up on Public Universal Pharmacare Program," March 1, 2021.

405 Jennifer Cole, "Time to Free Canada's Long-Term Care System from Its Backward History," *Canadian Dimension*, September 29, 2020.

406 Amy Twomey, "Pursuing Different Paths in Long-Term Care: Manitoba, Ontario and the Politics of Commercialization," (PhD thesis, Trent University, May, 2014).

407 Ibid., 62- 64.

408 Ibid., 72.

409 Jennie Russell, "After Decades of Systemic Issues, Time to Finally Overhaul Alberta Long-Term Care, Experts Say," *CBC News*, May 12, 2020.

410 Albert Banerjee, "An Overview of Long-Term Care in Canada and Selected Provinces and Territories," *Research Gate*, October 2007, 4.

411 Ibid., 5.

412 Kelly Grant, "No Place to Grow Old," *The Globe and Mail*, January 21, 2022.

413 Canadian Institute for Health Information, "Pandemic Experience in the Long-Term Care Sector: How Does Canada Compare with Other Countries?" Ottawa, ON: CIHI, June 2020.

414 Adam Miller, "Canada Failed to Protect Elderly in First Wave of Covid-19–Will the Same Mistakes be Made Again?" *CBC News*, September 26, 2020.

415 Canadian Institute for Health Information, "Pandemic Experience in the Long-Term Care Sector: How Does Canada Compare with Other Countries?" Ottawa, ON: CIHI, June 2020.

416 Adam Miller, "Canada Failed to Protect Elderly in First Wave of Covid-19–Will the Same Mistakes be Made Again?" *CBC News*, September 26, 2020.

417 Marcelo Tonelli, Kwok-Cho Tang, and Pierre-Gerlier Forest, "Canada Needs a "Health in All Policies" Action Plan Now," *CMAJ* 192, no. 3 (January 20, 2020): E61–E67, https://doi.org/10.1503/cmaj.190517.

418 Abdul Malik and Duncan Kinney, "Exclusive: Alberta Government Quietly Gave the NHL $4 Million During Pandemic," *Progress Report*, November 29, 2020.

419 Chandler Walter, "Alberta Drops Corporate Tax Rate to 8% a Year-and-a-Half Earlier Than Planned," *DH News*, July 2, 2020.

420 Dylan Short, "Alberta Asks for Federal Help Dealing with Covid-19 as Nearly 1,000 People Are in Hospital," *Calgary Herald*, September 21, 2020.

421 Alec Warkentin, "Greg Price: Slipping Through the Health care System," *Calgary Journal*, June 18, 2018.

422 Vanessa Milne, Joshua Tepper, and Maureen Taylor, "Anatomy of a Referral: Why Wait Times for Specialists are Still Too Long," *HealthyDebate*, February 9, 2017.

423 Ibid.

424 Vanessa Milne, Joshua Tepper, and Sachin Pendharkar, "Four Ways Canada Can Shorten Wait Times For Specialists," *HealthyDebate*, February 23, 2017.

425 Ibid.

426 *Canadian Institute for Health Information*, "How Canada Compares: Results from the Commonwealth Fund's 2016 International Health Policy Survey of Adults in 11 Countries," Ottawa, ON: CIHI, 2017.

427 The Canadian Nurses Association and Canadian Medical Association, *Integration: A New Direction for Canadian Health Care*, (Ottawa: Canadian Nurses Association, Canadian Medical Association, and Health Action Lobby, November 2013).

428 McMaster University, "Health Tapestry," *McMaster University Department of Family Medicine*, last modified September 20, 2022, https://

ENDNOTES

fammed.mcmaster.ca/research/research-projects-programs/projects/health-tapestry/.

429 Sandie Rinaldo, "How a Powerful Organization Protects Doctors from Medical Error Claims," *CTV News*, March 13, 2021.

430 Ibid.

431 Ibid.

432 Kathleen Findlay, "Taxpayers Should Stop Subsidizing Doctor's Liability Costs," *HuffPost*, June 11, 2016.

433 Theresa Boyle, "Suing a Doctor? Your Tax Dollars Will be Used Against You," *The Toronto Star*, September 15, 2015.

434 Sandie Rinaldo, "How a Powerful Organization Protects Doctors From Medical Error Claims," *CTV News*, March 13, 2021.

435 Kathleen Findlay, "Taxpayers Should Stop Subsidizing Doctor's Liability Costs," *HuffPost*, June 11, 2016.

436 Centre For Public Impact, "*Levensloopbestendige* (Apartments for Life) in the Netherlands," August 3, 2018.

437 Tiffany Cassidy, "Successful Care for Aging Populations Around the World," *Saskatchewan Seniors Mechanism*, November 2020, 7.

438 Steven E. Waldron, Thomas Agresta, and Theresa Wilkes, "Technology Tools and Trends for Better Patient Care: Beyond the EHR." *Family Practice Management* 24, no. 5 (September–October 2017): 28–32.

439 Independent Age, "Technology to Keep You Safe at Home," last modified September 15, 2022, https://www.independentage.org/get-advice/support-care/help-at-home/technology-to-keep-you-safe-at-home.

440 Catharine Tunney, "Canada Hires Company For $1.14M to Bring Trash Back Home from the Philippines," *CBC News*, May 22, 2019.

441 Amanda Connolly, "Why is Loblaw Getting $12M to Install New Refrigerators? McKenna Under Fire for New Funding," *Global News*, April 9, 2019.

442 Julia Horowitz, "IMF Slashes US and China Growth Forecasts," *CNN News*, January 25, 2022.

443 CBC, "Brian Gallant Halts Nursing Home Fee Changes," *CBC News*, September 9, 2015.

444 "Guardians of Public Health," Canadian Health Coalition, accessed September 21, 2022, https://archive.healthcoalition.ca/guardians-of-public-health-care/.

445 "About," BloodWatch, last modified September 19, 2022, https://bloodwatch.org/about/.

446 "We're Here to Help You Get An Important Message Out," PatientProtection.Health care, last modified July 27, 2022, https://www.patientprotection.health care/helping-the-media/.

447 "Our Story," Canadian Doctors for Medicare, last modified September 15, 2022, https://www.canadiandoctorsformedicare.ca/story.

448 Noam Chomsky, *Requiem for the American Dream* (New York: Seven Stories Press, 2017), 150

449 Ibid.

450 B. Singh Bolaria and Harley D. Dickinson, *Health, Illness, and Health care in Canada* (Scarborough: Nelson Thompson Learning, 2002), 453.

451 Ibid., 448

452 Michael Bradley, *Crisis of Clarity* (Toronto: Summerhill Press, 1987), 49.

453 James Gorman, "Ancient Bones That Tell a Story of Compassion," *The New York Times*, December 17, 2012.

454 Ibid.

455 Andy Coglan, "Hunter-Gatherers Cared for First Known Ancient Invalid," *New Scientist*, October 11, 2010.

456 Jacquelin Bhabla, "Half a Century of a Right to Health?" *UN Chronicle*, January 31, 2017.

457 Rachel Carson, Man is a part of nature, and his war against nature is inevitably a war against himself," Nieman Foundation, last modified April 25, 2018, https://nieman.harvard.edu/stories/man-is-a-part-of-nature-and-his-war-against-nature-is-inevitably-a-war-against-himself/.

458 Antonia Maioni, *Health Care in Canada* (Don Mills: Oxford University Press, 2015), 7.

459 Bradley, 219–220.

460 Bradley, 220.

461 Shirley Abbott, *Womenfolks: Growing Up Down South* (United States: University of Arkansas Press, March 15, 2017), 1.

462 Alas Elassar, "A Nurse Revealed the Tragic Last Words of His Coronavirus Patient: 'Who's Going to Pay for It?'" *CNN*, April 11, 2020.

Index

Please note that the italicized "*n*" following page numbers refers to an endnote and its relevant number.

A

Abbott, Shirley, 283, 283*n*461
ABC News, 39*n*67
Abdelmalek, Mark, 39, 39*n*67
"About" (bloodwatch.org), 273*n*445
Abrams, Melinda K., 30*n*42
"Absurdly High Cost of Insulin Explained: Why Americans Ration a Drug Discovered in the 1920s, The" (Belluz), 36*n*56
accountability, 59, 89, 93, 250, 252, 270, 271
"Action Not Excuses on Drug Coverage" (Picard), 238*n*395
Adams, Owen, 224*n*367, 225*n*368, 225*n*370, 226*n*372
Adler, Nancy, 233
Advisory Council on the Implementation of National Pharmacare, 241
Aetna health service company, 44
affordability argument, 154, 270
costs *vs.* benefits of, 154–156
healthcare and, 156–157
Affordable Care Act (2010, U.S.), 30
Afghanistan War, financial losses from, 89
"After Decades of Systemic Issues, Time to Finally Overhaul Alberta Long-Term Care, Experts Say" (J. Russell), 245*n*409
"After One Year, Pay-for-Plasma Clinic in Moncton Sees Almost 300 Visits Weekly" (Weldon), 99*n*170
aging population, growth of, 64–65
lack of community infrastructure for, 65–66
Agresta, Thomas, 267*n*438
Agriculture Canada, 88
Akbulut, Bengi, 222
Akerlof, George, 175
Alberta,
corporate tax rate dropped and effects of in, 152–153, 253
Covid-19 hospital admissions in, 253
failures of private long-term care during Covid-19, 167–168
financial wastage in, 88
Kenny's claim of new jobs in, 153–154
misuse of tax dollars in, 253
privatization of health care in, 83–84, 216
problems with for-profit long-term care homes in, 119
restructuring of health services

by Ralph Klein, 79
  surgeries cancelled during Covid-19, 201
"Alberta Asks for Federal Help Dealing with Covid-19 as Nearly 1,000 People Are in Hospital" (Short), 253*n*240
"Alberta Drops Corporate Tax Rate to 8% a Year-and-a-half Earlier Than Planned" (Walter), 253*n*419
Alberta Health Services, 245
Alberta Netcare eReferrals, 255–256
Alcock, Susan, 133
Alexander, Frank, 192
Alini, Erica, 180*n*280
Alker, Joan, 31*n*45
Alperovitz, Gar, 175
Alternet, 38*n*65
American Broadcasting Company (ABC), 39
American Medical Association (AMA), 28, 176–177
"Americans Stage 'Caravan to Canada' to Buy Cheaper Insulin" (CBC), 35*n*55
analysis-paralysis culture, 61
"Anatomy of a Referral: Why Wait Times for Specialists are Still Too Long" (Milne, Tepper & Taylor), 254*n*422–*n*423
Anbang insurance group, 115
  chairman jailed, 115, 118
"Ancient Bones That Tell a Story of Compassion" (J. Gorman), 280*n*453–*n*454
Angus Reid survey, 239
"Another Person Has Died After Rationing Insulin" (Jones), 36*n*58

Anti-Tuberculin League, 11
anti-war protests, 72
archeology of health care, 279–281
Archives of Internal Medicine, 46
Armstrong, Pat, 182*n*288
Armstrong, Peter, 156*n*257
As It Happens (CBC), 35*n*55
Associated Press, 113
"Astonishing High Administrative Costs of U.S. Healthcare, The" (Frakt), 48*n*80
Athabasca Extendicare, 119
"At Least 29 Long-Term Care Residents Killed by Fellow Residents in 6 years" (Mancini), 193*n*311–*n*312
atrial fibrillation, 239–240
"Atrial Fibrillation" (Heart and Stroke Canada), 240*n*399
Auditor General's Office, 250, 251
Australia,
  hybrid model of public and private healthcare in, 160–161
  private insurance tiering in, 161–162
"Authorities Ignored Early Warnings from Northwood's Long-Term Care Workers and Unions" (McCracken), 188*n*304
autonomy argument (for the rich buying care), 168–170, 174–175
"Average Tuition Fee for Full-Time Canadian Undergraduate Students in Canada in the 2021/22 Academic Year by Province" (*Statista* Research Department), 219*n*359
Ayers, Tom, 219*n*357

INDEX

B

"Bad Medicine: Trade Treaties, Privatization and Health Care Reform in Canada" (Grieshaber-Otto & Sinclair), 95n159, 96n160
Bains, Camille, 81n138
Banerjee, Albert, 246, 247, 247n410–n411
Bank of Canada, 74, 146
  wastage by, 88
Bank of Montreal (BMO), 91
Banting, Sir Frederick, 4, 175, 176
Barnett, Jessica C., 30n43, 31n46, 177n276
Barrette, Leon, 184
BC College of Physicians, 103
Beaudet, Dr. Alain, 154
Bedford, Rita, 140, 141
  disintegration cost loss of personal dignity, 143–144
"Bedlam Over Beds: We Can No Longer Ignore Our Long-Term-Care Crisis" (Picard), 65n106, 66n107–n108
Beers, Randi, 127n211
Bégin, Monique, 61, 64, 244
Bell, Dr. Bob, 160, 160n261, 161, 161n262–n263
Bellon, Pierre, 85
Belluz, Julia, 35, 36n56
Benefits Pro, 177n274
Bennett, Dean, 83n143
Bennett, Lucy, 221n362
Berchick, Edward R., 30n43–n44, 31n46, 177n276
Bergman, Brian, 79n135
Best, Charles, 175, 176
Beveridge, Sir William, 18
Bhabha, Jacqueline, 281n456
Bigelow, Dr. Wilfred G., 176
Big Pharma, 36, 148, 178
Bird, Hilary, 126n210
Blackwell, Richard, 75n120, 147n236
"Blood Safety and Availability" (WHO *Database on Blood Safety*), 98n169
blood selling (Canada),
  concerns about for-profit clinics, 99–100
  dangers of for-profit clinics and desperate donors, 101
  deregulation of blood system led to, 98–99
  privatization of, 273
blood selling (U.S.), 38–39, 97
  questionable screening processes in, 101
bloodwatch.org, 273, 273n445
"Bloody Mess, A: The Story Behind Paid Plasma in Canada" (Kingston), 98n167–n168, 100n172, 101n173
Blumenkranz, Erik, 43n74
Bobcaygeon's Pinecrest for-profit nursing home, 185
Bogart, Nicole, 200n326
Bolaria, B. Singh, 228, 228n375, 275, 275n450, 276n451
Bond and Botes Law Offices, 32n48
"To Boost Investments, End S.E.C. Rule That Spurs Stock Buybacks" (Lazonick), 146n235
Boozary, Andrew, 224n367, 225n368, 225n370, 226n372, 249
Boreal Health Partnership, 125
Boyce, Tom, 228
Boyle, Theresa, 262n433

Braddock, J. C., 282
Bradley, Michael, 10, 10*n*15, 12*n*17–*n*18, 13*n*19–*n*20, 14*n*21–*n*24, 15*n*25–*n*27, 16*n*28, 17*n*29, 19*n*31, 224*n*365–*n*366, 277, 277*n*452, 282, 283, 283*n*459–*n*460
Brady, Jennifer, 227*n*373, 228*n*374, 232*n*387
Brampton Civic Hospital, 123–125
   health care emergency from overcrowding in 2020, 125
   mired in controversy, 123–125
   as Ontario's first P3, 123
"Brampton Council Declares Health-Care Emergency Amid Hospital Overcrowding Wait Times" (Westoll), 125*n*208
Breen, Kerri, 197*n*31
Brewer, Dr. Rebecca, 68
"Brian Gallant Halts Nursing Home Fee Changes" *(CBC News)*, 271*n*443
"Brian Sinclair Inquest Recommendations Slammed by ER Doctors" *(CBC Manitoba)*, 134*n*220
Brief History of Canada, A (Reindeau), 1181*n*285
British Columbia,
   for-profit homes and public funding of, 167
   health service workers' strike in, 80
   long-term care homes sold then taken back by local health authority, 115–117, 190
   new beds needed in, 66
   public money going to for-profit homes not spent on resident's care, 118
   regulatory attempts to monitor for-profit clinics, 102
   slash and burn tactics to health care in, 80–81
   surgery cancellations during Covid-19, 200
British Columbia Care Providers Association Report, 66
British Medical Journal, 121
British Vogue, 217*n*354–*n*355
Broadbent Institute, The, 75*n*122
Brock, Stan, 41–42
"Broken Homes" (Curry), 190, 190*n*307
Brooks, Neil, 174, 175*n*272
Brown, Patrick, 125
Bruyére Research Institute, 237, 237*n*394
Bryan, Don, 119
Bryan, Sheila, 119
Buchman, Dr. Sandy, 194
"Budget 2019: Massive Boost for Mental Health" (L. Bennett), 221*n*362
Bulletin on Aging & Health, National Bureau of Economic Research, 45*n*77
"Bull Moose Party", 27
Burgon, Anne-Marie, 140, 141
Burial 9, 279–280
Burlington Laser Eye Centre, 105
"Buying Our Way Out of Pandemic Malaise is Hurting the Planet, Experts Say" (Mayer), 222*n*364

INDEX

C

Cable News Network (CNN), 271
Cadmean victory, 8
Calgary Herald, The, 200n325, 253n420
Calgary Journal, 254n421
Callaghan, Brian, 37
Callaghan, Dr. John C., 176
Calvary United Church, Weyburn, Saskatchewan, 12
Cambie Surgeries Corp., 80, 102, 105
Cambridge Health Alliance, 40
Campbell, Archie, 188
Campbell, David, 218
Campbell, Gordon, 80
"Campbelton Hospital Takes Extreme Steps After Running Out of Beds" (Fraser), 69n112, 198n321
Campbelton Regional Hospital, New Brunswick, 68, 198, 202
Canada,
   budget cuts reduce acute-care beds in, 64–65
   children's healthcare compared to the US, 31
   concerns about pre-Covid infrastructure in, 197–198
   corporate investments rates drop, 153
   corporate tax rates drop, 75, 78, 81–82, 89–90, 153
   cost of Medicare compared to US healthcare, 30–31
   federal budgets 1985–95 scaled back or froze health transfers, 225
   federal funding transfers reduced starting in 2016–17, 75
   federal government financial wastage by, 88, 89
   federal transfer payments for health care, 76, 77, 81–82
   40%–50% of budgets for health-care costs, 148–149
   government deficit reductions in mid to late-1990s, 263–264
   government expenditures 2016–17, 156
   harsh climate and isolation in, 19
   health care as provincial/territorial responsibility, 223–224
   occupancy rates in hospitals, 68–69
   pandemic preparation limited by lack of flexibility pre-Covid-19, 201–202
   patient care in delivered from provider focus, 257–258
   perfect storm in hospitals in, 64–65
   personal bankruptcy rate in from medical costs, 45
   pioneers' survival required interdependence, 19
   political ties to Britain, 17
   premiers asking for health care funding in 2020, 215–216
   profits of top five banks in, 91
   69% of public funding for health care in 2018, 76
   tax loopholes for elite, 91, 92, 93
   wasteful and erratic spending by governments in, 87–89
Canada Emergency Response Benefit (CERB), 239
"Canada Failed to Protect Elderly in First Wave of Covid-19—Will the Same Mistakes be Made Again?" (Miller),

249n414, 250n416
Canada Health Act (1984) (CHA), 76, 101, 182
   charter challenge by Brian Day in BC, 80–81
   exclusion of long-term care from, 244
   home care services not included in, 266–267, 268
   interconnectedness between federal and provincial governments, 223–224
   long-term care not incorporated into as insured service, 182
   long-term care stand-alone status outside, 248
   prohibits user-fees and extra-billing in theory, 101–103
Canada Health and Social Transfer (CHST) program, 77–78, 225
   block funding for long-term care, 245
Canada Health Transfer (CHT), 156
   frozen or cut back between 1985 and 1995, 225
   Harper reduced the escalator, 226
   increases in from 2004, 225–226
   reduced between 1995/6 and 1998/9, 225
"Canada Hires Company For $1.14M to Bring Trash Back Home from the Philippines" (Tunney), 269n440
"Canada Needs a 'Health in All Policies' Action Plan Now" (Tonelli, Tang & Forest), 251n417
"Canada Needs Universal Medicare" *(The Lancet)*, 237n393
"Canada Pays Too Much for Generic Drugs: Study" (Goodman), 237n394
Canada Revenue Agency (CRA), 91, 269
"Canada's Hardest Hit Nursing Homes Lost 40% of Residents in just 3 Months of the Pandemic" (Carman), 185n293, 185n295
"Canada's 'National Shame': Covid-19 in Nursing Homes" (Samuel), 181n284
Canada Social Transfer (CST), 156, 225
"Canada's Transformation Under Neoliberalism" (Stanford), 72n116, 73n117–n118, 74n119
"Canada's Unemployment Rate Reaches 13.7%" *(The Canadian Press)*, 180n282
"Canada Tops 100,000 Reported Coronavirus Cases" *(CBC News)*, 180n281
Canada West Foundation, 77n127
Canadian Association of Emergency Physicians, 134
Canadian Blood Services, 99
Canadian Broadcasting Corporation (CBC), 3, 35, 84, 115, 134, 143, 180n281, 197, 218, 271n443
   Douglas voted greatest Canadian by, 3–4
Canadian Centre for Policy Alternatives (CCPA), 90n152, 91, 91n156, 95n159–n160, 120n203, 182n288
Canadian Dimension, 6n4–n7, 7n8–n9, 72n116, 73n117–n118,

INDEX

74n119, 242n405
Canadian Doctors for Medicare, 81, 106, 274, 274n447
"Canadian Doctors Help Critically Ill Pregnant Woman Survive and Save Baby's Life" (Favaro, St. Philip & A. M. Jones), 155n256
Canadian Encyclopedia, The, 8n10–n11, 79n135
"Canadian Federal/Provincial/Territorial Funding of Universal Health Care: Fraught History, Uncertain Future" (Naylor, Boozary & Adams), 224n367, 225n368, 225n370, 226n372
Canadian Federation of Nurses Unions, 235
Canadian health-care policy, 94–96
  commercialization concerns for, 95–96
Canadian Health Coalition, The (CHC), 241n401, 250, 273, 273n444
Canadian Health Services Research Foundation (CHSRF), 159n258
Canadian Immunization Research Network (CIRN), Halifax, 154
Canadian Imperial Bank of Commerce (CIBC), 91
"*Canadian Income Survey 2019*" (Statistics Canada), 219n360
Canadian Institute for Health Information (CIHI), 77n126, 78, 78n130–n131, 81, 119, 181n283, 212, 212n348, 247, 248, 248n413, 249, 249n415, 257, 257n426
Canadian Institutes of Health Research (CIHR), 154, 154n255
Canadian Journal of Hospital Pharmacy, The, 59n85
Canadian Medical Association (CMA), 9, 194, 200, 244, 251, 255, 260n427, 269
  attacks on Medicare, 16
  task force created by to study health care resources, 182, 183
Canadian Medical Association Journal (CMAJ), 189n305, 224n367, 225n368, 226n372, 230, 231, 231n383–n385, 251n417
Canadian Medical Protective Association (CMPA), 261–262
  money saved from law firms could go back to Medicare, 262–263
  protection of doctors against malpractice claims, 261–262
  subsidized by Ontario taxpayers, 262
Canadian Museum of History, 79n134
Canadian Nurses Association, 260, 260n427
Canadian Plasma Resources (CPR), 99
Canadian Press, The, 58n83, 81n138–n139, 82n141, 83n143, 132n217, 133n218, 134n219, 180n282, 199n324, 210n343, 216n353, 237n394
Canadian Survey on Disability, 236
"Canadians Want Health Care to be the Focus for Political Parties in the Lead Up to the Election This Fall" (2019, Ipsos Canada), 3n2

Canadian Taxpayers Federation News Release, 89n150
Canadian Union of Public Employees (CUPE), 128n214
Cancer Care Manitoba, 216
cancer-drug coverage, 238
Cancer Olympics, The (McGee), 136, 136n222, 137n223–n224, 138n225–n228, 140n229
Cannings, Richard, 232n386
"Cape Breton Boasts 3 of Canada's Top 5 Public Golf Courses" (Tattrie), 218n356
Cape Breton Regional Hospital, 219
 Emergency Department, 67, 90
capitalism,
 arguments to promote profit accumulation, 146–147
 monopolies and abuse of workers in, 147
 rise of European linked to rise in Atlantic slave trade, 147
 as threat to Canadian Medicare, 287
cardiac stress tests, 110–111
Cardinal Meat Specialists Ltd., 88
Carillion plc, 125, 126, 127
caring characteristic of Canadians, 157, 279
Carling Manor, Ottawa, 196
Carman, Tara, 185n293, 185n295
Carmichael, Kevin, 75n120, 147n236
Carney, Mark, 74, 146
Caron, Guy, 232
Carr, Brendan, 202
Carrollian logic, 57
Carson, Rachel, 282n457, 457
Cascades senior care home,
Chilliwack, BC, 140, 141
Cassidy, Tiffany, 266n437
Cassista, Cecile, 272
Cauchon, Dr. Natalie, 198
Cave, Rachel, 202n329, 205n335
CBC Manitoba, 134n220
CBC News, 59n86, 60n87, 60n90, 60n92, 61n92, 64n101, 68n111–n112, 69n113, 70n114, 75n124, 79n133, 81n138–n139, 83n143, 84n145–n146, 92, 92n157–n158, 98n166, 99n170, 100n172, 101n173, 112n190, 115n195, 116n196, 117n199, 118n200, 119n201, 120n202, 125n209, 126n210, 127, 127n211, 127n212, 134n219, 141n230, 143, 143n231, 149n242, 150n243, 156n257, 160n260, 167n269, 180n281, 182n286, 183n289, 185n293, 185n295, 188n301–n302, 190n306, 191n308, 193n311–n312, 194n313, 195n315, 196n316–n317, 197, 198n320–n321, 202n329, 205n335, 215n350, 216n351, 218n356, 219n358, 222n364, 230n382, 241n400, 245n409, 249n414, 250n416, 269n440, 271n443
CBS News, 34n53, 35n54
Cecere, David, 40, 41n68
Center for Children and Families, Georgetown University, 31
Center for Patient Protection, The, 262, 273–274, 274n446
Centers for Disease Control and Prevention (CDC), 40, 188
Centre for Public Impact, 266n436
Chaleur Hospital, Bathurst, New

INDEX

Brunswick, 198
Champlain BASE e-Consult service (Ontario), \256
"Changing Nova Scotia's Healthcare System: Creating Sustainability Through Transformation" (Corpus Sanchez Consultancy), 60n88, 60n91, 61, 61n93, 61n95
Chapin, Christly Ford, 176
Charter of Rights and Freedoms (Canada), 80
CHCH News, 184n291
Chiasson, Paul, 81n139
Chin, Dr. Elaine, 108
Chomsky, Noam, 25, 26, 26n32, 27, 27n34–n35, 29, 274, 274n448–n449
Chrétien, Jean, 245
chronic diseases, 260–261
CHSLD-Ste-Dorothee, Quebec, 210
CHSLD Vigi Mont-Royal retirement home, Quebec, 195
Cigna health service company, 42, 44, 177
Cité-de-la-Santé Hospital, Laval, Quebec, 202–203
City News (Halifax), 199n323
City University, New York, 26
"Civil Case in Joan Rivers' Death Settled" (Winter), 114n192
civil rights marches, 72
class-action lawsuits on behalf of long-term care residents, 210–211
Cleveland Clinic Canada, 107, 108
Cliff, Sarah, 31
Clinton, Bill, 28
Cloutier, Paul-Émile, 197
CMAJ News, 204n333

CNBC News, 37n60–n61, 45n78, 178n277
CNN News, 271n442, 285n462
Coalition for Seniors and Nursing Home Residents' Rights (New Brunswick), 272
Coast, The, 188n301–n302, 188n303, 208n339–n340
code orange, 62–63
Coglan, Andy, 281n455
Cohen, Joshua, 43n75
Coldwell, M. J., 3, 13
Cole, Jennifer, 242n405
collectivism, 2
 compared to individualism in US, 24
College of Family Physicians, 3
Collip, James, 176
Columbia Broadcasting System (CBS), 34
Columbia University, New York, 166
commercialization of public health, 95–96
commercial trade treaties as danger to healthcare, 95, 96
Commonwealth Fund study, The, 2016, 30n42, 31
community health services, 85
 incorporation of long-term care into, 265–266
 success of integrated community clinics, 259–260
Community Medicine Service clinic, 62
Comox Valley Seniors Village, BC, 116
"Comparison of Hospital Administrative Costs in Eight Nations, A: US Costs Exceed All Others

321

by Far" (Himmelstein et al), 34*n*51–*n*52
computed tomography (CAT) scan, 254
Concordia University, Montreal, 222
Connolly, Amanda, 269*n*441
Constitution Act, 1867 (Canada), 223
Conversation, The, 96*n*162, 97*n*163, 221*n*363, 225*n*369, 225*n*371, 236*n*392
Conway, Claire, 228*n*376, 233*n*388
Cooke, Alex, 150*n*243
Cooke, Stephen, 235*n*390
"Coon Calls for Public Inquiry in Wake of Fredericton Teen's Suicide" *(CBC News)*, 70*n*114
Cooper, Christian H., 229*n*380, 230*n*381
Co-operative Commonwealth Party (CCF), 8
　beginnings of, 13–14
　campaigned for provincial health care in Saskatchewan, 223–224
　focussed on implementation of health insurance, 15
　implemented Hospital Insurance Plan in 1947, 15, 224
　as most popular party during WWII, 14
　opposition to, 14
　as party of the people, 29
　won 1944-Saskatchewan election, 14
Corbella, Licia, 200*n*325
"Corbella: Alberta Man Died from the Lockdown, Not Covid-19" (Corbella), 200*n*325
"Coronavirus: Canada Lost 1 Million Jobs in March" (Alini), 180*n*280
"Coronavirus Is About to Reveal How Fragile Our Health System Is" (Woolley), 203*n*332
"Coronavirus Pandemic Put's Canada's Supply of Ventilators in the Spotlight" (Breen), 197*n*319
"Coronavirus: Toronto Hospital Nurse Who Died by Suicide Remembered as Caring, Dedicated" (McDonald), 212*n*347
corporate greed, 74, 146–147, 148
"Corporate Tax Cuts, Lost Revenues and Lagging Business Investment" (Jackson), 75*n*122
"Corporate Tax Cuts Have Made Canada a Poorer Country" (Yiu), 78*n*132, 82*n*140
corporatization of healthcare system, 85, 94
Corpus Sanchez Consultancy, 60, 60*n*91, 61, 61*n*93, 61*n*95, 64
"Cost of Living, The: The Skyrocketing Price of a Lifesaving Medication" (Pohlman), 36*n*57
Cottrell, Linda, 207
Council of Canadians, The, 96, 96*n*161, 97*n*164, 239*n*398
counterculture, 72–73
Cove, Grace, 114, 115
Cove, Wyman, 114, 115
"Covid-19 Cases and Deaths in Health Care Workers in Canada" (CIHI), 212*n*348
Covid-19 pandemic, 31, 139, 154
　see also H1N1 virus; severe acute respiratory syndrome (SARS)

INDEX

announced by WHO as international public health emergency, 179, 180
Canadian seniors disproportionately ravaged by, 181
concerns about infrastructure in Canada highlighted by, 197, 211
deaths of seniors transferred from hospitals because of, 204, 205, 207
demonstrated need for national pharmacare plan, 239
as demonstration of failures of buying health, 170–171
effects on Canada, 179–181
emergency programs from federal government during, 232
ethical dilemma created by, 201–202, 206–207
etiology of, 179
exposed years of defunding, defrauding and deregulation, 201, 211
failure of private long-term care and, 167–168
frantic attempts to create space for patients across Canada, 200–204
illustrated vitalness of public healthcare systems, 270–271
impact of on regular operational procedures across Canada, 199–201
jobs loss during and loss of drug overage during, 239
lack of flex in pre-Covid Canadian system, 201–202
long-term care challenges in Canada and, 181–182, 248–249
number of health care workers who died during g, 211–212
overcrowded hospitals across Canada prior to, 200–203
PPE required for asymptomatic transmission, 188–189
protection of scarce hospital beds for, 206–207
second wave of, 215
shortages of PPE and staff treatment in Canada, 196–197, 211–212
short supply of staff and equipment in acute care, 211–212
staffing shortages and burnout in care homes, 186–187
worsened situation for seniors, 203, 205
"Covid-19 Shows That Pharmacare is Needed Now" (Malek), 239n398
"Covid Lockdown Leaves Long Surgical Delays in Nova Scotia" (Vibert), 198n322
"Covid-Strained Health Care Led to 4K Deaths. How Do We Stop It From Happening Again?" (D'Andrea), 201n327
Cox, Cynthia, 43n74, 44n76
Cribb, Robert, 108n187, 109n188, 110n189
Crime and Abuse Against Seniors: A Review of the Research Literature With Special Reference to the Canadian Situation (2009, Research and Statistics Division, Justice Department of Canada), 191
crisis intervention *vs.* disease prevention, 258
Crisis of Clarity (Bradley),

9n12, 10n15, 12n17–n18, 13n19–n20, 14n21–n24, 15n25–n27, 16n28, 17n29, 19n31, 224n365–n366, 277n452, 283n459–n460
"Crisis of Privatized Care in Ontario, The" (Ritt), 182n287
Crowley, Mike, 198n320
Cruise, Candice, 154, 155
CTV Atlantic News, 68, 68n110, 210n344
CTV eNews, 114n193
CTV News, 63, 63n100, 155n256, 195n314, 200n326, 210n343, 235n389, 261n429–n430, 262n431, 262n434
CTV News Toronto, 211n345
CTV News Winnipeg, 133n218
CTV Television Network, 262
Cullen, Terri, 46n79
Curie, Marie, 175
Current Oncology, 238n396
Curry, Paul, 190n307

D

"Daily Bed Census May Not Capture Full Extent of Hallway Health Care" (Lee-Shamrock), 69n113
Dajia Insurance Group, 118–119
Daken, Lexi, 69, 70
Daley, Lew, 175
D'Andrea, Aaron, 201n327
Dartmouth General Hospital, 51
Davis, Don, 82
Davis, Jack, 59
Day, Dr. Brian, 80
Deadly Spin (Potter), 42, 42n70–n71, 43n72–n73
"Death of Woman Hospitalized for 'Horrific' Bedsore Sparks Criminal Investigations" (M. Gorman), 120n202
DeerField's Wellness Centre, 107
defensive medicine, 46
defrauding,
  Covid-19 exposed in Canada, 201
  as essential component of neoliberalism, 76, 86–94
defunding,
  Covid-19 exposed in Canada, 201
  as essential component of neoliberalism, 76–86
  of health care in Nova Scotia, 151–152
deinstitutionalization of mental hospitals, 243
Delaney, Arthur, 41, 41n69
"Delayed Cardiac Surgeries Due to Coronavirus May Have Caused 35 deaths in Ontario: Minister" (A. Jones), 199n324
deliberate disintegration,
  Brian Sinclair's death as example of, 132–133
  defunding, defrauding and deregulation create measured form of, 130
  as essential component of neoliberalism, 76, 94–128
  exposed by Covid-19 in Canada, 201
Delolitte Canada, 200
"Depleted National Stockpile Leaves Canada Reliant on China For Masks, Gowns and Other Supplies During Pandemic" (Leo), 194n313
deregulation,
  Covid-19 exposed in

INDEX

Canada, 201
  as essential component of neoliberalism, 76, 94–128
"Devastation of Manitoba, The: An Autopsy of Pallister's Austerity Regime" (Wilt), 216*n*352
Devlin, Dr. Reuben, 67
Dewy, John, 27
Dey, Sujata, 96, 96*n*161, 97, 97*n*164
DH News, 253*n*419
diabetes, 33–34, 36, 37, 176, 178
Dickel, D. N., 280
Dickens, Bernard, 109
Dickinson, Harley D., 228, 228*n*375, 275, 275*n*450, 276*n*451
Dickson, Courtney, 117*n*199
Dion, Karine, 211
direct-acting oral anticoagulants (DOACs), 239–240
disability adjusted life years (DALY), 43–44
disabled persons, 5, 235–236, 279, 281
"Disaster in the Making. The Quiet Erosion of Canada's Regulation System" (Hennesy), 120*n*203
"Disingenuous demands of Canada's Premiers for $28 Billion in Health-Care Funding, The" (McIntosh), 225*n*369, 225*n*371
Djuric, Mickey, 160*n*259
"Doctor's Suicide a Tragic Wake-Up Call" (Hanes), 211*n*346
Donovan, Fabian, 235
Doran, G. H., 280
Doran, Wendy, 114, 115
Doucette, Keith, 63*n*100

Douglas, Thomas "Tommy" Clement, 3, 8, 19, 24, 29, 181, 216, 224
  advocated for including long-term care in Medicare, 242
  aware of enemies of Medicare, 72
  belief in pooling collective resources, 217–218
  birth of and parents, 11
  community involvement, 12
  dedicated to equality for all, 277
  elected as federal MP in 1935, 14
  elected as Saskatchewan premier in 1944, 14
  entered Baptist ministry, 12
  fought for concept of health as a human right, 281
  involvement in Estevan Mine Strike, 12–13
  knee surgery, 12
  voted by CBC as greatest Canadian, 3–4
Dr. Everett Chalmers Hospital emergency department, New Brunswick, 69
drug patents, 96
Dubinsky, Zach, 92, 92*n*157–*n*158
DuBreuil, Brian, 79*n*133
Dunham, Jerry, 199–200
Dunn, Fred, 245
Dunnington Chrissy, 119–120
Dutton, Paul, 105

E

Ebola epidemic, West Africa, 2013–14, 154
  Canadian experimental vaccines for, 154, 155
Economic Bill of Rights (1944, U.S.), 28
"Economics of Healthcare, The"

(Making), 163*n*264
Edmonton Journal, The, 168*n*270
Effective Public Healthcare Panacea Project, 77*n*125
"Effects of Rising Health Insurance Premiums on Employment, The" *(Bulletin on Aging & Health),* 45*n*77
Eggertson, Laura, 189*n*305
"80M Allocated for Health Super Board Startup Costs" *(CBC News),* 60n86
Elassar, Alas, 285*n*462
"Elderly N.S. Couple Hard-Pressed to Pay $309 to Access Medical Records" (Files), 114*n*193
Eli Lilly and Company, 36, 37, 178
"Eli Lilly Falls 5 Per Cent on Sluggish Growth in Animal Health, as it Weighs Options for the Unit" (Lavito), 37*n*61
"Eli Lilly Sees 2019 Profit, Revenue Above Estimates; Shares Rise" *(CNBC News),* 37*n*60
Elliott, Christine, 199
El-Sayed, Abdulrahman, 166, 167*n*268
Embassy West Senior Living, Ottawa, 247
emergency department,
  ambulance offload times for, 63
  to be seen (TBS) screen in, 288
  Brian Sinclair's 30-hour wait for treatment, 131–132
  Brian Sinclair's death sent shockwaves through all, 133
  closure of local, 67, 68
  code orange in Halifax, 62–63
  collapse of across Canada, 64–65
  consultancy reports on, 63–64
  culprits of decline in, 64–65
  early warnings from, 52–53
  effects of collapse of Canadian healthcare system on, 51–53
  effects of overcrowding of on other services, 53, 54
  as first point of contact for community, 53
  inward collapse of, 65–66, 69–70
  lack of primary-care services leads to more visits to, 69
  overcrowding of begins thirty years ago, 64–65
  pressures on across Canada, 66–68
  regionalization costs effects on, 59–60
  signs of deterioration in, 58
  utopian promises to repair, 54–58
"Emergency Room Overcrowding: Causes and Cures" (Milne, Tepper & Patch) 53*n*81, 64*n*103
employer health insurance, 44–45
  labour-market effects of increases in, 44–45
Enns, Dr. Charmaine, 116
equality for all, 277
Established Programs Financing Act (EPFA) (1977, Canada), 224
Estevan Mine Strike, 1931, 12–13
Etches, Dr. Vera, 106
evergreening (drug patent extensions), 96
"Exclusive: Alberta Government Quietly Gave the NHL $4 Million During Pandemic" (Malik & Kinney), 253*n*418
Executive Health Care, York Mills, Ontario, 108
"Explosive Changes in Klein's

Alberta, 1992–2000" (Canadian Museum of History), 79*n*134
Express Scripts, 177
Extended Health Care Services Program (ECHS), 243–244
extra billing (in for-profit health clinics), 102–107
   enforced by government, 103–104
extracorporeal membrane oxygenation (ECMO), 154–155
"'Extremely Concerned': Protesters Decry Ontario Health-Care Cuts, Changes" *(CBC News)*, 215*n*350

F

"Family of Brian Sinclair, Who Died During 34-Hour ER Wait, Says Racism Still an Issue" (Malone), 134*n*219
Family Practice Management, 267*n*438
Farm Security Act (1944, Saskatchewan), 14, 15
Favaro, Avis, 155*n*256
fecal occult blood test (FOBT), 137
federalism (Canadian), 19–21
   bonds provinces in provision of health care services, 76
   policy developments and, 19–20
Federal/Provincial/Territorial Working Group on Home Care, 247
"Field Visits by Phone, Locked-Up PPE Flagged by Nursing Home Staff in 1st Wave, Documents Show" (Ireton), 196*n*316

"Fifty Hospital Patients Waiting for Nursing Home Beds Have Been Transferred, Says Province" (Cave), 202*n*329
Files, Amy Stoodley, 114*n*193
Finance Canada, 153
financial accountability regarding expenditures (FARE) council, 250
   definition of, 250, 251
   to hold federal provincial governments to account, 253
   operation of under provincial/territorial offices of auditor general, 252
financialization of long-term care, 182–183
"Finding a Primary Care Provider in Nova Scotia—March 2021" (Nova Scotia Health), 58n84
Finlay, Kathleen, 262, 262*n*432, 263, 263*n*435, 274
First World War. *See* World War I (First World War)
Fitch Report, 64
"Five of Toronto's Most Exclusive Private Medical Clinics" (McKeon), 107*n*186
"5 Pharmacare Questions and Answers" *(CBC News)*, 241*n*400
"Five Reasons Free Markets Don't Work in Health Care" (El-Sayed), 167*n*268
"Five Reasons to Say No to More Corporate Tax Cuts" (Yalnizyan), 89*n*151
"Five Times Provincial Governments Failed with P3 Hospitals" (CUPE Nova Scotia), 128*n*214

Florida State University, 280
Fogarty, Grace, 235
Forbes, 43, 43*n*75, 88–89
Ford, Doug, 83, 215, 215*n*349, 216
Forest, Pierre-Gerlier, 231*n*383–*n*385, 251*n*417
Forgotten Generation, The: An Urgent Call for Reform in New Brunswick's Long-Term Care Sector (New Brunswick Nurses Union), 190–191, 190*n*306
for-profit consortiums, 120–121
"For-Profit Homes Fail to Deliver on Direct Care Funded by the Public, BC Seniors Advocate Says" (Lindsay), 118*n*200, 167*n*269
"For Profit Medical Companies are Making Tons of Money Taking Poor People's Blood" (*Alternet* & Posner), 38*n*65
"$40M Class Action Lawsuit Alleges Ontario Long-Term Care Home Did Not Follow Provincial Covid-19 Orders" (Katawazi), 211*n*345
"Four Ways Canada Can Shorten Wait Times For Specialists" (Milne, Tepper & Pendharkar), 254*n*424, 257*n*425
Fox, Terry, 4
Frakt, Austin, 48, 48*n*80
Franco, E.L., 238*n*396
Fraser, Dr. Margaret, 67, 90
Fraser, Elizabeth, 69*n*112, 198*n*321
free market, 145–146
 bankruptcies from health debt in US, 173–174
 core tenets of cannot be applied to health care, 162–163
 false notion of autonomy in US system of health insurance, 172–173
 health care not a competitive commodity in, 168
 innovation due to government financial support, 166–167
 monopolistic structure of health care distinguishes it, 165–166
 neoliberalism's obsession with, 169
 profits and healthcare services in, 148–149
 requires regulation, 146
 slave trade and, 147
 supply and demand model unworkable for healthcare, 162–163
 unpredictability in health care distinguishes it from, 163–164
 unworkable in drug market, 166
"Free Market Ideology Doesn't Work for Health Care" (Potter), 166*n*267
free-trade agreements, 73, 85
"Free up 'Dead Money,' Carney Exhorts Corporate Canada" (Carmichael, Blackwell & Keenan), 75*n*120, 147*n*236
Fuller, Colleen, 75*n*121, 85, 86*n*148
Fyfe, Dr. Murray, 115

G

Gabor, Thomas, 191*n*309
Gallant, Brian, 272
Gantz, Sarah, 32
Garratt, Barbara, 69
General Assembly of United Nations, 282
George, Judy, 37, 37*n*62–*n*63
Georgetown University Center for

INDEX

Children and Families 2018 report, 31*n*45
Gerster, Jane, 131*n*215, 132*n*216, 135n221
Gillis, Neil "Charlie", 285, 286
Gindin, Sam, 75
globalization, 73
  reduction of regulations with, 120
Global News, 60*n*88, 125*n*208, 131*n*215, 132*n*216, 135*n*221, 151*n*247–*n*249, 152*n*250–*n*251, 160*n*259, 180*n*280–*n*281, 197*n*319, 199*n*324, 201*n*327, 212*n*347, 235*n*391, 237*n*394, 269*n*441
Globe and Mail, The, 62, 62*n*97–*n*98, 63*n*99, 65, 65*n*104–*n*105, 65*n*106, 66*n*107–*n*108, 75*n*120, 82*n*141, 89*n*151, 102, 103, 103*n*175, 104, 104*n*176–*n*177, 105, 105*n*178–*n*179, 106*n*180, 114*n*194, 123*n*206, 147*n*236, 184*n*290, 197*n*318, 202*n*330, 203*n*331, 204*n*334, 206*n*336, 207*n*337–*n*338, 208*n*341, 210*n*342, 238*n*395, 248*n*412
Goldman, Brian, 230*n*382
Gonzales, Selena, 44*n*76
"Good, the Bad, and the Ugly on NAFTA 2.0, The" (Dey), 96*n*161, 97*n*164
Goodman, Lee-Anne, 237*n*394
goods and services tax (GST), 91, 156
"Gordon Campbell—Canada's Arch Health Care Privateer and Author of the Worst Cuts in BC's History" *(Ontario Health Coalition),* 80*n*137

Gorman, James, 280*n*453–*n*454
Gorman, Michael, 64*n*101, 84*n*146, 120*n*202, 219*n*358
"Government Must Come Clean About Yarmouth Ferry Costs" (MacPherson), 89*n*150
government regulations,
  deregulation of, 94
  examples of deregulation of, 95
  for large corporations to self-regulate, 120
  public safety due to, 94
  risk-based handling of in USMCA, 97
  shift in for blood-brokering business, 98–100
Grant, Kelly,   65*n*104–*n*105, 202*n*330, 203*n*331, 204*n*334, 206*n*336, 207*n*337–*n*338, 208*n*341, 210*n*342, 248*n*412
Great Bengal Famine of 1770, 147
Great Britain,
  abandonment of P3 model in, 121–122
  one of first to embrace P3 hospital model, 121
  political ties to Canada, 17
  post-second world war reconstruction, 17–18
  social welfare system in, 18
Great Depression, 8–9
  demand for social support, 9–10
  as social turning point for Canada, 9
Greenberg, Zoe, 97*n*165
Greenseid, Lija, 35
"Greg Price: Slipping Through the Health Care System" (Warkentin), 254*n*421
Gretzky, Wayne, 4
Grieshaber-Otto, Jim, 95,

329

95*n*159, 96*n*160
Grinspun, Doris, 212
gross domestic product (GDP), 29, 30, 32, 34, 72, 75
　criticism of use of, 220
　as degrowth, 222
　as retrospective measurement, 221
gross national product (GNP), 224, 225
Guaranteed Income Supplement (GIS), 156
Guardian, The, 72*n*115, 75*n*123, 174*n*271
"Guardians of Public Health" (CHC), 273*n*444
Gupta, Shikha, 235, 236*n*392
Guthrie, Rosalia, 103, 104

H

H1N1 virus, 194
Ha, Th Thanh, 184*n*290, 202*n*330, 203*n*331, 204*n*334, 206*n*336, 207*n*337–*n*338, 208*n*341, 210*n*342
Haig, Matt, 217, 217*n*354–*n*355
Haines, Avery, 195*n*314
Hajdu, Patty, 194
"Half a Century of a Right to Health?" (Bhabha), 281*n*456
Halifax Chamber of Commerce, 150
"Halifax Doctor Defends Use of 'disaster alert' for Overflow in Emergency" (Tutton), 62*n*97–*n*98, 63*n*99
Halifax Examiner, The, 202*n*328
Halifax Index, 151, 152
Halifax North End Community Health Centre, 260
Halifax Partnership, 152
"Halifax Women Blames Slow Ambulance Response in Death of Husband" (Doucette), 63*n*100
hallway healthcare, 67–68
"Hallway Health Care: A system under strain" (Ontario Ministry of Long-Term Care), 68*n*109
Hanes, Allison, 211*n*346
Harari, Yuval Noah, 145, 146*n*232–*n*234, 147, 147*n*237–*n*240, 148
Hardcastle, Lorain, 168*n*270
Harper, Stephen, 75, 226
Harris, Mike, 79–80
Harte, Paul, 262
Harvard Gazette, 39*n*68
Harvard School of Public Health, 46, 46*n*79
Harvard University, 163*n*264
Hasselback, Dr. Paul, 116
Havien, Judy, 187*n*296–*n*297
health, definition of, 228–229
Health, Illness, and Health Care in Canada (Bolaria & Dickinson), 228*n*375, 275*n*450, 276*n*451
Health Action Lobby, 260*n*427
Health Affairs, 33, 34*n*51–*n*52, 48, 48*n*80
health as human right (International Covenant on Economic, Social and Cultural Rights, UN General Assembly Resolution), 282
"Health Authority Handling Backlog of Colonoscopies" (Stoodley), 199*n*323
"Health Authority Takes Over Operations at Private Seniors Care Home in Okanagan Town" (Dickson), 117*n*199

INDEX

Health Canada, 98, 99, 239–240, 239n397, 241n402–n403
  private health clinics and, 108–109
Healthcare 365 clinic, 107
"Health Care as a Commodity" (Heath), 165n265
"Health Care Battle in Judge's Hands but Expected to Land in Canada's Top Court" (Bains), 81n138
health care consultancy, 60
  in Alberta, 84
  costs of, 60, 61
  golden age of, 78–79
  recommendations and reports, 60–61
"Health Care Costs Number One Cause of Bankruptcy for American Families" (Woods), 32n48
Health Care in Canada (Maioni), 9n13, 11n16, 28n38, 29n40, 77n128, 78n129, 282n458
health care inheritance, 174–176
healthcare pioneers, 174–175
health care plutocracy in US, 27, 41, 48, 147–148
Healthcare Profile System, 160n261, 161n262–n263
"Health Care Spending in the United States and Other High-Income Countries" (Papanicolas, Woskie & Jha), 33n50
healthcare system(s),
  see also Medicare (Canadian); Medicare (U.S.)
  abandonment of public systems by political institutions, 147–148
  administrative costs a country comparison, 33–34, 164–165
  adverse effects of private health clinics on public, 109–110
  affordability and, 156–157
  Canada's influenced by Britain, 17–18
  crisis in 1930s, 9–10
  cuts in Canada between 1980 and 1990, 78–79
  dangers to, 2
  defunding of, 2
  divergent paths in Canada and US towards, 29
  effects on emergency departments of collapse of Canadian, 51–53
  emergency department as seismograph for, 52, 132
  expensive operational and maintenance costs of, 148–149
  failure of supply and demand in, 168–169
  importance of public, 3
  isolated from social welfare state, 277–278
  limited resources for private and public, 158–159
  lowest life expectancies in US compared to OECD countries, 43–44
  market allocation of very inefficient, 165
  before Medicare, 5
  overcrowding prior to Covid-19 in Canadian hospitals, 197–198
  per-historic peoples', 279–281
  political infringement on structure and administration of, 61–62
  political system required to

ensure trust in, 146
poor health outcomes linked to poverty, 227–228
private payments in Canada for services not covered by Medicare, 77
regionalization in Canada of, 58–59
restructure of in mid to late-1990s in Canada without funding, 264–265
restructuring of from hospital-care to community-care model, 92–93
universal health care common in Western countries, 279
wars and interplay with, 15
healthcare workers, 268–269
"Health Cost of Being Poor, The" (Goldman), 230n382
health determinants, 228–229
"Health District Merger Costs Jump to $9 Million" (Walsh), 60n88
"Health in All Policies" (HiAP) federal action plan (CMAJ), 231, 231n385, 251, 252
"Health Insurance Coverage in the United States: 2017" (Berchick, Hood & Barnett), 31n46
"Health Insurance Coverage in the United States: 2018" (Berchick, Barnett & Upton), 30n43, 177n276
health-promotion strategies, 258, 259
Health Reform Transfer (2003, Canada), 225
Health Sciences Association of Alberta (HSAA), 83

"Health Spending Fails to Keep Pace with Inflation, Population Growth" (Chiasson), 81n139
healthsystemtracker.org, 43–44
"Health Tapestry" (McMaster University), 260n428
Healthy Debate, 53n81, 64, 64n103, 182n287, 254n422–n424, 257n425
Heaps, Toby A. A., 90n153–n154, 91n155
Heart and Stroke Canada, 240n399
Heart and Stroke Foundation, 240
Heath, Joseph, 165, 165n265
Henderson, Jennifer, 202n328
"'He Never Got a Chance': B.C. Man Dies After Surgery Cancelled Due to Covid-19" (Bogart), 200n326
Hennessy, Trish, 90n152, 120, 120n203
"Hennessy's Index, Tax Cuts 101" (Hennessy), 90n152
Henry, Geraldine, 104, 105
Hepburn, Bob, 82n142
"Herron Long-Term Care Residents Died of Thirst and Malnourishment Quebec Coroner's Inquest Told" (Ha), 184n290
Higgs, Blaine, 83
"High Cost of Low Corporate Taxes, The" (Oved, Heaps & Yow), 90n153–n154, 91n155
Himmelstein, David U., 26, 34n51–n52, 174
Hirsch, Dr. Greg, 198
"History of Tax Exemptions, Credits, and Loopholes in Canada" (Macdonald), 91n156

INDEX

"History of Why the US is the Only Rich Country Without Universal Health Care, A" (Merelli), 26n33, 27n36, 28n39, 29n41

Hoffman, Daniel R., 177n273

home care services, 254–255
  Apartments for Life (A4L) as example of, 255–256
  episodic and non-integrated, 264
  as integrative and holistic, 267–268
  privatization of, 264
  restructuring of health care systems to without funding, 264
  technology to help with, 267
  variations of across Canada, 266–267

Hood, Emily, 31n46

Hopps, Dr. John, 175, 176

Horowitz, Julia, 271n442

Hoskins, Dr. Eric, 239, 239n397, 241n402–n403

Hospital and Diagnostic Services Act (1957, Canada), 224–225

Hospital Employees' Union, BC, 116, 118

Hospital Insurance Plan, The (1947, Saskatchewan), 15, 224

"Hospital Overcrowding has Become the Norm in Ontario, Figures Show" (Grant), 65n104–n105

"Hospitals Empty Beds Before Wave of Covid-19 Admissions" (Henderson), 202n328

"Hospital Trends in Canada—Results of a Project to Create a Historical Series of Statistical and Financial Data for Canadian Hospitals Over Twenty-Seven Years" (CIHI), 78n130–n131

Houston, Tim, 189

"How a Powerful Organization Protects Doctors from Medical Error Claims" (Rinaldo), 261n429–n430, 262n431, 262n434

"How Canada Compares Results from the Commonwealth Fund's 2016 International Health Policy Survey of Adults in 11 Countries" (CIHI), 257n426

"How Much Does Canada Spend on Healthcare?" (Effective Public Healthcare Panacea Project), 77n125

"How Prepared are Our Hospitals for the Coronavirus Outbreak?" (Keller), 197n318

"How Private Long-Term Care Facilities Handled Covid Needs Scrutiny" (Lightman & Hardcastle), 168n270

"How Shoring up Hospitals for Covid-19 Contributed to Canada's Long-Term Care Crisis" (Grant & Ha), 202n330, 203n331, 204n334, 206n336, 207n337–n338, 210n342

"How Today's Corrupt Health Care System is About to Get Worse" (Hoffman), 177n273

"HSSA Criticizes Kenney's Plan for Potential $1.2B Cut to Health Care" (Parker), 84n144

Huddle, 150n244, 151n245–n246

HuffPost, 41n69, 78n132,

82n140, 167n268, 185n292, 262n432, 263n435
"Huge 'Pandora Papers' Leak Exposes Secret Offshore Accounts of Politicians, Celebrities, and Billionaires" (Dubinsky & International Consortium of Investigative Journalists), 92n158
human Immunodeficiency virus/ acquired immunodeficiency syndrome (HIV/AIDS), 97–98
humanitarianism, 2
Humanitas, 256
"Hundreds Attend Rent Control Rally in Halifax's Parade Square" (S. Cooke), 235n390
"Hundreds of Canadians Die Every Year Because They Can't Afford Medications: Nurses' Union" (Young), 235n391
Hunt, Michael, 81
Hunter, Adam, 127n212, 160n260
Hunter College, New York, 174
"Hunter-Gatherers Care for First Known Ancient Invalid" (Coglan), 281n455
hunter-gatherer societies' health-care, 281
Huskey Energy, 153

I

identity drive, 282–283
Ikea company, 88
Iliadis, Christos, 165, 166n266
"'I Live on the Streets Now': How Americans Fall into Bankruptcy" (Sainato), 174n271
"IMF Slashes US and China Growth Forecasts" (Horowitz), 271n442
immigration, 5
Imperial Oil, 153
Improving Healthcare and Ending Hallway Medicine, Ontario, 67
Independent Age, 267n439
Indigenous Canadians, life expectancy rates for, 229
poverty and, 228–229
unemployment rates for, 228–229
industrialization, 19
"Inquest Hears ER was Short Three Nurses the Night Brian Sinclair Died" *(CTV News Winnipeg),* 133n218
insulin, 34–36, 37, 175, 176
"Insulin Prices Killed Josh Wilkerson. Now His Mother is Taking on Big Pharma" (Pitt), 37n59
integrated health care systems, 257–258
community clinics as best option for, 258
consistent and harmonious management of, 259
driven by patient-centred care, treatment and oversight, 259
goal of, 258
importance of funding for, 259
inter-professional teams for, 259
many care models in existence already, 260
success of integrated community clinics, 259–260
Integration: A New Direction for Canadian Health Care (Canadian Nurses Association, CMA & Health Action Lobby), 260, 260n427

Intelligencer, 36*n*58
"Inter- and Intra-provincial Inequities in Public Coverage of Cancer Drug Programs Across Canada: A Plea for the Reestablishment of a Pan-Canadian Pharmacare Program" (Sorin, Franco & Quesnel-Vallée), 238*n*396
Interim report from the Premier's council on Improving health care and ending hallway medicine (2019, Ontario Ministry of Long-Term Care), 68*n*109
International Consortium of Investigative Journalists, 92*n*158
International Monetary Fund (IMF), 270–271
"In This PPP, Taxpayers are the Ones Who Paid" (Picard), 123*n*206
Inuit Tapiriit Kanatami, 247
Ipsos (Canada), 3*n*2
Ireton, Julie, 196*n*316
Isai, Vjosa, 108*n*187, 109*n*188, 110*n*189
"Island Health Takes Control of Nanaimo Seniors Home; Cites Inadequate Care of Residents" (Kines), 116*n*197–*n*198
"Is Neoliberalism Destroying the World?" (Livesey), 75*n*124
"It Cost $130K to Renovate Seven Steps at Province House" (Laroche), 148*n*242

J
Jackson, Andrew, 75*n*122
Jha, Ashish K., 33*n*50
Johnson, Erica, 119*n*201, 141*n*230
Jones, Alexandre Mae, 155*n*256
Jones, Allison, 199*n*324
Jones, Sarah, 36*n*58
Joseph, Andrew, 179*n*278
Journal of Health Care Communications, 166*n*266
Journal of the American Medical Association (JAMA), 33*n*50
Julian, Peter, 241

K
Kaiser Permanente, 177
"Kaiser Permanente Tripled Income in 2019" (Reuter), 177*n*275
Kamal, Rajah, 43*n*74
Katawazi, Miriam, 211*n*345
Keele, Jeff, 133*n*218
Keenan, Greg, 75*n*120, 147*n*236
Keller, James, 197*n*318
Kelly, Sharon, 32
Kenneth E. Spencer Memorial Home, Moncton, 202
Kenney, Jason, 83–84, 152, 153, 215, 216, 253
Kent State shootings, 73
"Key Lesson from SARS That Canada Failed to Heed When Covid-19 Hit" (Miller), 188*n*301–*n*302
Keynesianism, 72
Kiedrowski, John, 191*n*309
Kines, Lindsay, 116*n*197–*n*198
Kingston, Anne, 98*n*167–*n*168, 99*n*171, 100*n*172, 101*n*173
Kinney, Duncan, 253*n*418
Kirby, Jason, 88*n*149
Klein, Ralph, 79, 84
Klippel-Feil syndrome, 279
Knowles, Stanley, 243
Koehler, Billy, 41

Koehler, Georgeanne, 41
Konish, Lorie, 45*n*78
Kotierk, Aluki, 248
Krever, Horace, 98, 101
Krever Inquiry. See Royal Commission of Inquiry on the Blood System in Canada (1997) *(a. k. a. Krever Inquiry)*,

L

Labonte, Ronald, 96*n*162, 97*n*163
Lachance, Renaud, 128
Laconic, William, 146, 146*n*235
Lalonde Report (1974), 233, 243
Lancet, The, 237n393
Laroche, Jean, 149*n*242
Larsen, Karin, 115*n*195, 116*n*196, 190*n*306
Laurie, Wilfred, 4
Laval, Quebec overpass collapse, 2006, 95
Laval lee, Dr. Barry, 134
Lavito, Angelica, 37*n*61
"Lawsuits Over Covid-19 Handling in Nursing Homes Raise Questions About Standards of Care" *(CTV News)*, 210*n*343
"Leaving out Long-Term Care was Medicare's Original Sin—and We're Paying For It Now" (Wherry), 182*n*286, 183*n*289
Lecher, Paul, 149
LeClair, Suzanne, 173, 174
Lee-Shamrock, Philip, 69*n*113
left-without-being-seen (LBS) rates, 54
Legatee, Francois, 215, 216
Leo, Goff, 194*n*313
Levensloopbestendige (Apartments for Life (A4L)), 265–266
based on autonomy, "yes"

culture, family-centred approach and "move it or lose it" values, 265–266
"*Levensloopbestendige* (Apartments for Life) in the Netherlands" (Centre for Public Impact), 266*n*436
life expectancy,
Indigenous *vs.* non-Indigenous populations, 229
lowest in US compared to other OECD countries, 43–44
Lightman, Naomi, 168*n*270
Lindsay, Bethany, 118*n*200, 167*n*269
Livesey, Bruce, 75*n*124
load shedding, 204
"Long-Awaited Report into N.S. Ambulance System Released" (M. Gorman), 64*n*101
long-term care homes, 115–118
aggression in crowded facilities, 191, 192
alarm bells about disintegration of after 1983, 183
class-action suits against, 210–211
complaints across Canada, 190–191
Covid-19 effects of on, 181, 182, 183, 265
examples of Covid-19 deaths in for-profit, 183–186
financialization of, 182
homicides in Canadian, 192–193
police and military called in in Ontario and Quebec, 184–185
privatization of, 182, 183
problems with for-profit homes in Alberta, 119
problems with for-profit homes

INDEX

in BC, 116–119
problems with for-profit homes in New Brunswick, 119–120
problems with for-profit homes in Nova Scotia, 119–120
public money going to for profits not spent on resident's care, 118
shocking number of deaths during Covid-19, 185–186
sub-standards provided by for-profit companies, 115–118
"Long-Term Care Homes Feeling Impacts of Budget Cuts" (M. Gorman), 84n146
long-term care in Canada,
absent mandate period from 1980s and beyond, 244–245
"ad-hocism" period from 1970–80s, 243–244
aversion of by federal government between 1945–70, 242–243
Covid-19 deaths in, 248–249
dire circumstances in northern communities, 247–248
Douglas advocated for inclusion in Medicare in 1976, 242
downsides of community care models, 245–246
examples of federal indifference to, 245
exceptions for First Nations, Inuit and veterans, 245
regional variations in, 246–247
shift from institutionalized to community care, 245–246
"Look Back at Canada's Tainted Blood Scandal, A" *(George Stroumboulopoulos Tonight)*, 98n166

Lovelace, Berkeley, Jr., 178n277
Lui, Dr. Derek, 104, 105

M

MacCormick, Dr. Keith, 68
Macdonald, David, 91, 91n156
MacDonald, David, 147
MacDonald, Rodney, 60
machine learning, 267
Mackenzie, Hugh, 153
Mackenzie, Isobel, 118, 167
MacKinnon, Bobbi-Jean, 191n308
MacKinnon, Janice, 84
"MacKinnon Report Gives Kenney Roadmap for Klein-Style Cuts" (Thomson), 84n145
Maclean's, 87–88, 88n149, 98n167–n168
MacLellan, Ainslie, 195n315
MacPhee, Kelly, 63, 70
MacPherson, Paige, 89n150
Madonna Care Community, Orleans, Ontario, 196
magnetic resonance imaging (MRI),
as covered under *Canada Health Act*, 109
illegal charging for, 102, 107
postponements due to Covid-19, 201
in Saskatchewan, 159–160
Maioni, Antonia, 9, 9n13, 11n16, 28, 28n38, 29n40, 77n128, 78n129, 282, 282n458, 283
Malek, Jan, 239n398
Malik, Abdul, 253n418
Malone, Kelly Geraldine, 134n219
"Malpractice Liability Costs U.S. $55.6 Billion a Year" (Cullen), 46n79
Malpractice. *See*

337

medical malpractice
Maltais, Reno, 196
Mancini, Melissa, 193n311–n312
"Man is a part of nature, and his war against nature is inevitably a war against himself" (Carson), 282n457
Manitoba,
   financial wastage in, 88
   private care in leads to longer wait times for public health, 159
   public health funding cuts in, 216
Mankiw, N. Gregory, 163n264
"Man's Death After 34-hour ER Wait Must Be Ruled Homicide, Family's Lawyer Tells Inquest" (The *Canadian Press*), 132n217
"Man was Ignored to Death in an ER Ten Years Ago, A. It Could Happen Again" (Gerster), 131n215, 132n216, 135n221
Maple Leaf Foods tainted-meat outbreak, 2008, 95
Marques, Manuel, 207
Marsh, Leonard, 18
   as pioneer of social welfare in Canada, 18
Martin, Dr. Danielle, 109, 232
Martin, Dr. Debra L., 280
Martin, Paul, 73, 81, 225
Matters of Life and Death (Picard), 61n96, 62n94, 64n102, 229n377–n379
Mayer, Andre, 222n364
McCarter, Jim, 123
McColl, Mary Ann, 235, 236n392
McCracken, John, 188n304
McDonald, Catherine, 212n347
McEwen, Dr. Jill, 134

McGee, Robin, 136, 136n222, 137n223–n224, 138n225–n228, 139, 140, 140n229, 150
   disintegration cost significant portion of her life, 143
   as example of system disintegration, 136–139
   medical errors in case of, 136–13
McGill University Health Centre, Montreal, 128
McIntosh, Tom, 225n369, 225n371
McKenna, Frank, 79
"McKenna Retires" (Bergman), 79n135
McKeon, Lauren, 107n186
McManus, Theresa, 241n404
McMaster's Tapestry, 260
McMaster University, Hamilton, Ontario, 260n428
McNeil, Stephen, 84, 85, 128, 150, 187
McQuaig, Linda, 10, 10n14, 18n30, 38, 38n64, 174, 175n272
Medcan, Toronto, 108
MedCity News, 177n275
Medical Care Act, The (1966, Canada), 224, 225
medical malpractice, 46
   costs of, 46
   insurance coverage for Canadian doctors, 261–262
   malpractice lawsuit (for death of Joan Rivers), 113–114
medical records, 114–115
   increase in fees for, 114–115
   privatization of, 114
   secure electronic records, 259
medical referrals, 254–255
   antiquated systems make for unsafe wait times, 257

INDEX

central intake (or pooled) systems, 256–257
consistency across country of, 257
disorganization in, 255
general guidance required from, 256–257
paperless e-referrals in Alberta, 255–256
Medical Services Insurance (MSI), 17
Medicare (Canadian),
see also healthcare system(s)
administrative costs compared to the US system, 47–48
all of Canada implemented by 1972, 17
appreciation for, 3
attacks on, 16, 281–282
capitalism as threat to, 287
CHC dedicated to saving, 273
collapse of emergency departments as warning for, 53–54
costs of compared to US healthcare, 30–31
defrauding system of, 93–94
detractors, 71
Douglas as founder of, 4
in early years medical access important, 228
embryonic developments of, 11
entrenched into national identity, 282
final step initiated after 1948 election, 15
financing of, 86–87
focus on from value- to corporate-driven, 71
ground-breaking work done by, 154–156
health care before, 5
historical evolution of, 4
initiatives that formed groundwork for, 224
labour movement and social reforms factors in start of, 6
launched in Saskatchewan in 1962, 16
limits of GDP as quality indicator in saviour of, 223
long-term residential care not a priority for, 181–182
money saved from CMPA could be returned to, 262–263
neoliberal attacks on, 72, 77–78
neoliberal so-called solutions to, 71–72
network of social policies required for existence of, 277–278
not kept pace with socioeconomic changes, 257–258
poverty eradication to stop decline in, 230
prioritization of, 2
as provincial responsibility, 76
requires serious transfer program from federal government, 226–227
salvaging of as collaborative effort, 216–218
strike by Saskatchewan doctors at start of, 16–17
transition to fully integrated care model, 260
Medicine Hat Regional Hospital, 200
Medisys Health Group, 107
MedPage Today, 37n62–n63
Mehra, Natalie, 80n136, 106n181–n183, 107n184–n185, 124, 124n207, 193, 204

Menard, Jean Pierre, 208
"Mental Health Wins Record Funding in New Zealand's First 'Well-Being Budget'" (Sutherland), 221n363
Merck & Co., 178
Merelli, Annalisa, 26n33, 27, 27n36, 28, 28n39, 29n41
Metcalf, Stephen, 72, 72n115, 75, 75n123
"Military Says it Found Disturbing Conditions in Ontario Care Homes" (Paling), 185n292
Miller, Adam, 188n301–n302, 249n414, 250n416
Miller, Dr. Rob, 68
Milne, Vanessa, 53n81, 64n103, 254n422–n424, 257n425
Mississippi bubble of 1917, 146
"'Mistake Was Made, A': Man Left Behind During Evacuation of Hamilton Retirement Home" (Vize), 184n291
Monitor, The, 85n147
Montreal Gazette, The, 211n346
Moore, Stephen, 151
Mou, Haizhen, 77n127
"Mould Clean Up at Yellowknife's New Hospital Could Have Put Patients at Risk, Warn Staff" (Beers), 127n211
Mount Sinai Hospital, Toronto, 52, 155
MQO Research, 151
Mulroney, Brian, 73, 82
multinational corporations, 73
multiple sclerosis (MS), 37
Munro, Ian, 151
Mykyta, Larissa, 30n43–n44
"Myth: A Parallel Private System Would Reduce Waiting Times in the Public System" (CHSRF), 159n258

N

Nanaimo Seniors Village, BC, 116
National Bureau of Economic Research, 45, 45n77
"*National Health Expenditure Trends 2020*" (CIHI), 77n126
National Hockey League Enterprises Canada, 253
National Institute on Aging, 188
National Institutes of Health (U.S.), 166–167
National Microbiology Laboratory, Winnipeg, 154
National Observer, The, 153n252–n254, 187n296–n297
National Post, The, 132n217, 185n294, 216n353
National Research Council of Canada, 176
National Union of Public and General Employees, 84n144, 124n207
"Nation's Progress on Children's Health Coverage Reverses Course" (Alker & Pham), 31n45
Nautilus, 229n380, 230n381
Naylor, C. David, 224n367, 225n368, 225n370, 226n372
NBC News, 114n192
neoliberalism, 71, 72
  activism as *bête noir* of, 130
  affordability argument, 270
  aim of to reduce welfare state, 75
  believe everything should be left to free market, 145–146
  believe in protecting rights of capital at all costs, 145

INDEX

created new social order, 74–75
cutting social programs, 73
defrauding as essential component of, 76, 86–94
defunding as essential component of, 76–86
deliberate disintegration as essential component of, 76, 129–144
deregulation as essential component of, 76, 94–128
economic governance as priority of, 73–74
free-market obsession of, 169
greed and, 271
growth of in 1980s, 73
in Mulroney's supply-side economics in 1980s, 82
as name for pro market policies, 75
in scorched-earth tactics of Liberals in 1990s, 82
strengthening power of wealthiest 1% in Canada, 90
unions as targets of, 73–74
united Canadians against, 278–79
"Neoliberalism: The Idea that Swallowed the World" (Metcalf), 72n115, 75n123
New Brunswick,
attempt in 2015 to raise capped cost of nursing home care, 271–272
cuts to health care services in, 83
disintegration of long-term care in, 190–191
for-profit nursing homes in, 191
healthcare spending dropped from 10% to under 1%, 79
problems with for-profit long-term care homes in, 119–120

protests against plans to raise seniors' nursing home costs, 272
New Brunswick Nurses Union, 190
Newfoundland and Labrador,
financial wastage in, 88
premier Danny Williams uses US healthcare, 157–158
New NAFTA's Assault on Public Health, The (Labonte et al), 96n162, 97n163
New Scientist, 281n455
"New Study Finds 45,000 Deaths Annually Linked to Lack of Health Coverage" (Cecere), 41n68
"New Westminster-Burnaby MOP Not Giving Up on Public Universal Pharmacare Program" (McManus), 241n404
New York Times, The, 48n80, 97n165, 146n235, 280n453–n454
New Zealand,
mental health at centre of its budgets, 221
Nicholas, Trevor, 150n244, 151n245–n246
Nieman Foundation, 282n457
"99 Stupid Things the Government Did with Your Money: Parts I, II, and III" (Kirby, et al), 87–88, 88n149
"Noam Chomsky: The US Health System is an 'International Scandal'—and ACA Repeal Will Make It Worse" (Polychroniou), 26n32, 27n34–n35
"'No Heart Medication, No Food':

N.S. Woman Says That Will Be Her Choice After Rent Increase" (Petracek), 235n389
Nolan Reilly, J., 8n10–n11
Nolen, Stephanie, 186n298, 187n299–300, 188n303, 208, 208n339–n340
"No Place to Grow Old" (Grant), 248n412
Norovirus, 195
North American Free Trade Association (NAFTA), 85
see also United States-Mexico-Canada Agreement (USMCA)
   dangers to Canada's health-care policies, 95–96
   revamping of in 2018 into USMCA, 94, 96
North Bay Regional Health Centre, 127
Northern Kentucky Tribune, 31n47
"Northwood, a Blueprint for How Covid-19 Raged Through Long-Term Care Homes" (Havien), *187n296–n298*
Northwood long-term care facility, Halifax, 185–187, 188, 189, 202, 207, 208, 210, 246, 249
"Nothing is more important than health care" (Ford), 215n349
Nova Scotia,
   child poverty rates in, 219, 221
   corporate tax reduced in 2020, 150–151, 152
   as golf destination, 218
   highest child poverty rates in Canada, 149
   limited supplies of PPE in, 195–196
   lowest median after-tax income, 219
   new Inverness airport proposal in 2019, 218–220
   problems with for-profit long-terms care homes in, 119–120
   recommendations for long-term care in, 190
   so-called economic boom while defunding healthcare, 150–152
   waiting lists increased during Covid-19 in, 198–199
   wasted tax dollars but reduction on healthcare spending in, 149–150
   wasteful spending in, 87
   Yarmouth ferry debacle, 89
Nova Scotia Advocate, The, 188n304
Nova Scotia Golf Association, 218
Nova Scotia Health, 58n84, 149n241, 198
   consultancy in, 60
   funding cuts to healthcare services in, 84–85
   long-term care patients in, 66
   loss of 3,127 beds between 1993–99, 79
   regionalization of, 59
Nova Scotia Health Authority (NSHA), Halifax, 143, 198–199
   emptying hospital beds during Covid-19, 202
"Nova Scotians Made to Wait for the Trickle-Down That Will Never Come" (Saulnier), 85n147
Nova Scotia Nurses Union, 190, 190n307
"Nova Scotia Premier Announce Business Tax Cuts" (Nicholas), *150n244, 151n245–n246*
"Nova Scotia Sees Spike in

INDEX

Child Poverty Rates" (M. Gorman), 219*n*358
Nova Scotia Senior's Pharmacare Program, 239–240
Nova Scotia Standing Committee on Law Amendments, 251
Now, 32*n*49
"Numbers of Doctors Per Capita in Canada Reaches Record High" *(The Canadian Press)*, 58*n*83
Nunavut,
   elderly sent to Ottawa retirement hotel, 247–248
   long-term care in, 247–248
Nunavut Tunngavik Inc., 248
"Nurse Revealed the Tragic Last Words of His Coronavirus Patient, A: 'Who's Going to Pay for It?" (Elassar), 285*n*462
"Nurses' Union Calls for Independent Inquiry into Long-Term Care Sector" (MacKinnon), 191*n*308
"Nursing Home Rationed Diapers While Residents Suffered Rashes, Infections" (Johnson), 119*n*201
nzherald.co.nz, 221*n*362

O

Obed, Natan, 247
Off, Carol, 35
offshore tax havens, 92
Old Age Security (OAS), 156
"103 Ways to Fix Health Care in N.S." *(CBC News)*, 60*n*90, 60*n*92, 61*n*92
"$140 Billion the *New York Times* Says Americans Owe in Medical Debt is Just the Tip of the Iceberg, The"

(Potter), 32*n*49
"167 Canadian Health Professionals Call for a Basic Income" (Brady), 227*n*373, 228*n*374, 232*n*387
Ontario,
   cancellations and cutbacks from Covid-19, 199–200
   cut funding to public health services, 83
   hallway healthcare in, 67–68
   halted transfer of seniors from hospitals in 2020, 209
   privatization of some health services in, 79–80
   public health funding cuts in, 215–216
   results of bed losses and increase in sick seniors in, 65
   waitlist for long-term care in, 66
Ontario Health Coalition (OHC), 80*n*136–*n*137, 106, 106*n*181–*n*183, 107*n*184–*n*185, 121–122, 121*n*204, 122*n*205, 124, 192–193, 204
Ontario Hospital Insurance Plan (OHIP), 104, 105
"Ontario Will Pay $3.5 Billion Over 25 Years for One P3 Hospital" (Mehra), 124*n*207
Orchard Villa long-term care, 205–206, 210, 211
Organization for Economic Co-operation and Development (OECD), 30, 43, 63, 181, 197, 249
offshore assets list, 92
Orlikow, David, 244
"Our Promise Strategy" (Capital Health), 58*n*82
"Our Story" (Canadian Doctors

for Medicare), 274n447
outcome linked to time, 1–2
"Out-Of-Pocket Costs Go Through the Roof for Neurology Drugs—MS Patients with private insurance paid 20 times more in 2016 vs 2004" (George), 37n62–n63
outsourcing, 85–86
Oved, Marco Chown, 90n153–n154, 91n155
Ovens, Howard, 52
"Overview of Long-Term Care in Canada and Selected Provinces and Territories, An" (Banerjee), 247n410–n411

P

Paling, Emma, 185n292
Pallister, Brian, 215, 216
Palmer, Karen, 26
Panama Papers, 92
"Pandemic Experience in the Long-Term Care Sector: How Does Canada Compare with Other Countries?" (CIHI), 181n283, 248n413, 249, 249n415
Pandora Papers, 92
Papanicolas, Irene, 33n50
Paradise Papers, 92
paramedics, 63–64
Parker, Mike, 83, 83n144
Parkview Place long-term care home, Winnipeg, 192
Patch, Jeremy, 53n81, 64n103
patient offloading, 204–205
Patrick, Melissa, 31n47
Patten, Jim, 141, 142, 143
  disintegration cost life on dialysis, 144

Patten, Raquel, 143
Payne, Emily, 177n274
Pearle, Lauren, 39, 39n67
Pearson, Lester B., 4, 77
Pendharkar, Sachin, 254n424, 257n425
Pentland, H. Clare, 6, 6n4–n7, 7n8–n9
personal protective equipment (PPE), 185, 187
  complaints about quality and rationing of, 194–195
  for Covid-19 for asymptomatic transmission, 188–189
  shortage of when Covid-19 began, 193–194
  substandard, 194
Peterson-KFF Health System Tracker, 43n74, 44n76
Petracek, Heidi, 210n344, 235n389
Pfizer Inc., 178
Pham, Olivia, 31n45
pharmacare,
  see also direct-acting oral anticoagulants (DOACs); Warfarin medication
  cost of medications, 233–235
  costs of results in prescriptions going unfilled, 238–239
  Covid-19 demonstrated need for national plan, 239
  disabled Canadians and, 236–237
  excessive drug costs in Canada, 237–238
  to help severely disabled individuals, 236–237
  jurisdictional variations reduces access to medications, 238
  misconceptions about drug insurance coverage, 236

patchwork program in Canada for prescriptions, 237–238
premature deaths from lack of prescription drug coverage, 234–236
savings from universal system of, 240–241
standing committees' endorsements of universal public, 241–242
"Pharmacare" (CHC), 241n401
Pharmacare Now Statement (2019), \241
Philadelphia Inquirer, The, 32, 177n273
Phoenix pay system debacle, 89
Physicians for a National Health Program (U.S.), 176–177
Picard, André, 61n96, 62n94, 64n102, 65, 65n106, 66n107–n108, 114n194, 123n206, 229, 229n377–n379, 238, 238n395
Pinecrest Nursing Home, Bobcaygeon, Ontario, 207
Pitt, William Rivers, 37n59
"Plasma Centers Profit Off the Working Poor" (Scheffler), 38n66
Pohlman, Duane, 36n57
Policynote, 75n121, 86n148
Policy Options, 203n332
"Political Heavyweights Back Campaign for Airport Near Inverness Golf Course" (Ayers), 219n357
Polychroniou, C. J., 25, 26n32, 27n34–n35
"Poor Health: When Poverty Becomes Disease" (Conway), 229n376, 233n388
Posner, Liz, 38n65

Possamai, Mario, 188
Potter, Wendell, 32n49, 42, 42n70–n71, 43, 43n72–n73, 166n267
poverty, 227–228
amongst Indigenous Canadians, 228–229
breaking cycles of, 230
complexities of reduction in, 231–232
disabled people and, 236
eradication of to slow decline in Medicare, 230
lined to poor health outcomes, 227–228, 233
as social determinant leader regarding health, 228–229
stresses from can change people's biology, 229–230
as transgenerational in Indigenous communities, 229
poverty-associated stress, 229–230
"PPE Shortages Persist at Quebec Long-Term Care Home with More Than Half of the Residents Infected" (MacLellan), 195n315
"Prescription for Canada, A: Achieving Pharmacare for All" (Hoskins et al), 239n397, 241n402–n403
prevention of diseases strategy, 258
Price, Greg, 254, 255
Princess Margaret Cancer Centre Lodge, Toronto, 139
prioritization of healthcare funding, 149
"Private Clinics and the Threat to Public Medicare in Canada. Results of Surveys with Private Clinics and Patients" (Mehra), 106n181–n183, 107n184–n185

private health clinics, 101
　adverse effects of on public medicine, 109–110
　cardiac stress tests in compared to public hospital, 110–111
　charging for MRIs, 107
　difficulties in regulating, 102
　guidelines requested for Quebec, 111–112
　higher costs at, 105–107
　membership fees, 102, 107–108, 109
　proliferation in Canada of, 101–102
　research into by OHC, 106
　standards of compared to public healthcare, 110–112
private/public/partnerships (P3s), 79, 80
　as alternative way to deliver infrastructure, 120–121
　Brampton Civic Hospital as Ontario's first, 123–125
　Britain abandoned after decades of over-costs and disasters, 121–122
　Britain as one of first to embrace, 121
　British Medical Journal called it "perfidious financial idiocy", 121
　Canada's dismal track record with, 122–123
　examples of Canadian projects with serious problems, 125–128
　reasons for continual support of, 122
　Saskatchewan Hospital North Battleford problems, 127
　Stanton Territorial Hospital, Yellowknife as problematic, 125–126
"Private Public Partnerships (P3s) or Private Over Patients. The Facts About For-Profit Hospitals" (The Ontario Health Coalition), 121n204, 122n205
privatization (of health care), 2, 66
　bankruptcy as economic effect of, 45–46
　began in Canadian hospitals in late 1990s, 120–121
　Canadian and US support for, 44
　commercial trade treaties as part of, 95–96
　cost cutting sacrificed quality services, 114
　failure of in US, 29
　for-profit care homes and public funding of, 167
　free-trade deals set stage for, 73
　indictments of, 23–24
　insurance conglomerates difficulties with, 47
　long-term care homes in BC taken back by local health authority, 115–117
　long-term care in Canada and, 182
　medical malpractice in US as warning about, 46
　pitted various society segments against each other, 176–177
　reward puppets in US, 176–177, 178
　shift from funded hospital care to unfunded community care as, 93
　tactics to ensure US system remains, 177

INDEX

in United States, 24–27
US health insurance conglomerates and Canadian healthcare, 94–95
warnings about, 44–45
workplace violence after heath care, 191
Procurement and Sole Sourcing Policy (Alberta), 253
"Progressive Party (United States, 1912)" *(Wikipedia)*, 28*n*37
Progress Report, 253*n*418
"Proposed $200M Private Orthopedic Surgery Facility Would Be Largest in Alberta's History" (C. Russell & J. Russell), 216*n*351
"Proposed Northwood Lawsuit Expanded to Seek Damages from Nova Scotia Government" (Petracek), 210*n*344
"Provinces Irate Over Health Funding Talks with Morneau" (Tang), 82*n*141
provincial cutbacks in health services, 78–86
Provincial Health Services Operational Review (PHSOR), 60, 61
Public Health Agency of Canada (PHAC), 154
Public Opinions, 165*n*265
"Public Protected from Potential Collapse of Company Part of Stanton Hospital Project, Says N.W.T. Government" (Strong), 125*n*209
pulmonary hypertension, 154
purple saxifrage flower of Nunavut, 217

"Pursuing Different Paths in Long-Term Care: Manitoba, Ontario and the Politics of Commercialization" (Twomey), 243*n*406. 244*n*407, 245*n*408

Q

Quartz, 26*n*33, 27*n*36, 28*n*39, 29*n*41
Quebec,
federal government threatened to cut health care funds to, 216
government guidelines about long-term care residents, 208–209
halted transfer of seniors from hospitals in 2020, 2089
load shedding in hospitals in, 204–205
Quebec College of Physicians, 112
"Quebec Coroner Urges Stricter Rules for Private Clinics After Man Dies in Wait Room" *(CBC News)*, 112*n*190
Queen Elizabeth II Health Sciences Centre, Halifax, 61, 63, 120
redevelopment of as P3 project, 128
Queen's University, Kingston, Ontario, 235
Quesnel-Vallée, A., 238*n*396
Quinte Health Care, Belleville, Ontario, 206–207

R

Rapid Access to Consultative Expertise (RACE) (British Columbia), 256
Reagan, Ronald, 26, 73
"Reality Check: Are Hospital Bed Claims Accurate?" (DuBreuil), 79*n*133

records. *See* medical records
Record Storage and Retrieval Services Inc., 114
Redelmeier, Donald, 197, 198
referrals. *See* medical referrals
Regina Manifesto (Douglas, Woodsworth, Coldwell), 13
regionalization, 58–59
   of Alberta health care services, 79
   costs of, 59–60
Registered Nurses Association of Ontario, 212
registered retirement savings plan (RRSP), 91
Reindeau, Roger E., 181*n*285
Remote Area Medical (RAM) travelling medical clinic, 41–42, 43
Report on Social Security for Canada, The (1943) (Marsh), 18
Requiem for the American Dream (Chomsky), 274, 274*n*448–*n*449
Research and Statistics Division, Justice Department of Canada, 191, 191*n*309
Research Gate, 247*n*410–*n*411
Residence Herron, Montreal, 183
Retirement Concepts, Vancouver, 115, 117, 118, 119
Retirement Homes Act (Ontario), 204
Reuter, Elsie, 177*n*275
Reuters, 37*n*60
"Review Uncovers Fatal Flaws in Long-Term Care Infection Control" (Eggertson), 189*n*305
Richer, Jocelyn, 216*n*353
Riches, Samuel, 185*n*294
Ridgeley, Carolyn, 126
Rinaldo, Sandie, 261*n*429–*n*430, 262*n*431, 262*n*434

Ritt, Madeleine, 182*n*287
Rivers, Joan, 113
Rivers, Melissa, 113
Romanow Report (2002), 81, 182, 225, 245
Ronaldo, Sandie, 192*n*310
"Roof Replacement for New $400M North Battleford Hospital 'ridiculous,' Says Sask. NDP" (Hunter), 127*n*212
Roosevelt, Franklin, 28
Roosevelt, Theodore, 27, 28
Ross, Dr. John, 62, 63
Rosslyn Retirement Residence, Hamilton, 184
Royal Bank of Canada (RBC), 91
Royal Canadian Mounted Police (RCMP), 8, 13
Royal Commission of Inquiry on the Blood System in Canada (1997) *(a. k. a. Krever Inquiry)*, 98, 99, 101, 273
Royal Ottawa Mental Health Centre, 127–128
Rudderham, Inez, 150, 151, 152
Rudel-Tessier, Catherine, 111
Russell, Charles, 216*n*351
Russell, Jennie, 216*n*351, 245*n*409
Ryerson School of Journalism, 108, 108*n*187, 109*n*188, 110*n*189

S

Sadoway, Meyer, 193
Sagkeeng First Nation, 131
Sainato, Michael, 174*n*271
Saltwire News, 198*n*322, 235*n*390
Samuel, Sigal, 181*n*284
Sanger, Toby, 153*n*252–*n*254
Sanger-Katz, Margot, 32
Sapiens (Harari), 146, 146*n*232–*n*234, 147*n*237–*n*240

INDEX

SARS Commission (2007, Ontario), 188
Saskatchewan,
  experiment of universal health care as Canadian success, 20–21
  Farm Security Act passed in 1944, 14, 15
  as first province to provide free tuberculosis care, 11
  labour strife in, 6
  launched first government-run health insurance in 1962, 16
  MRI waitlists in, 159–160
  universal medical services insurance pioneered in, 224
Saskatchewan College of Physicians and Surgeons (SCPS), 16, 17
Saskatchewan general election, 1944, 14
Saskatchewan general election, 1948, 15
Saskatchewan Hospital North Battleford, 127
  problems with as P3 project, 127
Saskatchewan Medical Association, 9
  lobbied for health insurance in 1933, 11
Saskatchewan Seniors Mechanism, 266n437
"Saskatchewan's MRI Wait-List Doubled From 2015 to 2019" (Hunter), 160n260
"Saskatchewan's Private MRI System Not Meeting Provincial Requirement Auditor Says" (Djuric), 160n259
Saskatoon News, The, 127n213
Saulnier, Christine, 85n147
Sauvageau, Jean-Jacques, 111, 112, 113
Savage, John, 79
Scheffler, Nicholas, 38, 38n66
SCOREGolf magazine, 218
Scotiabank, 91
Scotland,
  personal growth and environmental stewardship in, 220
Seaton, Brenda, 104
Second World War. *See* World War II (Second World War)
Selkirk Seniors Village, Victoria, BC, 115–116
Senate Special Committee on Aging (1966), 242
"Seniors' Home Confines 94-Year-Old Blind Woman to Bedbug-Infested Room for Two Weeks" (Johnson), 141n230
"'Serious Bone of Contention, A': Emails Reveal Details About Faulty Sask. Hospital Roof" (Woodward), 127n213
severe acute respiratory syndrome (SARS), 188
Shakeel, Maham, 108n187, 109n188, 110n189
Shanidar 1, 280
Shannex Inc., 119
Shea, Victor, 202
Short, Dylan, 253n420
"Should the Wealthy be Allowed to Buy Their Way to Faster Health Care at Private Clinics?" (Cribb, Isai & Shakeel), 108n187, 109n188, 110n189
"Showcasing a Canadian Success Story: The Ebola Vaccine" (CIHR), 154n255
Sibbald, Barbara, 204n333
Sick Children's Hospital,

Toronto, 155
Sienna Senior Living, 140, 141
Silas, Linda, 79
"Of Silos and Systems: The Issue of Regionalizing Health Care" (Simpson), 59n85
Simm, Janet, 84
Simon, Herbert A., 174, 175
Simon Fraser University, 26
Simpson, Chris, 256
Simpson, Scot H., 59n85
Sinclair, Brian, 131, 139, 288
  death from 30-hour ER wait, 131–132
  death of as reminder of healthcare disintegration, 136
  disintegration cost his life, 143
  inquest into death of, 134–135
  racism involved in death of, 134–135
Sinclair, Scott, 95, 95n159, 96n160
Sinha, Dr. Samir, 188
slavery, 147
Smith, Alec, 34, 35, 36, 37
Smith, Derrick, 284, 285
Smith, Dr. R. H., 12
Smith-Holt, Alec, 34
Smith-Holt, Nicole, 34, 36
Smylie, Dr. Janet, 134
SNC-Lavalin Group Inc., 127
Social Security Act (1935, U.S.), 28
social welfare systems, 17–18
  in Canada compared to US pro-capitalist system, 24
  interconnected with healthcare systems, 277–278
socio-economics,
  changes in 1930s, 9–10
  changes in 1970s demand for long-term care, 243
  crash after Roaring Twenties, 8–9
  demand for government social support during Great Depression, 9–10
  Great Depression and, 8–9
  Medicare not kept pace with changes in Canada, 257–258
  new reality of Depression, 10
  struggles in early 20th century Canada, 4–5
socioeconomic status as health predictor, 228–229
  changes in compared to little change in social programs, 230–231
Sodexo food services and facilities management company, 85
Softchoice Corp., 147
Solow, Robert, 174
"Some Doctors are Charging Both Government and Patients Privately in Illegal Double-Dipping Practice" (Tomlinson), 103n175, 104n176–n177, 105n178–n179, 106n180
"Some of Ontario's Biggest Hospitals are Filled Beyond Capacity Nearly Every Day New Data Reveals" (Crowley), 198n320
Sorin, M., 238, 238n396
Sourtzis, Litsa, 192n310
Southbridge Care Homes, 210
Southlake Hospital emergency department, Ontario, 69
Specialist Link (Calgary), 256
"square deal" Theodore Roosevelt reform policy, 27–28
Stanford, Jim, 72, 72n116, 73, 73n117–n118, 74n119
Stanton Territorial Hospital,

INDEX

Yellowknife, 125–126
contracted out as P3 project, 125–127
project contractor replaced, 126–127
property taxes on new building not checked out, 125–126
water and sewage leaks at, 126–127
Star & Corporate Knights Project, The, 90n153–n154, 91n155
Statista, 219n359
Statistics Canada, 91, 153, 219n360
Stat News, 179n278
St. Michael's Hospital, Toronto, 257
Stoneridge Manor, Ontario, 196
Stoodley, Chris, 199n323
St. Philip, Elizabeth, 155n256
Stringer, Christopher Brian, 281
Strong, Walter, 125n209
St. Thomas University, Fredericton, 191
"Study Finds More Than 1/4 of Adults in the U.S. are Underinsured Because of High Deductibles" (Patrick), 31n47
Sturgeon, Nicola, 220, 220n361
subprime mortgage crisis, 2007, 74, 146
"Successful Care for Aging Populations Around the World" (Cassidy), 266n437
Summerland Seniors Village, Summerland, BC, 117
Suncor Energy, 153
super-health boards, 59–60
Superina, Stefan, 160, 160n261, 161, 161n262–n263
supply and demand model, 162–163
features of, 163
Supreme Court of Canada, 81
"Survivor Stories from a Deadly Covid-19 Outbreak at a New Brunswick Nursing Home" *(CBC News),* 196n317
Sutherland, Dougal, 221n363
Suzuki, David, 4
Swissair Flight 111 crash, 1998, 62
syndicalism, 7

T

Taft, William H., 27
tainted-blood scandal (1980s & 1990s), 97–98
Tang, Justin, 82n141
Tang, Kwok-Cho, 231n383–n385, 251n417
Tattrie, Jon, 218n356
tax gap, 91–92
"Taxpayers Should Stop Subsidizing Doctor's Liability Costs" (Findlay), 262n432, 263n435
Taylor, Maureen, 254n422–n423
TD Bank, 91
"Technology to Keep You Safe at Home" (Independent Age), 267n439
"Technology Tools and Trends for Better Patient Care: Beyond the EHR" (Waldron, Agresta & Wilkes), 267n438
Telehealth technology, 267
Telemedicine technology, 267
"10 Eternal Reasons to Feel Hopeful, According to Matt Haig" (Haig), 217n354–n355
Tepper, Joshua, 53n81, 64n103, 254n422–n424, 257n425

Thatcher, Margaret, 73
"The 1919 Winnipeg General Strike" (Pentland), 6n4–n7, 7n8–n9
"Theories of Supply and Demand, Problems of Peculiarities in the Healthcare Sector: Its Effects on Health Policy" (Iliadis et al), 166n260
They Deserve Better: The Long-Term Care Experience in Canada and Scandinavia (Pat Armstrong et al), 182n288
"Third BC Seniors Home Owned by Chinese Company Fails Standard of Care, Placed Under Health Authority Control" (Larsen), 115n195, 116n196, 190n306
"This is the Face of the Health-Care Crisis: Woman Issues Plea to N.S. Premier" (Cooke), 150n243
"This is the Real Reason Most Americans File for Bankruptcy" (Konish), 45n78
"This Man Lost His Leg After Seven Years Waiting for a Kidney in N.L.—and Now He's Losing Hope" (White), 143n231
Thomas, Jesse, 151n247–n249, 152n250–n251
Thomson, Alistair, 225
Thomson, Graham, 84n145
Thornton, Glen, 205
"$3.2M in Severance for Ex-CEOs of Calgary, Edmonton Health Boards" *(CBC News)*, 60n87
"Three Major Pharmaceutical Companies Just Reported Earnings—Here's How They Did" (Lovelace, Jr.), 178n277
Tikkanen, Roosa, 30n42
time linked to outcome, 1–2
Times Colonist, 116n197–n198
"Time to Free Canada's Long-Term Care System from Its Backward History" (Cole), 242n405
"Time to Take a Serious Look at Basic Income" (Cannings), 232n386
Tomlinson, Kathy, 103n175, 104n176–n177, 105n178–n179, 106n180
"Tommy Douglas Crowned Greatest Canadian" (2004, CBC), 3–4n3
Tonelli, Marcelo, 231n383–n385, 251n417
"Top Health Insurers' Revenues Soar to Almost $1 Trillion in 2019" (Payne), 177n274
Toronto General Hospital, 154, 155
Toronto Life, 107n186
Toronto Public Health, 209
Toronto Star, The, 82n142, 107, 108n187, 109n188, 110n189
Transitional Care Bridge Project, Netherlands, 266
"Treating Patients in Supply Closets Final Straw for ER Doctors in Kentville" *(CBC News)*, 68n111
Trent University, Peterborough, Ontario, 242, 243n406, 244n407, 245n408
Trouble with Billionaires, The (McQuaig & Brooks), 174, 175n272

INDEX

Trudeau, Justin, 179, 215, 227
Trudeau, Pierre Elliott, 51, 77, 224
Truman, Harry, 28
Trump, Donald, 96
Truthout, 25, 26n32, 27n34–n35, 37n59
Tunney, Catharine, 269n440
Tutton, Michael, 62n97–n98, 63n99
"20 Years Later: How Corporations Took Over Canada's Health Care System" (Fuller), 75n121, 86n148
"$22 Billion in Cuts to Funding for Public Services Planned by Mr. Ford, Worse than Harris, We are Extremely Worried" (Mehra), 80n136
Twitter, 215n349
Twomey, Amy, 242, 243, 243n406, 244, 244n407, 245, 245n408

U

UBI Works, 227n373, 228n374, 232n387
"UCP Leader Jason Kenney Wants to Explore Private Health-Care" (Bennett), 83n143
UN Chronicle, 281n456
underinsurance (health), 30–31
unemployment, 5, 14, 31, 180–181, 216, 229
"Uninsured Rate for Children up to 5.5 Percent in 2018" (Berchick & Mykyta), 30n44
unionism, 5–6
    attacked by neoliberal corporations, 73–74
    Estevan Mine Strike, 12–13
    gains of 1970s lost to neoliberalism in 1980s onwards, 74
    grew in strength in post-World War II in Canada, 72
    labour movement in US, 26
    labour share of GDP grew to peak in late 1970s, 72
    Western, 5–7
    in Western Canada after 1897, 5–6
United States (U.S.),
    administrative healthcare costs in, 33–34 47–48
    blood selling in, 38–39
    children's healthcare compared to Canada's Medicare, 31
    complex billing costs for healthcare in, 34
    core tenets of free market system in, 162–163
    deaths due to lack of access to heath care in, 40–42
    employer-based health insurance as most common in, 31
    failures in establishing national health service in, 27–28
    health insurance built on false notion of autonomy, 172–173
    individualism in compared to Canadian collectivism, 24
    infant mortality rate in, 43
    litigation costs of malpractice in, 46
    lowest life expectancy rates comped to OECD countries, 43–44
    medical debt as main source of personal bankruptcy in, 32, 45, 173–174
    medical-industrial complex in, 27–28
    medication prices in no-regulatory free-market system

in, 37–38
origins of corporate America and private health, 24–27
as outlier in healthcare services, 279
privatization expanded into Canada, 24
spending on healthcare compared to other OECD countries, 30
violent labour history in, 26
welfare state seen as handout, 18
United States Census Bureau, 31, 177n276
United States Census Bureau reports, 30n43, 30n44, 31n46
United States-Mexico-Canada Agreement (USMCA), 94
see also North American Free Trade Association (NAFTA)
patents of biologic drugs in, 96
trade takes priority over health regulations, 97
Universal Basic Income (UBI), 232
l'Université de Montréal, 128
University Health Network, Toronto, 104
University of California, San Francisco, 228, 233
University of California News, 229n376, 233n388
University of Maryland Baltimore County, 176
University of Massachusetts, Lowell, 146
University of Michigan, 37
University of Nevada, 280
University of Ottawa, 237, 237n394
University of Toronto, 109, 165, 176, 198
Upton, Rachel D., 30n43, 177n276
"U.S. Has Highest Rate of Disease Burden Among Comparable Countries, and the Gap is Growing, The" (Cox & Gonzales), 44n76
"U.S. Health Care from a Global Perspective, 2019: Higher Spending, Worse Outcomes" (Tikkanen & Abrams), 30n42
"U.S. Material and Infant Mortality: More Signs of Public Health Neglect" (Cohen), 43n75
USW 9460—Northlands Healthcare Workers Union, 38n66

V

Valiente, Alexa, 39, 39n67
"Valley Doctors Start Go-Fund-Me Page to Raise Awareness of Growing Health-Care Crisis" *(CTV Atlantic News)*, 68n110
Valley Regional Hospital, Kentville, Nova Scotia, 68
Vancouver Coastal Health, 85
Van den Hoonaard, Deborah, 191
Van Nguyen, Stephanie, 212
Vibert, Jim, 198n322
Victor, Peter, 222
Villa Renaissance, Dalhousie, New Brunswick, 196
Vize, Shayla, 184n291
Vox, 36n56, 181n284

W

W5, CTV News, 192, 192n310
"W5 Investigation Reveals National Crisis: Homicide in Care Homes" (Ronaldo & Sourtzis), 192n310
wait times for health procedures, 105–106

INDEX

Walcroft, Chris, 200
Waldron, Steven E., 267*n*438
Walkerton, Ontario water contamination, 2000, 95
Walsh, Marieke, 60*n*88
Walter, Chandler, 253*n*419
Wan, William, 180*n*279
"Want Your Medical Records? Be Prepared to Pay—a Lot" (Picard), 114*n*194
Warfarin medication, 239–240
Wark, Wesley, 194
Warkentin, Alec, 254*n*421
war(s),
  see also World War I (First World War); World War II (Second World War)
  interplay with health, 15
Washington Post, The, 113*n*191, 179*n*278, 180*n*279
waste, fiscal, 269–270, 271
Watt, Nina, 205, 206
Wealthy Banker's Wife, The (McQuaig), 10*n*14, 18*n*30, 38, 38*n*64
"Wealthy Canadians Hiding up to $240B Abroad" (Dubinsky), 92*n*157
Weaver, Erin, 36
Weldon, Tori, 99n170
Wellbeing Economies Governments (WEgo) Partnership, 220
  Canada and membership of, 221
  need to transform notion of progress, 222–223
"We're Here to Help You Get An Important Message Out" (The Center for Patient Protection), 274*n*446
Werner, Anna, 34
Western Canada,
  social climate for reforms in, 6
  unionism features in, 5–7
Westoll, NIck, 125*n*208
"'We Will Not be Dictated to': Quebec Premier Legault Warns Ottawa Over Health Care" (Richer), 216*n*353
"What Do We Know About Social Determinants of Health in the U.S. and Comparable Countries?" (Kamal, Cox & Blumenkranz), 43*n*74
"What Happened at Northwood" (Nolen), 186*n*298, 187*n*299–300, 188*n*303, 208*n*339–*n*340
"What Happened to Hospital Patients That Had Nowhere to Go?" (Sibbald), 204*n*333
"What is the Blood of a Poor Person Worth?" (Greenberg), 97*n*165
"What Now?/Canada Health Transfer: Background and Future" (Mou), 77*n*127
"What Went Wrong in Bobcaygeon: How Covid Killed 29 People in an Ill-Prepared Nursing Home" (Riches), 185*n*294
"What Went Wrong with Joan Rivers's Last Medical Procedure: Lawsuit" (Yahr), 113*n*191
"Where Your Tax Dollar Goes" (Armstrong), 156*n*257
Wherry, Aaron, 182*n*286, 183, 183*n*289
"Whistleblower Says Workers at Nursing Homes Aren't Being Given Protective Gear" (Haines), 195*n*314
White Jen, 143*n*231

Whiteside, Jennifer, 118
"WHO Declares a Pandemic of Coronavirus Disease Covid-19" (Wan), 180n279
"WHO Declares Coronavirus Outbreak a Global Health Emergency" (Joseph), 179n278
"Who Would Really Benefit from Kenney's Corporate Tax Cuts?" (Sanger), 153n252–n254
"Why Doug Ford's to Blame for Health-Care Mess" (Hepburn), 82n142
"Why Governments Should Prioritize Well-Being" (Sturgeon), 220n361
"Why is Loblaw Getting $12M to Install New Refrigerators? McKenna Under Fire for New Funding" (Connolly), 269n441
"Why Poverty Is Like a Disease" (Cooper), 229n380, 230n381
"Why Thousands of Low-Income Americans 'Donate' Their Blood Plasma to For-Profit Centers" (Valiente, Abdelmalek & Pearle), 39n67
Wikipedia, 28n37
Wilkerson, Josh, 36
Wilkes, Theresa, 267n438
Williams, Danny, 20, 157, 158
Wilson, Woodrow, 28
Wilt, James, 216n352
Winnipeg General Strike, 1919, 7–8
"Winnipeg General Strike of 1919" (Nolan Reilly), 8n10–n11
Winnipeg Health Sciences Centre's emergency department, 131
staff vacancy rates, 133
Winter, Tom, 114n192

"Without Pharmacare, Canadians with Disabilities Rationing Drugs Due to High Prescription Costs" (Gupta &McColl), 236n392
WKRC Indianapolis, 36n57
"Woman Says Her Son Couldn't Afford His Insulin—Now He's Dead" *(CBS News)*, 34n53, 35n54
Womenfolks: Grieving Up Down South (Abbott), 283n461
women's liberation movements, 73
Wood, Keith, 193
Woods, Ed, 32n48
Woodstock festival, 1969, 73
Woodsworth, J. S., 3, 13
arrest of in Winnipeg General Strike, 8
Woodward, Laura, 127n213
Woolhandler, Dr. Stephanie, 40
Woolley, Frances, 203, 203n332
workplaces (health), chaos in, 2
World Health Organization (WHO), 98, 98n169, 227
Covid-19 announced by, 179, 180
World Trade Organization (WTO) trade agreements, 85
dangers to Canada's health-care policies, 95–96
World War I (First World War), 9
medical services for unavailable after, 10
veterans returning from, 5
World War II (Second World War), 10
anniversary of Normandy Invasion, 283–284
Douglas against conscription, 14
economic transition from to

post-war, 5
effects of on universal health ins insurance, 15
post-war reconstruction in Europe, 17–18
Worsham, Antavia, 36
Woskie, Liana R., 33n50

Y

Yahoo News, 166n267
Yahr, Emily, 113n191
Yalnizyan, Armine, 89n151, 156
Yarmouth, Nova Scotia ferry debacle, 89
"Yellowknife's New Hospital Comis in Millions Over Budget Due to Property Tax Flub" (Bird), 126n210
"Yes, People Die When They Don't Have Access to Health Care" (Delaney), 41n69
Yiu, Gabriel, 78n132, 82n140
York University, 75, 222
Young, Leslie, 235n391
"Young People, Jobs are Coming Back to Halifax in Record Numbers" (Thomas), 151n247–n249, 152n250–n251
Yow, Michael, 90n153–n154, 91n155

Z

Zbogar, Vilko, 134
Zinn, Howard, 274

CPSIA information can be obtained
at www.ICGtesting.com
Printed in the USA
BVHW052201200123
656718BV00018B/736/J